POLITICAL MINEFIELDS

POLITICAL MINEFIELDS

The Struggle against Automated Killing

Matthew Breay Bolton

I.B. TAURIS

LONDON • NEW YORK • OXFORD • NEW DELHI • SYDNEY

I.B. TAURIS

Bloomsbury Publishing Plc

50 Bedford Square, London, WC1B 3DP, UK

1385 Broadway, New York, NY 10018, USA

BLOOMSBURY, I.B. TAURIS and the I.B. Tauris logo are trademarks of
Bloomsbury Publishing Plc

First published in Great Britain 2020

Cover design by danileighdesign.com
Cover image © Anadolu Agency / Getty Images

A catalogue record for this book is available from the British Library.

A catalogue record for this book is available from the Library of Congress.

ISBN: HB: 978-1-7807-6158-9
PB: 978-1-7807-6159-6
ePDF: 978-0-7556-1850-7
eBook: 978-0-7556-1849-1

Typeset by Deanta Global Publishing Services, Chennai, India

To find out more about our authors and books visit www.bloomsbury.com and
sign up for our newsletters.

For Emily, whose way out of a trap is
to question the society that set it.

CONTENTS

FOREWORD

Landmines are weapons of mass destruction in slow motion. They are inhumane, indiscriminate and cause unnecessary suffering, even decades after the forces that laid them stopped fighting. The landmine embodies a view of the world in which a human life can be snuffed out by an automated device. The person who placed and armed the mine may be on the other side of the world – even dead – when it finally explodes under the foot of a farmer planting rice, a child on the way to class, a refugee returning to their destroyed home. By the late 1980s, thousands of people in countries such as Afghanistan, Angola, Bosnia, Cambodia and Mozambique were being maimed and killed by landmines, while governments continued to act like they were 'normal' weapons. Millions of mines moved around the world in arms transfers that faced little scrutiny.

In the face of this dehumanized killing, though, humanity pushed back. Survivors, deminers, humanitarian workers, grassroots activists, human rights advocates and journalists raised the alarm. They demanded the world's militaries live up to their own principles in the laws of war. They called on the countries that had made a killing in the arms trade to help clear the deadly fruit of their irresponsible profiteering. Out of this groundswell emerged the International Campaign to Ban Landmines (ICBL), which I helped launch as its first coordinator in 1991. By 1997, the ICBL had persuaded the majority of the world's countries to adopt a treaty comprehensively banning anti-personnel mines and establishing obligations to clear contaminated land, assist victims and provide risk reduction education to affected communities. That year, the ICBL and I were jointly awarded the Nobel Peace Prize for starting 'a process which in the space of a few years changed a ban on anti-personnel mines from a vision to a feasible reality'.

The Nobel Committee recognized the ICBL for the 'unprecedented way' its global network of organizations had made it 'possible to express and mediate a broad wave of popular commitment', enabling 'governments of several small and medium-sized countries' to take up the issue and 'deal with it'. Indeed, the landmine ban treaty has been monumental success. Even countries that have so far refused to sign it – such as the United States, Russia and China – largely follow its prohibitions. The mass manufacture and trade in landmines have ground to a halt. Thousands of acres of contaminated land have been cleared; victims have received prosthetics, medical and socio-economic support.

The Nobel Committee was also prescient, seeing in the ICBL 'a model for similar processes in the future', saying that 'it could prove of decisive importance to the international effort for disarmament and peace'. Just over a decade later, a similar campaign – the Cluster Munition Coalition (CMC) – succeeded in pushing governments to negotiate a ban on cluster munitions. These insidious weapons spray explosive bomblets over a wide area; many fail to explode upon impact and become de facto anti-personnel landmines. And in 2017, the International Campaign to Abolish Nuclear Weapons (ICAN) was awarded the Nobel Peace Prize for persuading 122 countries to adopt a treaty banning the world's most destructive and inhumane weapons. ICBL, CMC and ICAN – standard bearers of what is known as the humanitarian disarmament movement – have shown that ordinary people, organizing across national boundaries and forefronting the voices of those most affected, can resist the seemingly inexorable march of violent technology.

Having seen the power of humanity over automated and indiscriminate killing, I am confident that civil society has the capacity to face the emerging threat of what diplomats have euphemistically called 'lethal autonomous weapons systems'. Weapons developers are seeking to pervert the power of information and communications technology for deadly ends, taking humans entirely out of the decision to kill. In the autonomous, weaponized robot, they are essentially designing mines that actively seek out their targets, that can follow you, that can fly. This is why I support the Campaign to Stop Killer Robots, which is using the humanitarian disarmament model to ban all weapons that fail to maintain meaningful human control over violence.

But even as we resist new threats of digitized slaughter and celebrate the successes of the humanitarian disarmament community, we cannot forget that landmines have not yet been eradicated. In fact, due to the horrifying carnage in Afghanistan, Myanmar, Syria and Yemen, the long-term decline in new landmine casualties has, since 2015, begun to reverse. Many governments have flagged in their commitment to clear all the world's minefields by 2025. And landmine survivors continue to struggle against the pervasive discrimination and stigma directed at people with disabilities. As this book went to press, the Trump Administration reversed longstanding US policy on landmines. Like many of his decisions, it is a step backward into a more cruel past. We must redouble our efforts to destroy all stockpiles of landmines and cluster munitions, demine all contaminated land, ensure every victim's human rights and universalize the landmine and cluster munition ban treaties.

In this book, Matthew Breay Bolton documents the story of these inter-locking struggles for humanity in this world riven by automated violence. In doing so, he draws on his extensive experience working in humanitarian fieldwork, diplomatic settings and academia. He approaches efforts to eradicate landmines and tackle other problematic weapons through the inclusive lens of human security as opposed to more narrowly focused national security concerns. Bolton examines the depersonalization of killing that has accompanied the use of unmanned aerial vehicles or drones and flags the need to tackle the multiple challenges posed by fully autonomous armed robots. Throughout, Bolton emphasizes the role of civil society to show how when ordinary people work together they can achieve extraordinary impact. He invites you to join the global struggle for peace and justice, refusing to leave decisions of life and death to a machine.

Jody Williams Chair, Nobel Women's Initiative 1997 Nobel Peace Prize Co-Laureate with the International Campaign to Ban Landmines Author of *My Name Is Jody Williams: A Vermont Girl's Winning Path to the Nobel Peace Prize.*

ENDORSEMENTS

'Matthew Bolton documents his experience working in humanitarian fieldwork, diplomatic settings, and academia. He approaches efforts to eradicate landmines and tackle other problematic weapons through the inclusive lens of human security as opposed to more narrowly focused national security concerns. Bolton examines the "depersonalization of killing" that has accompanied the use of unmanned aerial vehicles or drones and flags the need to tackle the multiple challenges posed by fully autonomous armed robots. Throughout Bolton emphasizes the role of civil society to show how when ordinary people work together they can achieve extraordinary impact.'

– Jody Williams, 1997 Nobel Peace Prize Laureate and Chair of the Nobel Women's Initiative, former coordinator of the International Campaign to Ban Landmines, author of *My Name Is Jody Williams: A Vermont Girl's Winning Path to the Nobel Peace Prize.*

'Matthew Bolton takes us on a very readable journey to what in Bosnia we used to call the Dark Side. He starts as an idealistic young aid worker and becomes almost by accident an expert on landmines and the politics of landmine clearance, which is minefield in itself. His account of unsettling experiences in Bosnia, Iraq, Afghanistan and South Sudan is a vivid snapshot of the dangerous times in which we live.'

– Martin Bell, OBE, Former BBC war reporter and independent UK Member of Parliament, UNICEF UK Ambassador, author of *In Harm's Way, An Accidental MP* and *Through the Gates of Fire*, and a published poet.

'Bolton's beautifully written book portends a dehumanized future in which smart weapons stray beyond our control and lack of regulation will be our undoing. Chilling.'

– Teresa Carpenter, Pulitzer-Prize winner and bestselling author of *Missing Beauty* and *The Miss Stone Affair.*

'An interesting philosophical and personal reflection on mines and demining that shows how even the best-intentioned interventions can fall victim to local political and economic forces.'

– Dr David Keen, Professor of Complex Emergencies, London School of Economics, author of *Useful Enemies: When Waging Wars Is More Important than Winning Them.*

Chapter 1

EXPLOSIVE TRAPS
AN INTRODUCTION

From the Second World War to the war in Iraq

My fascination with landmines began in Bosnia – with a bang. A pillar of grey dust shot up into the air. The concussive shockwave followed a moment later, smacking against my chest and knocking the air out of my lungs. As the dust column slowed its convulsive ascent, particles fell back towards the earth, creating a cap to the emerging mushroom. Adrenalin surged as the second blast hit me, this one creating the shape of two grey fans, morphing into a shapeless haze and drifting in the wind blowing across the open field before us. From a safe distance, I was watching deminers blowing up landmines and unexploded ordnance (UXO) in a field outside Brcko, the town in north-eastern Bosnia where I worked as a volunteer with a small agricultural aid programme. As the blasts reverberated across the countryside, I knew I had found my vocation. Lost in the complexities of Bosnia's post-war politics, I just wanted to do good. These deminers risked their lives every day saving the lives of strangers. Seeing them work was far more exciting than sitting in our office writing monthly reports no one would read.

I had leapt at the chance when Faris, an employee of a demining agency and acquaintance of my colleague Zijo, asked if I wanted to observe a demolition of the various defused mines, shells and grenades his group had collected in the past month. Zijo had introduced us, telling me that Faris's intimate local knowledge of the war meant he knew Brcko's minefields as well as anyone. Having escaped the Serb forces' capture of Brcko, running from his house under fire, Faris had served in the Bosnian Army on Brcko's frontlines for the whole war. He told me that he was often posted as a guard in a spot where he could see his abandoned house on the other side of the lines.

After we finished our coffee, I joined Faris in a convoy of vehicles as we travelled to a police training camp where, incongruously, they kept the mines and unexploded munitions next to the volleyball court. As his colleagues carried stacks of anti-tank mines to their vehicles, they had to dodge a ball flying at them from an officer's askance spike. Loaded up, we moved in a convoy of SUVs with flashing lights, an ambulance bringing up the rear, stopping traffic. I put on my sunglasses and glowered at the horizon – it felt like the appropriate thing to do. We turned onto a dirt road through the most desolate place I'd ever seen – uncultivated flatlands, bone dry, with a scattering of rough shrubbery. We pulled up next to a constellation of massive craters. Two US soldiers, Explosive Ordnance Disposal (EOD) specialists, were already there, standing next to a dark green Humvee. The NATO peacekeeping force liked to have its people around when the locals were blowing things up.

The American troops helped unload the ordnance and contributed a little of their own, picked up on patrols of surrounding villages. Arranging them into tight piles, one of the soldiers explained to me that the sundry mines, grenades, detonators, rockets and bullets all had to touch each other for the shockwave to be transmitted throughout the pile and detonate all the other devices. The pile was arranged to ensure that the explosive force was directed downwards, into itself and the ground, to avoid scattering munitions in the air. Katyusha rockets were placed at the bottom of the pile so they would be snapped in half by the blast; everything was topped off with a layer of C4 plastic explosives and fitted with radio-controlled detonators. Zijo, Faris and I beat a retreat down the road to an outcropping about a mile away. Radios crackled with procedure until it was clear that no one was left in the blast zone. The order finally came; then, bang.

After having sat through umpteen seminars for local farmers taught by some droning seed scientist – grasping for adjectives to make our work seem exciting to donors back home – demining seemed like a tangible way to make noticeable change in people's lives. Supporting deminers could be my small contribution to Bosnia's reconstruction. I threw myself into the world of landmines, racking up huge telephone bills as I scoured for reports on the internet with our dial-up modem. I took the bus to Sarajevo and criss-crossed all over the capital, meeting as many demining professionals as I could. For a wide-eyed naïf like me, fresh from a university in the quiet cornfields of Iowa, hanging with men like Faris made me feel macho. Working in demining gave me access to the cool stuff that attracts young men to the military – explosions, bravery, arcane acronyms, two-way radios, Kevlar jackets – without having to shoot anyone.

Given its strategic significance and brutal ethnic cleansing during the war, the Brcko District was one of the most mined areas in Bosnia. At the time I lived there, 12 per cent of its territory was considered hazardous.[1] A belt of deadly, overgrown wasteland cut across the District, following former frontlines, perpetuating its division, projecting the effects of the war into the peace. The region had once been a 'breadbasket' of the former Yugoslavia; now old mortars and unexploded grenades kept farmers from their fallow fields. Landmines prevented refugees and displaced people from returning to their burnt-out homesteads. Almost forty people had been killed by landmines and UXO in the Brcko District since the war. Living in Brcko, I developed a fear of grassy and overgrown areas, which tended to be mined. The vegetation was often about shoulder height, abandoned about the same time. To this day, I always think twice before walking on un-cut grass and my heart jumps if I see a piece of metal protruding from the ground. As I looked around me in Brcko, landmines and demining offered powerful symbols for the violence lying just below the surface, as well as efforts to defuse it. I could feel the tension beneath the apparent calm in the town, hinted at by the belligerent graffiti, the blacked-out windows of the Serb radical nationalist club, gunshots in the night.

To me, this made the work of deminers unquestionably heroic. They were literally tearing evil from the earth and destroying it. By helping others to dig out landmines, I could be doing my part to rid the world of violence. I was overjoyed when Zijo and I got permission from our NGO's headquarters to move forward with a pilot mine action programme 'intended to rehabilitate the environment, woodland, and agricultural land' in Brcko. I would finally be making a difference – doing something to make my mark on Brcko. For our first project, we selected a piece of farmland shown to us by Faris. It had been right on the frontlines. Around us lay the detritus of war: empty ration tins, discarded boots and a pile of unexploded mortar shells. Down the hill you could see the looming US Army base, built on the grounds of an old pig farm, straddling the former frontlines. Bored young men were running around the racetrack just inside the wire. Though we had heard muttered complaints about profiteering, all the major international demining NGOs had other commitments and so we used a commercial company.

But as I learned more about the demining sector, my heroic fantasies became increasingly unsettled. Unwittingly, I had walked into the midst of a scandal. Aid agencies were discovering that the demining sector in Bosnia – particularly the company we had selected – was dominated by people who had been deeply implicated in the conflict. A US diplomatic cable later cited claims that 'millions of dollars in international donor funds' had been 'embezzled' and used in a network of 'organized crime, and possible war criminal support'. [2]

*   *   *

Hurtling out of the sky in a tight corkscrew spiral – a countermeasure against potential anti-aircraft fire – I arrived in Iraq seven months later on a UN Humanitarian Air Service C-130 cargo plane. It screeched to a halt on the runway of 'Erbil International Airport', consisting of an airstrip, two 40-foot containers, a gravel parking lot and, evidently, big ambitions. I stepped onto the asphalt, blinking in the bright sun. UN trucks bustled around like ants. A couple of sand-coloured Humvees whizzed by, guided by unshaven American soldiers sporting Ray-Bans and deep tans. I stood, holding my backpack sheepishly, feeling out of place. The flight had carried the same motley bunch of expatriates I had hung around with in Bosnia. Clad in 'Aid Worker Chic' – khakis, epaulettes and pockets – smoking heavily and carrying kit bags decorated with aid agency logos (including one from the UN landmine agency in Sarajevo), they compared the myriad stamps in each other's passports, conversing in earnest world-weariness. Gathering my other belongings – I too had a bag full of moisture-wicking shirts – I boarded a bus and rode to Ankawa, a suburb of Erbil, the de facto capital of the primarily Kurdish northern Iraq. We weaved through a complex of UN buildings that had taken over whole city blocks, cordoning off roads with barbed wire, concrete barricades and armed guards. This was to be my home for the next three months, as I worked for an American humanitarian organization and assessed the needs of landmine survivors. The security situation in the Kurdish-controlled region was much better for foreigners than elsewhere in Iraq in 2003. Other than a hair-raising day in Mosul and ducking the celebratory gunfire following Saddam Hussein's arrest, I never felt directly threatened during my stay in Iraq. Nonetheless, there was pervasive and creeping fear; I shuddered with each report of explosive attacks on foreign aid workers.

A small cell of US Special Forces lived a few doors down from my new office in Erbil. As I was the only American in the team, my new boss sent me down the road to contact the soldiers, to serve as a kind of liaison. I was nervous about meeting them – I moved in different circles than the military. Three years earlier I had been arrested at an Air Force base for protesting the ongoing US bombing of Iraq. But I found the soldiers to be a relaxed bunch, mostly working in civil-military affairs rather than direct combat. They coordinated with the Kurdish government and NGOs on matters of governance and public services and channelled US funding to reconstruction projects aimed at winning 'hearts and minds'. The US military was especially interested in the landscape of landmines and UXO that surrounded them. Their experience of the invasion had served as a cautionary tale.

Speeding through the desert to Baghdad, the US Army's 3rd Infantry Division found their way blocked by the River Euphrates. To traverse the water, on 2 April 2003, Task Force 3-69 set out to capture 'Objective Peach', the Al-Kaed ('Leader') Bridge. Access to the bridge, which was sturdy enough to support crossing tanks, was crucial to pass through the narrow 'Karbala Gap', a 25-mile bottleneck between rivers that would allow the US military enter Iraq's capital. With mortars raining about them, reconnoitring American 'sappers' – combat engineers who set or defuse explosive traps – discovered that Iraqi troops had wired the bridge with demolition charges. They would need to decode and defuse the puzzle of a massive booby trap to be able to enter the city. Only a week before, Task Force 3-69's tanks had been crossing another bridge, Al-Kifl, when Iraqi engineers detonated a similar device. Luckily for the American troops, Al-Kifl had not collapsed. Chastened, Task Force 3-69 was more careful at Objective Peach, figuring out that Iraqi soldiers must be holding the trigger somewhere close. They called in artillery and air strikes, aiming to kill whoever might have the power to close this portal into Baghdad. A small group of American engineers jumped into three 15-foot inflatable Zodiac dinghies and, under small arms fire, attempted to motor into the river under the bridge. The first boat began to drift as the soldiers returned fire and stopped steering their craft. The engine in the second boat died, clogged with sand. Finally, the engineers found and began to cut the wires. One man almost drowned while severing an underwater cord. As they worked, Iraqi troops triggered the remaining charges, causing considerable damage; nonetheless, a span remained. The Americans charged through the Karbala Gap, capturing the airport and heading towards the city from the west. But Task Force 3-69's sappers found themselves needed again. Astride Highway 8, connecting Baghdad airport to what would become the 'Green Zone', was a 1,200 metre minefield, laid with Italian-made mines fitted with anti-handling devices to blow up anyone who tried to defuse them. Rather than waste time finding and deactivating all the mines, the engineers ploughed through, using an armoured bulldozer and more than 2,500 pounds of explosives, causing 'a mushroom-cloud explosion that shook the ground and blew out the windows of nearby buildings.'[3] On 6 April, US troops captured Baghdad.[4] But the city soon descended into looting and civil disarray. And as the American occupation tried to establish a semblance of control, they found themselves facing a bold and baffling rebellion.

The insurgents' weapon of choice was the improvised explosive device (IED), a kind of artisanal landmine, which became the main cause of American casualties. Local factions innovated methods of using mobile phones, walkie-talkies and infrared remote-control switches to remotely detonate roadside bombs. The sappers who had unravelled the puzzle of Saddam's booby-trapped bridges were now deployed to secure Iraq's increasingly tricky terrain. EOD specialists learned that, even when the technical solution seemed obvious, defusing a rigged shell was only a small element of dodging the IED threat. Insurgents would emplace easily decoded, hoax devices and watch US troops reveal their detection techniques, enabling the creation of ever more deadly traps. IEDs operate as a kind of 'weapon of the weak', a tool to subvert asymmetries and disrupt the plans of the powerful. The Americans desperately tried to read IEDs, seeking forensic clues that would lead them to 'capture or kill' the makers. As Michael Ondaatje wrote in *The English Patient*, in bomb disposal, 'you must consider the character of your enemy. ... People think a bomb is a mechanical object, a mechanical enemy. But you have to consider that somebody made it.' Ondaatje's sapper character Kip describes feeling 'watched' by the 'contraption' as he tried to untangle its 'maze'.[5]

Among the first soldiers I met in Erbil was the point person on demining. She was passionate about ridding northern Iraq of its mine problem and invited me to attend the coordination meetings. In a stuffy Kurdish government conference room, I was introduced to complex politics of northern Iraq's 'mine action' – efforts to manage the risk of landmines through education, stockpile destruction, data gathering, advocacy, survivor assistance and clearance. There were commercial demining companies that sold landmine clearance and bomb disposal services, mostly to the US government. A network of local and international do-gooders provided relief and minefield clearance to civilians affected by landmines and UXO. Focused on alleviating suffering, they generally preferred to remain impartial rather than challenge the occupation. Sometimes though, they found themselves drawn unwittingly into the war's dynamics, by doing projects that contributed to the US reconstruction effort or the Kurdish government's efforts to demonstrate autonomy.

Similarly, the US military and Iraqi insurgents became ensnared in an esoteric and deadly conversation, mediated by the enigma of the IED. Breaching Baghdad's minefields had drawn the Americans into a far more bewildering political minefield. In a pair of paintings from Sandow Birk's 2007 *Depravities of War* project, he depicted an American soldier – in helmet, camouflage and armed with an automatic rifle – standing before a Sphinx. In one, the Sphinx is recognizable as a fallen, disintegrating statue of Saddam Hussein. Satirizing nineteenth-century Orientalist works by Jean-Auguste-Dominique Ingres, Elihu Vedder and Jean-Leon Gerome, the paintings (entitled *Riddle of the Sphinx* and *The Questioner and the Sphynx*) evoke twenty-first-century news media images of Iraq while gesturing to a much older story.[6] On his way to conquer Thebes, Oedipus faced the Sphinx, a monster who kills all those trying to pass who cannot decode her riddle. Oedipus solves the puzzle, defeating the Sphinx, and, entering the city, ascends to the Theban throne. But in Sophocles' play, the protagonist's successful evasion of one trap only pulls him into the meta-level trap of his tragic fate.

* * *

After evacuation from Dunkirk in 1940, my grandfather, John 'Jack' Bolton, a mechanic in the British Army's Royal Electrical and Mechanical Engineers, was sent to Egypt via a treacherous passage through the Mediterranean Sea to train soldiers on how to fix the engines. In Second World War North Africa, armoured mobility – the tank – had become central to the conflict as armies tried to outmanoeuvre each other in what appeared to Europeans as a featureless sandy sea. Outnumbered and outgunned by the Allies who faced him at the Egyptian frontline of El Alamein – 250 kilometres from the Great Sphinx of Giza – Nazi general Erwin Rommel had ordered the construction of a 'Devil's Garden' across the desert.[7] This 5-mile-wide minefield – one of the largest ever made – was sown with half a million mines.

As they tried to maintain their vehicles in a punishing environment, both sides turned to landmines to stymie the other's tanks, demarcate frontlines, protect bases and project violence into the desert beyond their stretched supply lines. At one point, a British factory near Cairo was churning out 8,000 mines a day to feed the frontlines.[8] Initially, landmines were targeted at the tanks, aimed at slowing the march of mechanized warfare in places such as El Alamein. These 'anti-vehicle landmines' require considerable pressure to detonate and so generally do not hurt those on foot. However, they still pose a threat to civilian drivers. Sometimes they became oversensitive with time and can kill someone unfortunate enough to step on them. The advent of anti-vehicle landmines prompted militaries to train specialized 'counter-mine' or 'demining' units – ancestors of the EOD soldiers I met in Bosnia and Iraq. In response, anti-personnel landmines were developed to guard anti-vehicle landmines against deminers. They were designed to maim people rather than kill them. An injured soldier – who needs medical attention and evacuation – diverts more military resources than a dead one. The injuries caused by an anti-personnel mine are horrific. The blast will blow off a hand or foot, shredding flesh, sending vicious shockwaves throughout the body and jamming shrapnel, dirt and bacteria deep into the wound, causing serious infections.

But for Rommel, who advocated for a hyper-rationalist approach to combat (he titled his North Africa memoir *Krieg ohne Hass* – 'War without Hate'), the landmine seemed like the perfect replacement for human troops: they never got emotional, needed no sleep, never got bored, never hungered or pursued sexual misadventures. As such, minefields were expressions of deadly modernist architecture, form perfectly fitted to deadly function. Both sides developed mathematical algorithms to maximize autonomous killing for the least cost and wrote manuals to instruct regular troops on how to lay the minefields. Unlike baroque castles, they were brutally minimalist, with no pretention to art. However, in the shifting of sands, ever-changing frontlines and ingenuity of individual soldiers, the regularity of the Devil's Gardens soon devolved into a complex, fluctuating mess. As one landmine expert put it, in effect, 'the minefield changes sides'.[9]

The Allies eventually cut through this knot of minefields by advancing directly through them, initially in complete darkness, casualty rates be damned. A member of the Royal Engineers recalled what, 'with grim humor', was codenamed Operation Lightfoot:[10]

> Deliberate, continuous sweeping with detectors, each man going forward slowly and intently, eyes on the ground, earphones on the head, while the noise of battle crashes around; and the cold blooded investigation and lifting of mines, never knowing when some heathenish invention for catching one out would not blow the grubber to eternity.[11]

The Devil's Garden and similar minefields did little to alter the course of the war. Military forces could just blast their way through. Rommel's other project, the 5 million mines of the 'Atlantic Wall', failed to halt the D-Day landings.[12] But it is Bedouins – who have tried to live in harmony with the desert rather than conquer it – who now live with the explosive fruit of the Devil's Garden. Second World War minefields continue to maim and kill civilians in North Africa.[13]

Besides mines, soldiers and civilians alike faced the threat of thousands of unexploded bombs. Such explosive remnants of war are widespread wherever there has been an armed conflict, as about 5 to 30 per cent of munitions fail to detonate on impact. UXO function as de facto landmines because they remain unstable and can blow up if disturbed, tampered with or touched. In his remarkable Second World War memoir *Unexploded Bomb*, Major Arthur Bamford Hartley recalls the scramble to deal with the thousands of UXO scattered throughout Britain's cities during the Blitz:

> In many cases unexploded bombs were causing more disruption, delay and public inconvenience than those which went off …. Roads were closed, factories deserted, undamaged homes left empty while their inhabitants joined the flow of evacuees and added to the strain imposed on the relief organizations and essential services.[14]

Caught off guard, the British military scrambled together bomb disposal units with barely trained personnel. Major Hartely remembered the beginning of the war as 'a period of individual prowess when urgency and a lack of knowledge and equipment led to the taking of fantastic risks, to fantastic escapes, and to many, many deaths'.[15] The units would often dig 20 to 30 feet underground and 'when the bomb was exposed the officer alone, having sent the others to safety, descend[ed] the shaft and there, fumbling in mud which swallowed every object he dropped, struggled singly with his monstrous, recalcitrant enemy with nothing but his own cunning, skill and luck to rely on'.[16] Major Hartely pays tribute to the conscientious objectors, who made up around 12 per cent of the British bomb disposal personnel. 'At first', he recalls, 'they were received with very mixed feelings by their fellows in their companies, who often made their hostility plain enough. But … after a short settling down period such prejudice invariably disappeared, chiefly because the objectors were most punctilious about their duties and in general did excellent work.'[17]

Just as the new bomb disposal units figured out how to defuse the munitions, German arms manufacturers innovated anti-handling devices, booby traps that would detonate the bomb if someone tampered with the fuse. Major Hartley describes a complex game of moves and countermoves, as Allied forces hunted for intelligence on Axis fuses to decode each new iteration. Meanwhile, German agents spied on the bomb disposal units, relaying each fix to the engineers inventing new explosive enigmas: 'The only question was would the bomb disposer improve his technique faster than the bomb dispatcher.'[18] A key breakthrough occurred when bomb disposers abandoned their fixation on solving the puzzle of the fuse itself. Many German munitions could be made safer by injecting steam into the shell, liquefying the high-explosive TNT, which drained out through a hole.[19]

Most bombs only caused single explosions. However, cluster munitions – bombs or shells that divide into smaller 'sub-munitions' after being fired – first saw widespread usage in the Second World War. The German butterfly bombs – nicknamed 'Devil's Eggs' by the Luftwaffe – would be released from a canister holding up to around 100 of them. As it fell, the bomblet would unclasp two metal wings, causing it to spin and arm itself. These 'hideous little mobile booby-traps', as Major Hartely called them, were prone to becoming UXO and 'had an extraordinary aptitude for hiding themselves in garden hedges, long grass, and a thousand other places. ... The most dangerous ... were those caught in trees and overhead wires since blast and fragmentation were most effective from such a position.'[20] When dropped in populated areas, butterfly bombs caused many civilian casualties:

> To the populace in their shelters, most of whom were well accustomed to raids, the bombing did not seem particularly heavy. But after the all clear, when people began to emerge into the blackout, the butterflies began to take their toll. Numbers of men and women stumbled against them and were killed or wounded; many were blinded; ambulances ran over bombs lying in the streets and were wrecked; fire engines were damaged and their crews made casualties. ... [T]owns were brought almost to a standstill. Transport and other essential services were checked, shops could not be opened, repairs and rehabilitation were held up and children, among whom there were some terrible accidents, had to be kept at home. [21]

In North Africa, bomb disposal units faced major challenges. Just as on the Home Front, by 1940, the Allied forces had made 'No provision ... for unexploded bombs and no unit capable of coping with them existed' in the Middle East.[22] However, the quantity of 'unexploded bombs in town demanded the utmost efforts', wrote Major Hartely. 'Close packed ... as they often were, Arab and Egyptian dwellings frequently proved particularly susceptible to shock, and even where dwellings of sun-baked mud might have been replaced without much trouble it would have been politically unsound to risk detonations *in situ* among them.[23] The British military cobbled together units with a few specialists brought from the UK and a variety of 'volunteers from different arms of the service'.[24] Major Hartely writes that in North Africa, 'bombs were sterilized, explosive fillings burnt out and fuses dissected by men who were often more or less amateurs. ... the risks were often appalling and casualties were proportionately high; but the survivors learnt fast and passed on their knowledge'.[25] They struggled to deal with Italian ordnance whose 'clockwork fuzes were nightmarishly eccentric'.[26] Flows of technical information and equipment from the UK were stymied by the dangers of shipping in a hostile Mediterranean Sea. Operating over a vast area – 'from Beyrouth to Benghazi' – communications between the bomb disposers in a single company 'were often slow and difficult, and the distribution of vital information about developments in enemy bombs a source of perpetual worry'.[27]

In addition to the logistical and technical challenges, the bomb disposers came under tremendous pressure from the 'insatiable needs of Intelligence'.[28] In the rapid back and forth of desert tank warfare, Allied troops often captured caches of German and Italian munitions – 'valuable specimens' that were analysed to figure out countermeasures for anti-handling devices and time-delay fuses.[29] However, these could only be obtained 'at considerable risk since the enemy ... booby-trapped dumps before vacating them'.[30] As Rommel's forces began to retreat from El Alamein, the Allies' bomb disposers were 'stretched almost beyond capacity. Innumerable mined and booby-trapped areas and installations had to be cleared, and day by day the vast area for which it was responsible increased'.[31] Besides clearing for military purposes, the generals decided it was 'now politically and humanely expedient' to deal with the UXO in civilian areas, particularly when they discovered a 'lively trade in ammunition and explosives' from abandoned ammo dumps.[32] Towards the end of the North Africa campaign, Allied bomb disposal units were 'actually dealing with more British and American bombs than German and Italian ones'. However, Air Force 'security regulations' initially prevented the bomb disposers from knowing much about their own sides' bombs, leading to 'a number of unnecessary accidents'.[33]

After defeating the Axis in North Africa, Allied troops pursued them through the Mediterranean. My grandfather shipped to Italy, where he worked in the frenetic effort to keep tanks running, charging ever northwards. As the German troops retreated, they continued to lay explosive traps – both out of spite and to slow the Allied advance. Rather than using the standardized, 'regular minefields' of the Devil's Garden, they adopted the much more improvisational style of the booby trap and 'nuisance mining'. As a 1943 US Army mine warfare Field Manual put it, the 'effectiveness' of a booby trap is determined by 'ingenuity', not dull, rule following. Derived etymologically from slang for 'fool', the word 'booby' evokes the work of a seedy trickster, not a bureaucratic site plan. In *The English Patient*, a novel set during the Italy campaign, Michael Ondaatje's character Kip calls this the 'joke', the hidden trick that can send you to your grave.[34] Unlike the traditional minefield, which was (at least in theory) supposed to be fenced and marked with warning signs, the Field Manual warns that booby traps 'may be encountered under any circumstances'.[35] An American officer described it as a landscape of unrelenting anxiety, where even seemingly ordinary objects make one insecure:

> Booby traps were planted in bunches of grapes, in fruit and olive trees, in haystacks, at road blocks, among felled trees, along hedges and walls in ravines and valleys, hillsides and terraces, along beds and banks of streams, in tyre or cart tracks along any likely avenue of approach, in possible bivouac areas, in buildings that troops might be expected to enter … . Field glasses, Luger pistols, wallets and pencils were booby trapped as were chocolate bars, soap windows, doors, furniture, toilets, … even bodies of Allied and German civilians and soldiers.[36]

By the Second World War's end, there were an estimated 100 million landmines strewn across Europe and North Africa. In Europe, the governments that had mobilized masses of people and resources for war-making directed their attention to clearing minefields. Tens of thousands of Axis prisoners of war (POWs) were coerced into serving as deminers and the tolerance for casualties was high.[37] In Italy, 1,100 deminers were killed or injured clearing 3 million mines in the year after the war. Within three years, most of the problem in Europe was under control, though remnants remained.[38] The last landmines were cleared from Whitsand Bay in Cornwall, UK, in 1998.[39] However, the warring parties made little effort to clear up the deadly legacy of their minefields in what they saw as the world's peripheries, such as North Africa. Indicative were the racist objections of one Allied soldier who resented the 'enormously difficult and dangerous' work of clearing mines in Tunisia from 'thick bush and scrub that would only be trod on by Arabs and their beasts'.[40]

Grandad Bolton returned to the hills and valleys of northern England a shattered man, consumed by trauma and addiction, with a brittle intolerance of surprises. He calmed himself by tending orchids, listening to orchestral LPs and maintaining a strict routine. I only remember him talking to me about the war once, as a child. I remember less of his words, more that the blood had drained from his face, eyes wide with a fear that remained buried only just below the surface of everyday life.

* * *

Military strategists and self-described 'realists' argue that there is no lasting way out of the minefields we set for ourselves – both literally and metaphorically. We can only learn how to survive inside them by protecting ourselves within ever proliferating rings of defences, hiding within labyrinths of explosive traps, perhaps momentarily blasting our way through for a moment's respite from our enemy's atrocious riddling.[41] Well-intentioned humanitarians at best offer band-aids, and at worst make the situation worse by their naive delusion. However, in each of the above cases – in Bosnia, Iraq and the Second World War's European and North African theatres – there are hints of alternative possibilities. Community organizations, government agencies and the UN continue to manage the human devastation in the Egyptian desert, through demining, victim assistance and risk education programmes. Every year bomb disposal units and demining agencies recover hundreds of tonnes of abandoned and unexploded ordnance from former Second World War battlefields.[42] In Bosnia and Iraq, I have encountered landmine survivors and activists campaigning for a more humane, peaceful and just politics. They successfully persuaded their governments to join the global treaty banning landmines and address the human costs of minefields, UXO and IEDs.[43]

Indeed, belligerents and civilians are not alone on the battlefields and in the minefields. As the swashbuckling Swiss humanitarian and raconteur Dr Marcel Junod put it shortly after the Second World War, 'adversaries are apt to find that suddenly in their midst is a third combatant – a warrior without weapons' – such as the delegates of the International Committee of the Red Cross (ICRC). Imperfectly, often relying on troubling compromise with the warring parties, the ICRC sought to 'intervene on behalf of the victims ... to recall their very existence ... and to make the reality of their sufferings appreciated'.

Their standard was the Red Cross emblem and only weapon was the 'the spirit of the thing' – the 'principle of humanity' animating the dry words of the Geneva Conventions.[44]

After the war, having seen the lives shredded by Second World War mines, UXO and booby traps in their field hospitals, the ICRC promoted changes to the laws of war to limit the humanitarian costs of explosive traps. In the 1949 Geneva Conventions, the ICRC persuaded governments to ban the post-Second World War practice of coercing POWs to do minefield clearance.[45] They also proposed draft rules in the 1950s that would stigmatize using 'weapons with uncontrollable effects', especially those unable to distinguish between civilians and soldiers, including 'delayed-action weapons'. They called for militaries to keep records of the minefields they laid and to hand them over to 'authorities responsible for the safety of the population' at the 'close of active hostilities'.[46] By 1980, many of the world's governments had negotiated a Convention on Certain Conventional Weapons (CCW), regulating weapons that 'may be deemed to be excessively injurious or to have indiscriminate effects'. The CCW's second protocol placed some restrictions on the use of landmines.[47]

Nevertheless, landmines retained a seductive appeal. Critics argue that the new laws of war allowed governments to claim landmines and other explosive traps were legitimate weapons, as long as they were used 'appropriately', 'proportionately' and away from civilian settlements. With superpowers eager to give military aid to their client states and an arms industry able to pump out millions of cheap, lightweight, easily triggered weapons, landmines became ubiquitous and an unrelenting plague in the insurgencies, proxy conflicts and civil wars of the post-Second World War era. Guerillas, irregular forces and terrorists became masters of offensive nuisance mining: ambushing a platoon trudging along a forest path, surprising a supply truck or intimidating civilians whose houses are 'in the wrong place'. Meanwhile, the big military powers figured out how to spray thousands of mines from airplanes and helicopters. Despite being of questionable military utility, governments laid large defensive minefields along the Korean DMZ, the border between East and West Germany and in the Golan Heights.[48]

The human costs have been devastating. From 1999 to 2017 in Afghanistan, Angola, Bosnia, Cambodia, Colombia, Kosovo, Libya, Kashmir, Mozambique, Myanmar, South Sudan and many other conflict zones, there have been more than 120,000 casualties of landmines, UXO and similar victim-activated devices.[49] Minefields prevent refugees and displaced people from returning home. They pose obstacles to farming and the development of infrastructure, block roads and access to markets. Survivors of landmine blasts often struggle to make a living or find medical and psychological care in places with poor health systems. They are often marginalized by prejudices against people with disabilities.

In contrast with the efficient clean-up of Europe after the Second World War, few of the world's governments acknowledged or addressed the suffering of civilians living and working in areas contaminated by landmines and UXO during the Cold War. In the late 1980s and 1990s, non-governmental humanitarian agencies and private security companies developed the capacity to clear minefields themselves, becoming some of the world's most productive deminers and eventually persuading governments to fund them. Methods of clearing landmines and UXO have not changed much since their initial development during and after the Second World War. The development of 'humanitarian demining' in the 1990s has made changes in the process, management style and standards, but there are few major differences in techniques. Nevertheless, humanitarian demining has different purposes to and a lower risk threshold than military minefield breaching (often called 'counter-mining'). When faced with an enemy minefield in the heat of battle – like in the Karbala Gap or Second World War North Africa – the top priority of a military commander is to get through it as quickly as possible while minimizing casualties. With higher standards of safety, humanitarian deminers check and clear every square metre of a suspected hazardous area, aiming for near 100 per cent clearance.

In speaking to deminers around the world, I have learned that one of their pet peeves is the popular media's fixation on high-tech and bizarre demining innovations – everything from rats, bees and remote-controlled robots to air-balloons, radars and genetically modified mustard seeds. Given that importing sensitive, high-tech machines and organisms into mine-affected countries is often prohibitively expensive, deminers tell me that there are few 'quick fixes' to the world's landmine problem. The vast majority of demining programmes use a combination of low-tech techniques, by choice. The best detectors of landmines remain well-trained human deminers, dressed in protective gear, armed with a prodder and/or trowel, excavating the ground along a predetermined 'lane', carefully ensuring that they poke mines from an angle that will not detonate them. When deminers come upon a landmine, it is removed, defused or destroyed in situ. When deminers know that the mines used in a particular area have metal parts, and the surrounding earth is not too metallic, they may also use metal detectors to facilitate their work. New, high-tech hand-held detectors combine metal detectors with ground-penetrating radar, which increases the accuracy of the signals. Working in combination, along lanes safely spaced from each other, the deminers check every single square metre of the minefield. Demining agencies also often train dogs to sniff out and locate explosives, though within the demining industry there is some debate about how best to use them. The dogs are rarely heavy enough to initiate mines and so can sit on or near the mine to show their handler where to excavate. Inventors have developed a variety of machines to assist in the demining process, clearing vegetation, flailing the ground to explode mines or using radar and aerial photography to aid minefield survey. But, as yet, no machines have been able to match the accuracy and care of a good human deminer and so mechanical clearance methods are combined with other techniques.[50]

Between 1999 and 2017, demining agencies around the world had cleared almost 2,300 square kilometres of mined land in addition to a much larger area of former battle zones contaminated by UXO – an area more than 'twice the size of London'. Clearance efforts have secured, removed and destroyed almost 3.9 million anti-personnel landmines, 343,000 anti-vehicle landmines and millions of UXO. Since 1992, government and private donors have invested almost $7.4 billion in 'mine action' – efforts to manage the risk of landmines and other UXO through education, stockpile destruction, data gathering, advocacy, survivor assistance and clearance.[51] Unlike after the Second World War, when demining was solely a governmental matter, the mine action system is a complex, privatized and global system, comprising the UN, foreign aid donors, NGOs, commercial companies and local community organizations.

However, not everyone has been satisfied with clearing up landmines and UXO after the fact. Founded in 1992, the International Campaign to Ban Landmines (ICBL) mobilized a global network of survivors, human rights activists, faith groups and radical political organizations calling attention to the brutal and indiscriminate human costs of landmines. In contrast with earlier attempts to 'regulate' their use, the ICBL demanded that governments treat landmines like biological and chemical weapons. In the international laws of war, these weapons of mass destruction are considered such pariahs, so menacing to humanity, that they are declared *mala in se* (literally 'evil in themselves'). The campaign was adept at capturing the attention of the global news media, as shocking images of landmine injuries contrasted with the endorsements of celebrities like Princess Diana and moral authorities like Archbishop

Desmond Tutu. The ICBL found allies among diplomats of smaller countries who were eager to use the post-Cold War political opening to build a more humane and peaceful international order.

By the end of 1997, 122 governments gathered in Ottawa, Canada, to sign the Anti-personnel Landmine Ban Treaty, which prohibited the use, stockpiling, production and transfer of devices 'designed to be exploded by the presence, proximity or contact of a person and that will incapacitate, injure or kill one or more persons'.[52] The treaty negotiations were radically different from more traditional arms control talks. They were open to landmine survivors and ICBL activists and explicitly framed around humanitarian and human rights concerns. This new approach to international law on weapons was reflected in the text, which also obligated governments to clear all the world's minefields and 'provide assistance for the care and rehabilitation, and social and economic reintegration, of mine victims and for mine awareness programs'.[53] The ICBL and its coordinator Jody Williams were jointly awarded the Nobel Peace Prize in 1997 for demonstrating new possibilities for global advocacy and diplomacy against violence.

The success of the 'Ottawa Process', as it was called, has inspired similar campaigns to ban other automated and inhumane weapons. In 2008, the Cluster Munition Coalition successfully persuaded more than 100 governments to negotiate a Convention on Cluster Munitions that banned cluster bombs, obligated assistance to victims and clearance of unexploded bomblets from former strike sites. In 2017, at the urging of the International Campaign to Abolish Nuclear Weapons (ICAN), a conference of the UN General Assembly agreed to a treaty banning nuclear weapons that also included provisions on victim assistance and environmental remediation. In each of these cases, major military powers have boycotted or stymied the proceedings and refused to sign resulting agreements. However, the treaties have had a stigmatizing effect on the weapons they banned, as non-signatory governments have shifted their policies to align closer to the global norms and have given assistance to survivors, deminers and risk educators. Many of the people involved in these successful advocacy efforts are now working with the Campaign to Stop Killer Robots, aiming to achieve an international ban on autonomous robotic weapons systems that fail to maintain meaningful human control over the use of violence.

* * *

This book is a political history of explosive traps – landmines, booby traps, UXO, IEDs, automated bombing systems and killer robots. Listening to survivors, deminers, humanitarians, soldiers, mercenaries, activists and diplomats, I will tell you stories of people affected by the explosive legacies of war through a sort of travelogue through the world's minefields and UXO dumps. As an aid worker in Bosnia and Iraq in the early 2000s, I lived in mine-affected communities and began working with humanitarian efforts to address the impact of the minefields surrounding me. Later, in my graduate studies in political science and work as an academic, I conducted additional fieldwork in Afghanistan, Bosnia, Cambodia, Croatia, Kenya, Laos, Sudan, South Sudan and Vietnam.

As a white man in countries where my forebears did tremendous damage as colonizers, I recognize my presence has not been unambiguously helpful. Privileges of gender, nationalities, class, race and sexual orientation have shielded me from direct experience of the violence I write about here. But I have tried to listen carefully to those who know their own contexts, interviewing a couple hundred people employed in landmine and UXO clearance and related programmes, consulting relevant local archives and visiting demining projects. I've also been a participant observer in global policymaking processes at the UN on a variety of disarmament and arms control issues, including landmines, cluster munitions, the arms trade, killer robots and, most recently, with the 2017 Nobel Prize-winning campaign to ban nuclear weapons. I am lucky to work closely in this advocacy with my spouse, Dr Emily Welty, a peace studies scholar and vice-moderator of the World Council of Churches' Commission on International Affairs, whose expertise expands and challenges my understanding of these processes and the places we visit. Nevertheless, this book is not exhaustive and there are important parts of the story of landmines that I have not covered in depth here, including the role of mines in the Arab–Israeli wars, or the extensive use of IEDs by ISIS. This is because I have focused on those areas of the world where I have done field research in person and campaigns which I have personally observed at work.

Academic readers of this book might be surprised by my occasional use of first-person narrative. I use the genre of travelogue to introduce more general readers to scholarly thinking about war and humanitarianism. But, like many new writers in the field of international relations, I seek to encourage academics to connect with the human reality of the societies they are describing.[54] This includes not hiding behind the mask of the third person. I am writing this book because I care about the impact of landmines in the communities I have visited. I do not pretend to be objective, nor separate from the stories I share. My narrative is also political – all narratives are – taking the side of those affected by automated violence. I support efforts to ban inhumane weapons, remediate the harm they have done and assist victims. At times I will be particularly critical of the United States and Britain. This is not to suggest that the United States and United Kingdom are somehow worse than other military powers. But because I am a citizen of these two counties, I feel I have a responsibility to hold them to their rhetoric of democracy, humanity and the rule of law.

In my journeys, I have found that the violent enigma of the minefield can rarely be separated from complexities that trap those who, in aiming to clear landmines, fail to perceive the political minefields in which they are embedded. The landmine is not just a technical device passively placed or displaced at will. 'Infernal machines', as journalists in the US Civil War called early landmines, are always embedded in social, economic and cultural systems of violence. The mine does what scholars call 'discursive work' – even as it is being removed – shaping the terrain and context that surrounds it. Landmines enact a view of the world in which a victim is condemned to death simply by having triggered a tripwire or matched a 'target signature'; no chance for mercy, forbearance or discrimination. Efforts to mitigate their human impact – or clear them away altogether – falter when they lack an appreciation of the complexities of the social systems of violence – 'meta-minefields' – which have produced, planted, sustained and maintained the minefields.

The chapters that follow trace efforts to deploy and destroy technologies of disembodied violence from the Cold War to the present, aiming to answer an underlying question: *How do we free ourselves from the trap of automated killing?* Organized both chronologically and geographically, they advance around the world and through time to give the reader a sense of the continuity, change and scope of the problem from the 1960s to the present. Most chapters begin with a focus on a representative device (cluster munitions, landmines, UXO and killer robots), which is treated as an artefact of a violent context whose drama is unveiled through reportage, historical background and political analysis.

In the next chapter, I narrate the problems faced by American troops who tried to impose an external order on the Indochina region (Vietnam, Laos and Cambodia) in the 1960s and early 1970s. Guerillas' use of landmines and booby traps belaboured US soldiers' movements and created an environment of pervasive anxiety. In reaction, the Pentagon attempted to enclose the region into an 'electronic battlefield', aiming to automatically identify and engage targets, often with cluster munitions. This fantasy of remote control caused tremendous humanitarian harm; dud cluster bomblets – *bombies* as they are called in Laos – continue to maim and kill today. But there were American peace activists and humanitarian workers who refused to reduce Vietnamese and Lao people to pixels and bombing coordinates. They campaigned to stop the automated air war, aided victims and established the foundations of today's UXO clearance programmes and advocacy for the Convention on Cluster Munitions. More recently, Lao-Americans – refugees and their descendants – have successfully persuaded the US government to take increasing responsibility for addressing the harm caused by cluster munitions in Laos.

Acknowledgement of the devastation of the wars in Indochina and the Middle East prompted a Cold War détente, but this lull in hostilities did not last long. During the 1980s, following the Soviet invasion of Afghanistan and US president Ronald Reagan's reassertion of American military power, the superpowers sponsored a series of 'proxy wars' in what they dismissed as a peripheral 'Third World'. The borderlands between Soviet and American client states became clogged with minefields, injuring and killing thousands of civilians, especially when conflicts ended and refugees returned home. Chapter 3 looks closely at the impact of this humanitarian crisis in Cambodia, the result of treating people as proxies. Indicative of this attitude was the Khmer Rouge's description of landmines as 'perfect soldiers'; obedient and literally anti-personnel. However, landmine survivors, Catholic nuns and Buddhist monks – motivated by a profound conviction that people are inherently sacred – initiated a national movement against mines that catalysed the global campaign for the landmine ban. The resulting stigma against anti-personnel landmines has been remarkably persuasive, even changing the behaviour of superpowers.

The 1997 treaty's obligation to clear the world's minefields channelled billions of dollars of investment in humanitarian demining. However, this money flowed into regions often torn by the 'New Wars' of the 1990s, areas facing a post-Cold War fragmentation of state authority, domination by political–criminal networks and ethno-nationalist violence. Meanwhile, a global network of private security firms offered protection from landmines to the highest bidder. Some of them were very good at demining; they were efficient, safe and professional. Others, in the interest of the bottom line, cut corners, failing to protect their workers and skimmed taxpayer money. At times, these were the very companies that had manufactured landmines. In 'getting the job done', commercial deminers have often cut deals with armed groups and criminals to gain protection, access to labour and supplies. Chapter 4 explores the unexpected pitfalls faced by demining programmes in Bosnia, which became embroiled in the politics of the conflict. Government foreign aid donors, in thrall to a privatizing trend, contracted out landmine clearance to demining companies. This resulted in an ethnically polarized sector, stalked by allegations of graft and low standards. While many expatriate aid workers depicted this as the result of a uniquely Bosnian social pathologies, there were international demining companies that profited from doing business in this environment. They exacerbated the political tendencies that produced Bosnia's landmine crisis in the first place. Nevertheless, those donors who pulled funding and wrote off the whole sector as irredeemably corrupt overlooked the work of both local and international agencies that tried to move mine action from paramilitary profiteering to something more developmental, gender-equitable and inclusive.

This more humanitarian approach to clearing UXO was endangered, however, by the traumas of the 'War on Terror'. In Afghanistan, where the UN and demining NGOs had cultivated a cosmopolitan ethos of service, intervening US forces brought with them a different approach. Threatened by the extensive availability of UXO and abandoned munitions – which insurgents repurposed into IEDs – the United States gave millions of dollars to private security companies to dispose of munitions and demine military bases. I describe in Chapter 5 how these contractors, armed and engaging in behaviour that scandalized the local population, eroded respect for demining as a non-violent act of charity. They helped shape post-9/11 Afghanistan into an archipelago of walled 'green zones'. Inside these radically privatized enclaves, expats and the privileged elite were safe from landmines and UXO. Outside, local people remained profoundly vulnerable to the dangers of Afghanistan's explosive detritus. Humanitarian deminers, left unprotected, suffered from a terrorist backlash and ubiquitous criminality.

I would be remiss if this book ended up as uncritical propaganda for the humanitarian and human rights approaches to mine action. Mine action programmes, typically controlled by international staff on fixed-term contracts, have often found their work fraught with misunderstandings. Chapter 6 examines how in Sudan and South Sudan, UN and NGO demining projects struggled to perceive the boundaries between safe and unsafe land. In an emerging context that some have called 'Everywhere War', all moments, all roads, seemed like potential explosive traps, haunted by the possibility of killing. As the UN peacekeeping mission deployed following a 2005 peace agreement between the Sudanese government and South Sudanese rebels, they erred on the side of caution. Early UN maps overrepresented the extent of the mine contamination on major roads, which may have stymied already marginalized communities' access to aid. Technocratic minefield surveys suggested a level of precision that demining agencies lacked when they sought to define the edges of insecurity. The kind of abstraction that turned minefields into GPS points was not always combined with rigorous analysis of their social, cultural, economic and political dimensions. Demining programmes sometimes found themselves complicit in the political structures responsible for the violence. That said, when they paid close and careful attention to contextual factors, humanitarian mine action agencies were able to have a modest but nonetheless positive impact, building peace and alleviating the profound anxieties of 'Everywhere War'.

I have found that when talking about landmines to people in the world's more comfortable places of North America and Western Europe, they engage in a subtle psychic distancing. It is less unsettling to think about automated violence when it is seen as something that happens 'Over There' either to bad people who deserve it or to poor benighted 'women and children' to be saved by our philanthropy. But explosive traps linger in unexpected places, from the estimated 15,000 unexploded anti-aircraft munitions lying submerged in the New York Harbor to automated nuclear missile systems that once surrounded the city, part of the global trap of mutually assured destruction. And coercive technologies and techniques used by governments to control people in areas they consider the world's peripheries have a tendency to 'boomerang' back into the metropolitan core. Chapter 7 considers how high-tech remote and autonomous weaponry are replacing traditional landmines in the arsenals of industrialized countries. At the cutting edge of weapons development, there is an emerging class of robots that act autonomously, identifying 'enemy targets' and delivering a violent response without human approval. These killer robots are the landmines of the digital, globalized, mobile future, with weaponized networks extending a deadly trap throughout the earth, cyberspace and outer space. Critical computer scientists – 'robotic refuseniks' – have refused military funding and joined forces with philosophers, lawyers, social scientists and human rights activists to launch a Campaign to Stop Killer Robots, aiming to prevent a future of unconstrained digital warfare. But the success of disarmament campaigners in prohibiting several categories of inhumane weapons faces new political challenges as they seek to ban ever more complex manifestations of violence, including revival of lower-tech methods of slaughter in Syria, Yemen, Somalia and beyond.

I conclude with an epilogue, reflecting on the successful conclusion of the 2017 UN conference that negotiated a treaty banning nuclear weapons. Setsuko Thurlow, a survivor of the Hiroshima atomic bombing, reminded the conference of their obligation to the victims of nuclear violence. 'Each person who died' in the atomic bombings, she declared, 'had a name. Each person was loved by someone.'[55] She decided to speak out, she has said, because 'those who survived became convinced that no human being should ever have to experience the inhumanity and unspeakable suffering of nuclear weapons.'[56] Later that year, Thurlow received the 2017 Nobel Peace Prize on behalf of the International Campaign to Abolish Nuclear Weapons (ICAN), along with its executive director, Beatrice Fihn. Sitting in the audience in Oslo, I reflected on the underestimated possibility for agency in a world of explosive traps. I am inspired most by those who have survived indiscriminate violence and have dedicated their lives to mitigating and resisting it. Their witness demands our solidarity.

'Solving' the problem of explosive traps requires a commitment to a great humbling, putting the voices of those most affected by violence at the centre of the conversation, refusing to be complicit in sustaining the regime of perplexing violence, refusing to hide behind masks of 'objectivity'. We cannot defuse political minefields with force, manipulation, the profit motive, technological wizardry or even charity. In *Oedipus the King*, the answer to the Sphinx's riddle was '*anthropos*' – the human being. There is no quick fix, but the way out of the riddle starts with a recognition of our shared humanity with the Other, those people on the opposite side of the minefield, those cowering under a barrage of cluster bombs, those with whom we have mutually assured destruction, those flickering data points on the drone operator's screen.

Chapter 2

BOMBIES
AUTOMATED AIR WAR, LAOS

Lao People's Democratic Republic

'Turn off any electronic devices,' one of the MAG Community Liaison Officers (CLOs) instructed me and waited as I shut down my phone. After a couple hours with the MAG Lao team, I am learning a fastidious observance of Standard Operating Procedures. I am not to smoke and only take photos after asking permission. Getting into the vehicle after a stop, my guide pauses after inserting the key in the ignition, looking me in the eye as he waits for the click of my seatbelt. MAG – Mines Advisory Group International – is one of the oldest NGOs specializing in landmine and UXO clearance and has been working in Laos since 1994, funded by the United States, other governments and private donations.

'We will walk in single file, 10 meters apart,' the CLO, continued. 'If you see a device, stop and notify us. If at any point you feel uncomfortable, let us know and we will escort you back to the car.'

At that, a villager started down the hill, showing us the way.

For this farmer, the Vietnam War is not over. Nor was it contained to Vietnam. Shortly before we visited him, he found an unexploded cluster bomblet next to his new cattle stable, only 50 metres from a primary school and 100 metres from the road. This small village is not far from Phonsavan, the new capital of the Xiangkhouang province in the Lao People's Democratic Republic. Xiangkhouang has the dubious distinction of being one of the most intensely bombed regions on the planet, as the Americans tried to eradicate the communist Pathet Lao rebels. The guerillas eventually won, toppling a superpower-backed government in 1975. Phonsavan was built to replace Xiangkhouang town, which was levelled by US warplanes during what the CIA called the 'Other War' – an addendum to the Vietnam War, kept secret from the American public.

To get to the village, our white truck – MAG skull and crossbones logo, Lao and US flags decaled on the doors – left Phonsavan and passed Plain of Jars Sites 2 and 3, where ancient stone vessels lie scattered across the hills. Rounding a corner, I notice a sign to 'Spoon Village', where artisans melt down old ordnance and craft cutlery for the locals and key rings for the tourists. We are not far from Long Cheng, the former base of the CIA's proxy army recruited from the Hmong, a marginalized upland people. Given their clandestine collaboration with the Americans in the 1960s and 1970s, the post-war experience has been a gruelling one for many Hmong people: escape, refugee camps, exile or persecution in post-revolutionary Laos. My guide, a MAG staff member who is Hmong himself, tells me that we can't get much closer to the former base than where we are, even though it is populated and heavily impacted by UXO. Though welcoming MAG's work, the communist government remains nervous about a US government-funded organization searching for explosives in a former nexus of covert action.

We turn off the paved road and onto a bumpy dirt lane bisecting a village. The sides are lined with bamboo fences, electrical cables, grazing cattle and thatched stables. Beyond the homesteads, a ring of mountains is laddered with rice terraces. Two small boys wave to our vehicle as we park in front of a young man and woman, both in dark blue fatigues with MAG patches. They stand by identical red Honda scooters in front of a wooden house with an iron sheet roof. The young man has two pens peeking above his breast pocket, a long knife on his belt. The woman carries a notebook; a silver necklace dresses up her uniform. Introductions extended beyond the conventional niceties to my blood type – 'O Positive' – and my allergies – 'Amoxicillin but not other antibiotics' – radioed to MAG's base back in Phonsavan. The man and woman are both MAG CLOs, visiting villages in the rural areas of Xiangkhouang and conducting 'Non-Technical Survey'. They speak with local people, asking them if they have seen UXO or know about areas considered risky. As I gave my sanguinary particulars to the CLOs, the farmer came out of the house, greeting us with a *nop*, hands together as if in prayer just below the chin, a slight bow. He wished us good health – '*Sabadee!*' – and explained that he had found the *bombie* – a cluster munition bomblet – while tending cattle in his new barn.

The farmer's grey hoodie bounced up and down his back as he paced down the hill. We all waited in single file, while one of the CLOs regulated our spacing. She held her arm in front of her colleague until the farmer had gone ten steps. Lowering her hand with a quick nod she allowed him forward, but raised her arm again for the next in line. I fidgeted while waiting my turn until, satisfied, she alerted me; 'OK, go.' I had to keep my loping 6'5"stride in check to maintain my distance. At the bottom of the hill, we crossed into a meadow. Off to our left was a small primary school, chattering voices repeating an adult's calm tones. The school was about a decade old, with one teacher serving ten first- and second-year students. A water pump stood in the yard, shaded by a leafy tree, and a latrine block in the far corner. Our group turned to the right. As we neared the farmer's shiny-roofed stable on the rise of the next hill, I was instructed to stop in place. One CLO advanced up the hill, part of the way with the farmer, the rest of the way by himself, stopping at the corner of the stable. Cutting the surrounding undergrowth and pushing branches into the earth around an unseen object, he strung them with red and white tape. Extracting aerosol paint from his bag, he shook the can and sprayed the area red. The wind carried the tang of paint. He then engrossed his attention in gadgets, taking a GPS reading and a digital photograph. Meanwhile, the other CLO interviewed the farmer, writing careful notes in her pad. His old stable had stood not far from where we were standing. A couple months ago he had moved his cattle to the new spot.

Returning to our group, the paint-toting CLO offered to take me up to the stable to see the bomblet. As we scramble through the brush, my heart quickens and I catch myself gulping. He brings me close to the newly marked off area and gestures with pride to its centre. My eyes scan back and forth. I see red paint. I can see twigs and dirt. A piece of string. Some weeds; a purple wildflower. I stare harder. He watches me. 'Can you see it?' he asks. I can't. I feel disappointed and a little silly. Inadequate perhaps. Baffled. 'Yes, yes,' I lie, 'there, right?' I gesture vaguely.

Despite having researched landmines and UXO for fifteen years, I am not a deminer, nor have I ever been a solider. I have never had to suffer personally the impact of a bombie. I pull myself out of this hand-wringing moment, to remind myself that this is not about me; in my desire for the climactic reveal, I feel like the inconvenient war tourist I probably am. I ask if I can snap a few photos, hoping I will see the device when I can zoom in later on my computer (in the end, I still won't be able to see the bombie – it is invisible to my untrained eye).

We turn and head back up the road to the village. One CLO brings up the rear, spray painting 'benchmarks' on fence posts so that one of Roving EOD Teams will later be able to retrace our path and find the device. Back at the farmer's house, the CLOs inform me that I can now switch my phone back on, and should I like to, have a smoke. One of the CLOs tells me that she originally trained as a teacher in Phonsavan. While her family worries about her safety, she sees her work 'as a kind of charity. I am happy to make it safe for the community'. She likes to 'be the one who tells people they can build a better life' once the bombies are cleared. The morning had started out cold and foggy but now, 11 am, it is getting hot. Though the CLOs answer my questions patiently, they are starting to sweat. We bid them goodbye and hop back in the truck. I now know to fasten my seatbelt without dawdling.

The CLOs later fill out a six-page 'Dangerous Area Report' including information about the village, the location of the device, surrounding vegetation, a sketch map and the type of bombie. In attached photographs the bombie is marked clearly. Rusted, the device is the same colour as the earth in which it is three-quarters buried. A tell-tale ridge rises along a small, smooth sphere: it is a BLU-63. The BLU-63, a MAG supervisor told me as we drive to a restaurant for lunch of *pho* (Vietnamese beef noodle soup), is one of 'the most dangerous pieces of UXO and can kill people up to 25 meters away if it explodes'. Filing the report, MAG's Data Officer in Phonsavan coded it as an urgent task – given the proximity to the school, road and stable. Three days later, a MAG team retraced the benchmarks left by the CLOs. They protected the stable with sandbags, and put 100 grams of C4 plastic explosives on top of the device, inserting a detonator. After evacuating the village, they blew up the BLU-63. MAG Technical Surveyors would then return to the village to gauge whether the bombie was part of a broader pattern of contamination requiring more systematic clearance.

* * *

BLU-63 cluster munitions are 'about the size of baseballs', according to a 1972 US General Accounting Office report.[1] BLU stands for 'Bomb, Live, Unit'. They are made by enclosing an explosive charge and a fuse between two steel hemispheres. On the outside, the shell looks smooth, with 'aerodynamic flutes which catch the airstream to spin the bomblet', causing it to arm. Internally, the shell has been scored in a latitude/longitude grid to make it explode into more than 200 deadly fragments. The BLU-63 that the farmer found next to his stable would have been dropped in a 'dispenser', along with 649 others, from an airplane.[2] As it fell towards the earth, the dispenser – probably a CBU (Cluster Bomb Unit) 58/B – broke in half, spraying out its deadly cargo.

At the time of its descent, the BLU-63 now rusting half-submerged in the dirt of the village was at the cutting edge of lethal technology, representing a revolution in projecting explosive force through space and time. Most Second World War bombs were singular, unitary devices. They were dropped from a plane and usually exploded on impact with the ground. While they were certainly deadly, they only posed a danger to people in the immediate vicinity of the blast. By the 1960s, however, a single projectile – an air-dropped bomb, artillery shell or rocket – could separate into many smaller submunitions, each capable of dividing into hundreds of fragments. Dropping a CBU-58/B saturated an area with over an area with more than 600 explosions and sprayed a haze of almost 150,000 pieces of steel shrapnel.[3] This 'wide area effect' was more like a shotgun than a sniper rifle and had devastating 'collateral damage' on civilians and infrastructure in the vicinity of a cluster munition strike. But cluster munitions offered the illusive promise of projecting American power into new places without deploying actual American people there.[4] Cold War US and Soviet weapons engineers also stretched the explosive fourth dimension by delaying detonation. Vietnam War-era US 'scatterable mines' could lay in wait until initiated by a passer-by – whether soldier or civilian – years or decades into the future. Cluster munition strikes also left behind dangerously unstable unexploded 'dud' bomblets that acted like de facto landmines, capable of causing horrific injury or death if disturbed by a future user of the land. This meant the United States was able to render significant areas of Vietnam, Cambodia and Laos perilous for decades to come.

The US Air Force used the conflicts in Southeast Asia as an opportunity to test new ordnance; many of these innovations had unusually high dud rates.[5] The explosive deluge was particularly horrific in Laos. Between 1964 and 1973, the US military dropped more than 2 million tonnes of bombs on Laos – an average of one 'planeload of bombs' on Laos 'every eight minutes'[6] – more than it dropped in all Second World War theatres.[7] The 'heaviest aerial bombardment in history'[8] was kept secret even from Congress until 1970,[9] with officials issuing denials 'as village after village was leveled, countless people buried alive by high explosives, or burnt alive by napalm and white phosphorous, or riddled by anti-personnel bomb pellets'.[10] The vast majority of victims of the bombing – as many as 80 per cent – were civilians.[11] This was no accident. A 1972 Cornell University study on *The Air War in Indochina* asserted that classified US military documents described 'bombing civilian villages in communist-held areas "to deprive the enemy of the population resource"'.[12] 'The solution', to the inability of the US military to ferret out the illusive rebels in South Vietnam, Cambodia and Laos, opined one commanding US general, was 'more bombs, more shells, more napalm … till the other side cracks and gives up'.[13] The Joint Chiefs of Staff even drew up plans, thankfully never implemented, to use tactical nuclear weapons.[14] A comment by General William Westmoreland, commander of US forces in Vietnam, aptly sums up the US military's disregard for civilian lives in Indochina: 'Life is cheap in the Orient'.[15]

*   *   *

The Xiangkhouang Plateau in northern Laos, which was the stronghold of the Pathet Lao, is scattered with enormous ancient stone vessels, baffling archaeologists and intriguing tourists.[16] But now the lively local mythology of mystery, danger and romance associated with the Jars coexists with the modern tragedy of 'bombies', as Lao people call the unexploded submunitions. It is one of the most cluster munition-contaminated regions of the world. After interviewing people displaced from the Plain of Jars, a UN adviser wrote in 1971 that 'the intensity of the bombings was such that no organized life was possible in the villages. … Nothing was left standing. The villagers lived in trenches and holes or in caves. They only farmed at night. … [B]ombings were aimed at the systematic destruction of the material basis of the civilian society'.[17] A US Information Service survey of more than 200 people displaced from the Plain found that 97 per cent of them 'had seen a bombing attack' and 75 per cent said their 'homes had been damaged'.[18] By 1971, the per capita cost of bombing the country was more than 'eight times Laos' estimated per capita income' and was 'roughly twenty-eight times more' than US 'economic aid to the country'.[19]

The indiscriminate bloodletting did not end with the US withdrawal from Indochina. About 30 per cent of cluster munitions failed to explode, remaining scattered throughout the landscape.[20] After the war, the UN estimated that Laos remained contaminated by about 500,000 tonnes of UXO. An aid worker who observed the early post-war period told me, 'Almost every week children playing and farmers working in their fields accidently detonated explosives. As I walked in isolated, rural areas, setting up rehabilitation projects, amputees were a common sight.' By 2017, unexploded munitions had caused over 50,700 casualties in Laos, 20,000 of which occurred after the war ended in 1974.[21] Millions of dud cluster bomblets – metal balls small enough to fit in the palm of one's hand but powerful enough to kill – lay strewn across farmers' fields, roads and people's homes. A quarter of the villages in Laos are contaminated with UXO, stunting agricultural productivity and infrastructure development. Local and international agencies are still clearing tens of thousands of bombies every year.[22]

In the Lao capital, Vientiane, the Cooperative Orthotic and Prosthetic Enterprise (COPE) provides medical rehabilitation to survivors of bombie accidents and other persons with disabilities, both in Vientiane and in clinics and extension programmes throughout the country. Its visitor's centre is in all the guide books and attracts a steady stream of tourists – more than 17,000 a year. They come to learn about the impact of bombies and the challenges of living with disabilities in Laos and beyond. Immediately inside the entrance a CBU shell, breaking apart, is suspended from the ceiling. Hanging from almost invisible wire, hundreds of 'bombies' seem to cascade around you. It is unnerving. A small sign alerts you that these bombies are made from plaster by staff of the medical rehabilitation centre.

After walking through the exhibits, I sat outside in the sun with COPE staff. They tell me that COPE supports some 1,000 patients a year, a third of whom are survivors of UXO accidents. They provide prosthetics and also accommodation and travel since many survivors live in poor, rural communities with little access to health services. Physical rehabilitation is not enough. Survivors need help, they told me, battling the 'mindset of despair'. Struggling against stigma, many survivors 'feel very lonely'. Some worry about whether they did something bad in a past life. Survivors who were already poor before their accident lose income and face a host of new expenses, living, as they put it, 'hand-to-mouth'. COPE aims to encourage survivors that though 'you lost a limb, your life is not over'. But even as the bombie accident rate has 'gone down dramatically', there are still thousands of people who need regular replacements of prosthetics and long-term care. Unfortunately, the staff said, 'very few people in the world know about cluster munitions in Laos and the situation faced by people with disabilities. People should learn more about Laos and do something to support them.'[23]

* * *

The United States was drawn into the conflicts in Southeast Asia by a view of the world as a geopolitical contest. American foreign policy elite saw Vietnam, Laos and Cambodia, newly independent from France, as potential 'dominoes' that could fall to Soviet communism, with a knock-on effect across Asia, even the world. Initially, it was Laos that the United States was most concerned about. President John F. Kennedy asserted at a news conference in 1961 that while 'Laos is far away from America … the world is small' and the 'security of all Southeast Asia will be endangered' if Laos became communist.[24] As an authorized history of the CIA's involvement in Laos put it (apparently without self-awareness), 'The country had little intrinsic value', however, 'its geographical position placed it at the center of the Cold War'.[25]

But Laos, Cambodia and Vietnam were not singular 'pieces' in a global great game – they were complex societies, with histories, cultures and political ambitions. In reviewing US government documents from the time, Walt Haney, an academic and former aid worker in Laos, reflected that, 'one is left with the single overwhelming impression: that to U.S. policymakers, the *people* of Laos, the *people* of Indochina never mattered'.[26] As the United States became further drawn into supporting its puppet regime in South Vietnam, they found people resistant to being used as pawns in Cold War machinations. Unable to beat the United States head-to-head, the Vietnamese communists fought a guerilla insurgency, remaining mobile, hidden, dispersed. The South Vietnamese rebels were supplied by a continuously shape-shifting series of pathways – nicknamed the 'Ho Chi Minh Trail' – running south from communist North Vietnam through the borderlands of Laos and Cambodia, just beyond the reach of the South Vietnamese government and American soldiers. Throughout the war, the United States struggled to comprehend both the people it was fighting against and even those it claimed to be fighting for.

Landmines and booby traps were well suited to the insurgency. Cheap to deploy and difficult to detect, they were a subterranean, invisible enemy, generating unremitting anxiety for American soldiers. Vietnamese guerillas laid mines on crucial supply routes; deployed improvised grenade traps on jungle pathways; rigged gates, 'innocent looking souvenir[s]', their own flags and C-ration cans with tripwires. They even weaponized bicycles that detonated when moved. To add insult to injury, '16 per cent of Viet Cong mines…located by US troops had been lifted from US minefields. … The Viet Cong essentially used [US] minefields as ordnance depots'.[27] In what might serve as a description for America's missteps in Indochina, a 1967 US military manual on Vietnamese mine warfare chides 'inexperienced observers' who assume the guerillas' landmine 'techniques are haphazard and ineffective'. This 'completely erroneous' condescension led US soldiers into 'a false sense of security and tactical errors'. The 'facts of the matter', the manual asserts, 'are that the Viet Cong know what they are doing in mine warfare, and they do it well'. While they did not lay mines according to the 'standard pattern' American soldiers expected, the guerillas' surprising behaviour was precisely what made them so deadly.[28] As the literary theorist and Vietnam veteran Herman Rapaport put it, while the communist guerillas 'avoid direct, head-on contact … at the trap they are devastating'.[29] The very lack of climax or clear resolution to combat left American forces in disarray. After the mine blast, there is no one to shoot at; 'the trail is cold, the "other" has disappeared without a sound', leaving the GIs 'bound by the moebius strip' of an indistinct 'zone of violence which has no borders'.[30]

The Americans felt trapped, like a 'giant without eyes', unable to find what General Westmoreland called an 'elusive and cunning' enemy.[31] The US military was corroding from the pressure and faced widespread dissatisfaction at home. As Michael Herr wrote in his *Dispatches*, 'You could be in the most protected space in Vietnam and still know that your safety was provisional, that early death … could come in on the freakyfluky as easily as in the so-called expected ways.' Even the '*trees* would kill you, the elephant grass grew up homicidal, the ground you were walking over possessed malignant intelligence'.[32] Declassified US documents suggest that more than 65 per cent of the US Marines' casualties in Vietnam in 1965 were caused by mines and booby traps;[33] over the course of the war, mines caused 70 per cent of US 'vehicle casualties' and 30 per cent of 'personnel casualties'.[34] General Norman Schwarzkopf concluded that this experience of living in fear meant US soldiers were 'so demoralized by landmines and booby traps that they had lost the will to fight'.[35] The Pentagon hunted for methods to maintain control while physically disengaging from Southeast Asian society and terrain. US Army General Ellis Williamson explained, 'We are making unusual efforts to avoid having the American young man stand toe-to-toe, eyeball-to-eyeball, or even rifle-to-rifle against an enemy. … How less painful it is to use firepower to fight him at a distance.'[36]

In Laos, this desire for disembodied control motivated US covert support to Hmong militias, supported by Thai paramilitaries. But the reach of the Hmong militias was limited to the northern highlands. The United States was more concerned about the constant infiltration of supplies and fighters along the Ho Chi Minh Trail. It also needed to protect a Tactical Air Navigation transponder – Lima Site 85 – at Phou Pha Thi, which guided US bombers flying to North Vietnam.[37] However, the Trail – and the Pathet Lao – rarely offered obvious targets. Lao and Vietnamese guerillas had few fixed bases, were able to move in small groups, often on foot or in civilian vehicles. They provisioned from the society around them, avoiding long supply chains. And for much of the bombardment of Laos, the US targeting process was as unsophisticated as it was high-tech. Planes that were unable to drop their payload on North Vietnam – because of weather or other hostile conditions – would just dump it somewhere in Laos. It was considered easier than landing with their bombs still attached.[38] When, in 1968, President Johnson announced a halt in the bombing of North Vietnam, the excess capacity was merely diverted to Laos; one American official said, 'We couldn't just let the planes rust.'[39] This created a glut of bombers available to US war planners: 'There weren't enough targets to go around. The jets went into holding patterns, like passenger planes over a busy airport, circling and circling.'[40] Increasing the volume of bombing, the United States also reduced restrictions on protecting civilians and the town of Xiangkhouang was completely destroyed.[41] The secrecy of this 'Other War' attracted American soldiers, spies and mercenaries who disliked the 'bureaucratic' strictures in Vietnam – they longed for a more freewheeling war, in which they could fight without oversight from lawyers and policymakers.[42] Unsurprisingly, the heavy bombing did little to help US interests in Laos. The Pathet Lao remained a persistent threat and guns and guerillas flowed with little interruption from North to South Vietnam.

US secretary of defense Robert McNamara put this problem – stopping infiltration along the Ho Chi Minh Trail – to the 'JASONs', a group of prominent scientists who advised the Pentagon on tricky technical problems. Many had worked on the Manhattan Project that developed the atomic bomb. After a series of seminars in Massachusetts and California, they proposed to seal off the Lao–Vietnamese border with a vast complex of minefields and 'an invisible electronic network that would detect, identify and destroy any enemy seeking to cross it'.[43] The idea so enchanted the secretary of defense that despite its official codenames – Igloo White, Steel Tiger – it was known as the 'McNamara Line'. Over the next six years, the US Air Force seeded the Lao borderlands with thousands of electronic sensors, video cameras and listening devices. The Air-Delivered Seismic Intrusion Detector (ADSID) was disguised as a plant and would detect the vibrations of people walking or driving in its vicinity. 'People sniffers' that detected urine and tiny ACOUBOUY microphones were scattered throughout the jungle. Some devices were camouflaged to look like animal droppings. The sensors were interspersed with thousands of air-dropped small 'gravel' and 'dragontooth' mines – intended to both harass Vietnamese communist convoys and generate more sound and vibrations for the sensors. As one Air Force officer put it, 'We wired the Ho Chi Minh Trail like a drugstore pin-ball machine.'[44]

When these sensors detected the ostensible presence of people and vehicles – presumed to be North Vietnamese troops and convoys – they would send a radio signal to gigantic IBM 360-65 computers, located in an extra-secure Infiltration Surveillance Center on the Nakhon Phanom Air Force Base in Thailand. The computer was programmed to correlate the incoming data with other intelligence and produce a list of targets. These coordinates were forwarded to Phantom F4 warplanes, already in the air, whose on-board computers would fly the aircraft to the appropriate 'box' on the map and automatically release its payload of landmines, cluster munitions and other bombs on the area of supposed suspicious activity. As General Westmoreland put it, the United States tried to 'replace wherever possible the man with the machine', which 'located, tracked and targeted' the enemy with 'the almost instantaneous application of highly lethal firepower'.[45] According to technology scholar Paul N. Edwards, 'The pilot might do no more than sit and watch as the invisible jungle below suddenly exploded into flames.'[46] By the end of the war, the United States was experimenting with aerial drones to take human pilots out of the 'kill chain' altogether. In essence, the Pentagon sought to stretch the traditional minefield into the air, aiming to enclose the entire Vietnamese border region into a massive electronic trap. The Pentagon spent $6 billion on the McNamara Line – mostly in secret before the operation was disclosed to the American public in the 1971 Pentagon Papers leak.[47]

According to a history of the McNamara Line, the fantasy of an 'automated battlefield' – able to detect threats to the United States electronically and send a remote-controlled explosive retort – suggested 'a world in which human beings, with all their messy unpredictable traits, would be eliminated, except as targets'.[48] But the McNamara Line neither met expectations nor its own dubious statistical claims. Major General John Deane, head of the electronic battlefield programme, acknowledged that the detectors could not distinguish between Viet Cong infiltrators and 'a group of woodcutters coming … down the trail'.[49] In the retrospective assessment of journalist Andrew Cockburn, the automated battlefield – 'that appeared so complete and elegant on the beach at Santa Barbara' – could not 'prosper in contact with … a world that shifted and adapted even as the mighty computers struggled to make it fits the maps and patterns programmed into their memories'.[50]

* * *

The Traditional Arts and Ethnology Centre (TAEC), in Laos' former royal capital, Luang Prabang, focuses on the hundreds of ethnic groups and clans collectively known as Laos' 'hill peoples'. Among the clothing, baskets, crafts and cultural artefacts, a sign tells visitors that traditional Hmong weaving has been used to transmit messages in lieu of writing, which their myths say they lost in their ancient flight from China. But, from the air, the differences between Laos' hundreds of cultures disappear. You cannot 'read' the messages woven into textiles, people's conversations, minor dramas of family life or the intricate murals on temple walls. It all flattens into coordinates and computer code, a surface to be bombed into shape. In an exhibit on childhood, TAEC's curators tell us that 'members of the Yao Mien ethnic group place elaborately decorated hats on their babies to disguise the infants as flowers, tricking spirits looking down from above to leave them unharmed'. In looking down on the Lao, Vietnamese and Cambodian people – both literally and metaphorically – the US military failed to detect how their aerial delusions tricked them into thinking they were in control. As one scholar noted, the 'majority of Americans involved in the war in Laos never set foot on Lao soil'.[51] Because of the automated targeting and flight paths, many pilots bombing Laos did not even know they were no longer flying over Vietnam.[52]

In his Vietnam War *Dispatches*, Michael Herr wrote, 'Airmobility ... made you feel safe, it made you feel Omni, but it was only a stunt, technology'.[53] The societies of Indochina resisted attempts to simplify their complexity. The tragic flaw in the McNamara Line, writes Cockburn, was that it confronted not 'a fixed target that would faithfully behave as predicted but a living enemy skilled in camouflage and deception that could watch, think and adapt'.[54] Vietnamese communist fighters learned how to spoof the sensors, placing bags of urine near the 'people sniffers', playing tapes of vehicle noises near the microphones, running cattle down trails to test them and innovating new routes.[55] The Pathet Lao leadership moved into caves at Vieng Say, constructing a vast underground complex of offices, housing, medical facilities, a factory and even a movie theatre, immune from American bombing.[56] Meanwhile, some 13,000 people were displaced by the automated bombing and the Americans lost more than 300 aircraft.[57] When news of US clandestine bombing and automated battlefield broke, it became a 'global symbol of the soulless but deadly American war machine'.[58] In the political manipulations needed to keep the bombing of Laos and Cambodia secret, several commentators have seen the roots of the Watergate abuses that undermined the credibility of the American political system.[59]

US popular memory of the Vietnam War has depicted Indochina as a kind of primordial 'quagmire', entangling Americans in its duplicitous terrain. Even anti-war commentators adopted this discourse, suggesting that US politicians led the country steadily into the insurgency's snare. However, the McNamara Line reveals how the quagmire was in part created by American delusions. The bombardment probably hurt US strategic aims in Laos, but the gee-whiz technical wonders of airplanes, sensors, computers and bombs trapped the American leadership into thinking they were winning. The United States was trying to beat the Indochina of its imagination by pouring ordnance into the jungle. But to their surprise, all the ways that Indochina was different from the delusion crept back in. The hubris of American exceptionalism was a metaphysical booby trap of its own making. Flailing reprisals at a barely visible enemy provoked further subterfuge and ambush, drawing the United States into further dependence on a violent response. As George Orwell observed in Burma, imperial projects become trapped in a paradox: for a foreign ruler to seem credible, they must use violence, but that violence undermines their credibility: 'when the white man turns tyrant it is his own freedom that he destroys'.[60]

* * *

Faced with the constant harassment of Vietnamese communist mining and booby trapping, the US military improved landmine detection techniques, including training of mine dogs. While civilians certainly benefited from efforts to keep South Vietnamese roads open (a primary priority of the new countermining teams), the clearance efforts were largely for military purposes.[61] Similarly, while the US Air Force was pounding Laos with millions of tonnes of ordnance, its EOD teams occasionally supported covert 'hearts and minds' operations aimed at winning the support of the Laotian peasantry.[62] Based at the same base in Nakhon Phanom, Thailand, from which Air Force pilots flew their bombing sorties,[63] these EOD teams 'worked in civilian clothes with the CIA, picking up unexploded ordnance so the roads were clear and the farmers could work their paddies'.[64]

These efforts were less about humanitarianism than pursuing security interests – the US military needed roads open and the Air Force had an interest in discovering what ordnance was failing to explode in Laos. The instrumental logic of US demining is illustrated by the Ba Chuc scandal, in which South Vietnamese and American soldiers compelled local civilians into clearing a minefield at gunpoint. Apparently a common practice,[65] this case was revealed to the *New York Times* by two American aid workers with the International Voluntary Services (IVS). Initially affiliated with the American peace churches, IVS placed earnest young people with humanitarian and development projects mostly in Southeast Asia. The Pentagon ordered an end to the operation, which had already killed and injured several villagers. But IVS fired the whistleblowers.[66]

As the United States forced civilians to clear one set of traps, they trapped themselves into a relationship of hatred and distrust with the local population. And unlike the equally callous pressganging of POWs to clear Europe of landmines after the Second World War, it was ad hoc, on a limited scale. The Air Forces' EOD programme in Laos ended in 1974, withdrawn to comply with the 1973 Vientiane Peace Agreement.[67] Following the Lao revolution in late 1975, the United States tried to use the offer of aid for UXO clearance as an enticement to persuade the new communist government to let American forensic experts search for the bodies of pilots missing in action. However, negotiations broke down in mistrust.[68]

For its part, the Soviet Union sent 12 EOD experts to a state-owned farm in the Plain of Jars in 1979 as part of a broader package of economic and political support to the new Laotian communist regime. The Soviet technicians trained 120 local personnel to use jeep-mounted metal detectors and cleared 12,700 UXO from 5,000 hectares. But they left after eighteen months and, lacking funding, the programme disbanded.[69] In Vietnam, the communist government compelled political prisoners to engage in forced demining,[70] but there was no comprehensive clearance. This lacklustre, and often callous, response to the massive UXO contamination in Indochina was symptomatic of Cold War governments' lack of interest in the civilian impact of their military technology.

*   *   *

Fred Branfman arrived in Laos in April 1967 as an IVS volunteer. After growing up in the Long Island suburbs, he seemed determined to live an eventful life. By the age of twenty-five, he had lived on a kibbutz in Israel, graduated with degrees from the University of Chicago and Harvard and joined the anti-Vietnam War movement. He had also served as a volunteer teacher in Tanzania to avoid being drafted for what he saw as an unjust war in Southeast Asia. Before arriving in Vientiane, Branfman had no special affinity for Laos; it kept him out of the military after his assignment in East Africa. He knew nothing about the secret war, which was still absent from American news outlets. He soon bored of his new job as an educational adviser with the US Agency for International Development (USAID) and immersed himself in the local language and culture. As he spoke with Lao people and met fellow expatriates in bars, he heard troubling rumours of the war and tales of the US-supported regime's corruption. To IVS's chagrin, he began asking inconvenient questions of powerful people, including a visiting Congressman and the USAID country director. Branfman strained against the stifling conformity of the expat community. He experimented with the seedier side of Vientiane nightlife. Reading Pathet Lao educational textbooks, he found them better suited to the experience of the rural people around him than what he had been told to use.

I met Branfman only once, at the 2012 CODEPINK Drone Summit in Washington DC. He was seventy years old, dressed in an old t-shirt and baggy jeans, white sneakers. Friendly and unobtrusive, he told me he was concentrating lately on spirituality. I hadn't expected his genial affect, having read accounts of his *avant garde* militancy as a young man in Laos:[71]

> He became a familiar figure on his motorbike ... always dressed in black, a vague sartorial statement of sympathy toward the Viet Cong – black sandals, black chinos, a black peasant's shirt from northeast Thailand. On his wrists were scores of thin white strings from attending *bouns* and *baci* ceremonies.[72]

After completing his IVS assignment, now old enough to avoid the draft, Branfman moved to France. While there, he read a newspaper article on the aerial bombardment. Stunned and wanting to verify the reports, he unsuccessfully lobbied Pathet Lao representatives in Paris to let him travel to rebel-held areas. Nevertheless, he returned to Vientiane as a freelance translator, fixer, stringer and provocateur. He found that American reporters were beginning to question the US official line. But, like him, they couldn't get up-country to find out for himself.

The truth of the war soon found him. No longer able to survive the barrage of bombies, people from the Plain of Jars streamed into Vientiane, setting up camp in the gigantic plaza at That Luang. Dominated by monumental temples – today swarming with package tours – it is now hard to imagine the scene that Branfman and his journalist friend Tim Allman found there in September 1969. Together, they interviewed people who had lost everything but what they could carry – their homes, their land, their livestock. Branfman and Allman heard stories of people cowering in caves, of life on the run, of family members killed. One man, who introduced himself as Nguen, was a particularly compelling guide. Over the following days, Branfman returned to That Luang numerous times, persuading foreign journalists to come listen to the stories of those displaced by the air war. Empathizing with those displaced from the Plain, he said, 'I was shocked to the core of my being.'[73] The 'sheer horror of the bombing had broken through my defenses, mobilized me',[74] making him a 'completely different person'.[75] He felt compelled to end the atrocity of the bombing. 'As a Jew profoundly touched by the Holocaust,' he wrote, 'I not only strongly identified with the victims but found it impossible to turn away from their plight.'[76] Branfman felt 'as if I had discovered Auschwitz when it was still going on'.[77] In the next few years, Branfman interviewed more than 2,000 displaced people, as well as American pilots and officials responsible for the missions over Laos.[78] He and Allman published a series of articles that exposed the extent and human impact of the secret air war.[79]

His increasingly close friendship with Nguen – who, it turned out, had connections to the Pathet Lao – and associations with Russians in Vientiane raised suspicions. By February, he was arrested by Lao police and deported. Moving to Washington DC, Branfman threw himself into the anti-war movement as it crested, with 200,000 people rallying on the National Mall in April 1971. In a speech delivered at Yale University shortly after his expulsion from Laos, Branfman decried the 'Laser-guided bombs striking water buffalo; three-million-dollar jets bombing bamboo houses, infra-red scopes and complete radar sets tracking a man plowing his field. ... If any of our concepts of decency, morality, humanity have any meaning at all, we must not rest until this is stopped.'[80] A couple months later, Branfman was sitting in the audience of a Senate hearing on Lao refugees. Dissatisfied with the State Department's evasions, Senator Ted Kennedy unexpectedly called on him. Before the news cameras, Branfman told TV audiences across the country, 'There is good evidence the United States has been carrying out the most protracted bombings in history in Laos.'[81]

Nguen and Branfman collected drawings, songs, poems and first-person accounts of people who had lived through the bombardment. Back in the United States, Branfman published them as *Voices from the Plain of Jars,* writing in an introductory essay that 'after a recorded history of 700 years ... [the] Plain of Jars became the first society to vanish through automated warfare.'[82] He saw the secret war as a harbinger of a 'new type of warfare…fought not by men but machines'.[83] I came across the slim volume thirty-five years later, pages yellowing and torn. But the pictures and text had a queasy immediacy. The cover is a naïve but brutal drawing, sketched rapidly with coloured pencils. A severed head, a detached arm, tumbling through the air, overflown by

jets, a dead horse. A representative testimonial, from a Lao folk singer
– transcribed by Branfman:

Everything is dead and gone, disappearing without a trace
Because of the airplanes which bombed the length and breadth of
    Xieng
...
What terrible sadness
So many loved ones killed
...
So many loved ones forced to leave their native villages,
Leaving behind spacious ricefields and gardens now turned to dust.[84]

As one historian put it, 'Among the thousands of books on the Vietnam
War, this is the only one written by ordinary villagers ... . [The]
undeniable integrity of the eyewitness testimonies and the powerful
visual evidence of the drawings shattered the six-year silence that had
shrouded the secret bombing of Laos.'[85] Branfman established two non-
profit organizations – Project Air War and the Indochina Resource
Center – that publicized the impact of the aerial bombardment. He
submerged himself into 'a 24-hour workday, taking naps on the couch';
he continued investigative research in Southeast Asia, wrote op-eds,
lobbied Congress people and helped draft legislation.[86] Branfman
became a highly visible face of the peace movement, delivering speeches
and appearing on televisions news.
    His courage spurred others to acts of witness. Branfman persuaded
a top Air Force targeting officer to serve as the primary source for an
expose by Seymour Hersh.[87] Horrified by revelations about the secret
war, anti-war activists – the 'Hickam Three' – infiltrated Pacific Air
Force Headquarters in Hawaii in 1972 and poured their own blood
onto top secret files associated with the 'electronic battlefield'. In sworn
testimony at their trial, an Air Force officer admitted to seeing the
deliberate targeting of a hospital and other civilian infrastructure in
Laos.[88] After the 1973 Paris Peace Accords halted the bombing of Laos
and Vietnam, Branfman continued to investigate the ongoing bombing
of Cambodia, travelling to Phnom Penh and even talking his way into
the command centre of Nakhon Phanom air base. The evidence he
uncovered helped sway Congress to ban further bombing.[89]
    Years later, as the Cold War drew to a close, and after returning to
Laos to visit the Plain of Jars, Branfman reflected that 'history is usually
told from the air. ... . We reconstruct it from the top down ... . But I didn't

learn history that way in Laos. I learned it in the eyes of the Laotian peasants who didn't know where America was, let alone why its leaders dropped bombs that blew their grandmothers to bits.' But with time he began to see the 'monstrous acts' of the American leaders, officials and pilots not as an intrinsic characteristic of particularly monstrous people, but rather the consequence of a system of domination that automated slaughter and justified it with an ideological veneer. The people of Laos were not somehow benighted victims: 'They didn't have the technology to drop millions of tons of bombs as did we – if they had they might well have used it.' What is 'most significant' is that automated warfare entrapped 'decent, not evil men', enabling them to order 'whole rural societies wiped off the map'.[90]

When I spoke to Branfman in 2012, he was worried that the remote-controlled drone warfare in Pakistan, Yemen and Somalia was a continuation of the logic he had fought against in Laos. I told him that I had read *Voices* and admired his persistence in campaigning against the air war. He beamed sheepishly, expressing surprise that people were still reading it. He handed me a self-printed business card and to my regret, I put off asking for an interview until it was too late; he died of ALS in Budapest in 2014.

*   *   *

In 1966, dissatisfied with what they saw as the failure and passivity of the traditional peace churches in the face of US imperialism in Indochina, a group of radical Philadelphia Quakers vowed to 'apply nonviolent direct action as a witness against the war in Vietnam'.[91] Calling themselves A Quaker Action Group (AQAG), they began shipping humanitarian supplies to North and South Vietnam. For thirteen months, Bob Eaton was based in Hiroshima, Japan, with AQAG, loading medicines donated by doctors at the A-Bomb Casualty Hospital into a sailboat called the *Phoenix of Hiroshima*. AQAG opted for a wooden boat because of the danger of sea mines. Having grown up in Connecticut, sailing in Long Island Sound, Eaton captained the boat on two trips, via Hong Kong, in April 1967 and November 1968, just in time to get stuck in Haiphong Harbor during the Tet Offensive. The *Phoenix* voyages were illegal, breaking the US-imposed sanctions on North Vietnam.[92] But Eaton was used to breaking the law and disturbing social niceties. A Swarthmore-trained economist, he is surprisingly direct for a pacifist, peppering his sentences with colourful vulgarisms as he plays raconteur, narrating stories of living in a commune in West Philadelphia, getting arrested in Hungary for protesting the Soviet occupation of Czechoslovakia and serving prison time for draft resistance. Concentration camp survivor Martin Niemoeller was a character witness at Eaton's sentencing hearing, and he claims that Daniel Ellsberg was inspired to leak the Pentagon Papers after meeting him.[93]

I first encountered Eaton in the Washington DC suburb of Takoma Park, dubbed the 'People's Republic of Takoma Park' by enthusiasts and detractors alike. The local council had recently passed resolutions calling for the impeachment of President Bush, renewing itself as a nuclear-free zone and condemning the delicacy *foie gras* as a form of 'extreme animal cruelty'.[94] Hippies, new-agers, hipsters and college professors all mixed at a local farmers' market, independent video store and small shops selling knick-knacks. Finding Eaton, the bespeckled head of a mine action NGO and a Quaker peace activist, in this radical milieu was unsurprising. His office sported a Vietnam-era Doonesbury poster and a baby blue Afghan rug with a UN symbol woven into it. A bushy grey beard grizzled his chin; he is often told he looks like an elder Gregory Peck.

On his first *Phoenix* trip, North Vietnamese representatives took Eaton to a hamlet that had just been bombed; bamboo huts still smouldered and people wandered dazed as they began burying their dead. One of the guides, a North Vietnamese colonel, handed Eaton an unexploded cluster munition bomblet and, assuring him it was deactivated, asked him to take it back to America to illustrate the impact of the war on civilians. When Eaton returned to the United States, he used the bomblet as a prop in his talks with peace groups. This memento mori still occupies a prominent place on his shelf.

Several other peace-church-affiliated agencies provided aid to North and South Vietnamese people during the war and realized the impact of unexploded munitions and landmines on the civilian population. The Mennonite Central Committee (MCC) experimented with ordnance clearance efforts, using armoured tractors to till contaminated land. The American Friends Service Committee (AFSC), a humanitarian arm of the American Quakers, funded a physical rehabilitation centre for war victims in Quang Ngai province.[95] Both AFSC and MCC were also active in Laos, the only Western relief agencies permitted to remain there following the 1975 revolution. The new regime allowed the Mennonites and Quakers to stay, Eaton told me, because 'during the civil war, as a matter of humanitarian principle, they worked on both sides. They did as much work with the Pathet Lao communists as they did with the Royalists.' From 1980 to 1984, Eaton and his spouse, Wendy Batson, became the AFSC representatives in Laos. Other than a 'skeletal' US Embassy staff, with the couple from MCC, they were the only four Americans in the country.[96]

The MCC and AFSC couples decided to coordinate their efforts closely because of their shared pacifist convictions. They approached the new Lao government, saying they wanted 'to work on healing the wounds of war'. According to Eaton, government officials suggested they work in the areas of the Ho Chi Minh Trail and the Plain of Jars, where there was a 'bloodletting…in terms of people dying from UXOs'. Eaton and the other AFSC/MCC staff travelled to these regions and were shocked by what they saw: 'there was no electricity, no radio communications, it felt like the end of the world. You'd walk for days to get up in these areas and if you passed two days without seeing a freshly wounded person, it was rare. I mean, it was just appalling what was going on up there. It was just awful.' Batson recalls speaking with an elderly woman who asked her 'why did my village explode?' The large bombs would strike at faster than the speed of sound and so people often had no warning before their homes and communities erupted into flames.

The AFSC and MCC staff were scandalized by the scale of suffering, but when they tried to tell the American public what they had seen, they were discouraged to find little interest. Eaton recalled, 'We wrote these impassioned reports to alert the world to this heinous thing that was happening and everybody said, "Well, that's a military issue." The donors, they just didn't see it, didn't want to help.' Unusually for the Mennonites and Quakers, they even turned to the US Department of Defense: 'We asked them just for identification charts … [for the ordnance] that we were finding' but they found the US government uninterested in providing information about what it considered a military secret. There was a lack of 'political consensus that these things were bad,' reflected Eaton. 'People thought, "You always have this after war," and nobody cared.' As a result, MCC and AFSC cobbled together what funding they could, mostly from church-affiliated agencies, and experimented with ways to mitigate the impact of the bombies.

Since the Mennonites came from farming communities, they focused on the agricultural implications of the crisis. 'Those cluster bomb units were just littered in the paddy fields,' said Eaton. In the dry season the earth was very hard and farmers would use a heavy hoe, called a *jok*, swung from down over one's head, to break the soil and allow the rains to percolate into the ground. The force of the *jok* hitting the ground would detonate any hidden bombies and focus the explosion into the farmer's body. This 'created hideous blast wounds,' said Eaton, forcing 'dirt, buffalo dung and dirty clothes' up into the wound. Without access to antibiotics, 'people would die awful, lingering deaths from infections'. Having seen a photo of the tank-mounted flails used for military demining, some of the MCC workers tinkered with a Massey Fergusson tractor, trying to detonate the explosives from the safety of an armoured cab. They didn't have much luck, nor did their experiments with metal detectors come to much fruition. 'They played around to figure out how they could destroy the UXO but came to the conclusion that they couldn't,' Eaton recalled. 'Nobody would help us, nobody would give us technical advice and our efforts were pretty useless.'

They had much more success mitigating the impact of the bombies than they did clearing them. MCC and AFSC supported survivor assistance in partnership with a recently established French NGO, Handicap International (now Humanity and Inclusion, or HI). HI, which later became prominent voice in the ICBL, was founded in 1982 to provide orthopaedic services in the refugee camps of Southeast Asia.[97] By the late 1980s, HI had an office of its own in Vientiane and supported prosthetics workshops around the country. Wendy Batson later headed HI's DC office, down the hall from Eaton's landmine survey NGO in Takoma Park.

AFSC and MCC also discovered that when farmers used Western-style shovels, the bombies were less likely to detonate. 'A jok is like a hammer, a shovel is like a knife, you push it in with the gentle motion of your foot,' explained Eaton. 'If the shovel came across a bombie, it tended to slide on one side or the other and so they weren't blowing up the bombies.' MCC and AFSC decided that since they could not solve the UXO crisis, they might be able to reduce the number of casualties by distributing shovels. Initially, donors were sceptical, saying, according to Eaton, 'Farmers are very traditional, you're not going to get them to change what their father used, what their grandpappy used.' But while the farmers 'may be traditional, they're not stupid. And when they worked out that these shovels didn't give them fragmentation wounds, they couldn't get enough of them.' Since the cost of importing the shovels would be expensive anyway, AFSC and MCC decided to procure what they considered 'the best shovels money could buy', from Ames, a farm implement company with a Quaker connection. Between 1977 and 1991, AFSC and MCC distributed 30,000 shovels to farmers. They also helped a Lao manufacturer start domestic production. While the shovels project was less dramatic than AFSC and MCC's attempts at clearance with a tractor and flail, it was far more effective.[98] As Eaton explained, 'We cut through the casualty rates significantly by reducing people's exposure to the threat.'

However, other than some money from smaller countries such as Norway, MCC and AFSC were not able to persuade the United States or other government donors to chip in. Most of the funding came from private donors, NGOs such as Oxfam America or Quaker-affiliated groups.[99] One of the more high-profile donations came from the Honeywell Project, a coalition of Minnesotan and national anti-war groups that was among the first to raise alarm about the human impact of cluster munitions in Southeast Asia. The campaign, with Branfman's help, exposed Honeywell, a major employer in Minnesota, as a key manufacturer of landmines and cluster munitions.[100] Threatened by negative publicity, Honeywell collaborated with the FBI in the surveillance and infiltration of the Honeywell Project and other anti-war groups. These groups sued, and when the federal government and Honeywell finally paid out, the Honeywell Project donated a portion of the settlement to the Laos shovel programme.[101]

The cluster bomb advocacy efforts of AFSC, MCC and the Honeywell Project did not occur in a vacuum. They were part of a nascent global conversation within the peace movement, the ICRC and sympathetic governments about placing humanitarian limits on conventional weapons. In 1974, Sweden proposed to protect non-combatants by banning fragmentation cluster bomblets and aerially dispersed mines. While it received some support, it was dismissed as 'prohibitionist' by the bigger military powers. The Cold War climate placed security matters firmly in the hands of military and technological 'experts', rather than affected or concerned citizens.[102] It was also difficult for smaller countries to follow an independent diplomatic path. Eaton reflected that during the Cold War, the United States and USSR prevented a large-scale mobilization to deal with the crisis: 'There was no political consensus, there was no funding, and the world didn't want to know about it.' Compared with the massive clean-up efforts after the Second World War and in the post-Cold War era, attempts to mitigate the impact of mines and UXO in Southeast Asia – both by states and NGOs – were minimal, scattered and underfunded. Even the North Vietnamese government was uninterested in regulating mines and cluster munitions, stating that an 'imperialist weapon' became 'a sacred tool' when wielded by a 'liberation fighter'.[103] The 1977 Additional Protocols to the Geneva Conventions, which the United States did not even sign, included only vague and unenforceable prohibitions on weapons that caused 'superfluous injury' or 'unnecessary suffering'.[104] Similarly the 1980 Convention on Certain Conventional Weapons (CCW) placed weak and loophole-ridden restrictions on the use of landmines, but left cluster munitions unregulated.

But in the dogged advocacy of Branfman, the civil disobedience of the Hickam Three, in the Quaker and Mennonite aid projects, and diplomacy at the CCW, one begins to discern an alternative way out of the 'quagmire'. When reading Branfman's work and listening to Eaton's stories, it is clear that they saw Lao people not as instrumental to a grand strategic vision, but rather as people of intrinsic human value. Instead of flying over the complexity of Laos, Cambodia and Vietnam, they listened to local people, literally publicizing 'Voices from the Plain of Jars'. For them, the way out of the 'quagmire' is by seeking solidarity with those most affected by the quagmire. In doing so, they laid the groundwork for today's charitable mine and UXO clearance programmes in Southeast Asia and contributed to political efforts to change the global laws of war on landmines, cluster munitions and aerial bombardment. In 1994, MCC funded MAG to begin clearing unexploded bombies in Laos. It was soon joined by other NGOs and the government set up UXO Lao in 1996 to offer a more coordinated response. Today, MAG's CLOs visit the homes and stables of those most affected by the ongoing impact of the bombies. However, these life-saving efforts have been overwhelmed by the scale of the contamination. In the decade between 1994 and 2003, the United States only offered an average of $1.5 million a year in aid to help clear up the deadly legacy it had left behind.[105]

* * *

Late in 2003, Channapha Khamvongsa, a Lao-American Ford Foundation staffer, was meeting with John Cavanagh, the head of the Institute for Policy Studies, a progressive think-tank.[106] Upon learning of Channapha's Lao roots, he told her, 'It's really terrible what happened in the Plain of Jars!'[107] She was shocked. Channapha had encountered few Americans who knew much about the secret war. Even in her family, no one talked about it. 'I considered myself somewhat well-read and conscious of right and wrong,' she later told the *New York Times*, 'yet this major piece of Lao-American history was unknown to me.'[108]

Channapha lived in Vientiane until she was six, the daughter of middle-class businesspeople who, though outside of politics, moved in the same social circles as the US-backed regime. After the capital fell to the Pathet Lao in 1975, she and her family members escaped across the Mekong River into Thailand. They lived for a year in a

Thai refugee camp, before her uncle, who had worked with the US Embassy and lived in Washington DC, arranged visas. America was seen as 'the dream destination for those of us who were living in the camps' in Thailand, she told me. 'You would never have to worry about money or food – that was the mythology of America.' In 1980, they settled in northern Virginia, where they struggled 'with very little – that reality was very difficult for us'. While refugee families like hers felt an imperative to 'learn the language, get jobs and get off assistance', there was also lingering trauma and guilt, 'an emotional toll that was never addressed – a culture of silence and shame'. After graduating from George Mason University, she moved to Seattle, where she experienced a social awakening. 'I didn't have a political education,' she told me. But in Seattle, she encountered Asian-American politicians and community organizers, who helped her 'formulate an understanding of Asian-American history and identity politics'.

Working later with the Ford Foundation, she had the opportunity to travel around Southeast Asia – including Laos – and began to grasp the scale of the war's devastation and lasting impact. In this 'very formative' experience, she also learned about 'how change happens' from activists all over the world. In her serendipitous encounter with Cavanagh, he explained that he had worked as an intern for Branfman at the Indochina Resource Center in the 1970s. Clearing out the office when the organization shut down, Cavanagh came across the original drawings from the *Voices from the Plain of Jars*. Cavanagh saved them in his office for twenty-five years. Intrigued, Channapha asked if she could see the drawings. As she flipped through a tattered blue binder, she was moved by their powerful simplicity. Travelling around the United States for work, she began showing them to other Lao-Americans, discovering that many of her generation also longed to understand their history. Artists, she found, were among those wrestling most publicly with the Lao-American experience. They inspired her to organize a travelling exhibition centred on the *Voices* drawings, as well as contemporary representations of Lao-American life. Preparing for the exhibition, she was surprised by people's reactions to the art. She encountered white Americans – like Branfman – who had worked in Laos in the 1970s and, mobilized by the Iraq War, were eager to reconnect with the country that had awakened them to the peace movement. She met Mennonites and Quakers who had served with the MCC and AFSC programmes in the 1970s and 1980s. 'I had never heard of these people', Channapha told me. 'I never realized the extent of the effort that went on here to stop the bombing.'

By contrast, the Lao-American diaspora was initially ambivalent. Many resisted anything that seemed to support the communist government and others were reluctant to reopen old wounds. As a result, Channapha focused on a message of healing – between the United States and Laos, between different Lao political factions and between the Lao-American diaspora and Laos itself. In 2004, she founded a non-profit, Legacies of War and began lobbying US Congresspersons representing areas where many Lao-Americans lived.

I found Legacies of War's office on the top floor of a white-washed brick row house in DC's gentrifying Shaw neighbourhood. A nearby sign commemorated the area's character as 'a place between places', where 'races and classes bumped and mingled as they got a foothold in the city'. An eager intern gave me a spontaneous briefing, showing me a BLU-26 cluster bomblet and a *pétanque* bowling ball to illustrate how easy it would be for a child to mistake a bombie for a toy. Channapha pointed to the high bookshelf and said 'the pictures are up there, have a look!' On tip-toes, I gingerly eased a heavy archival box down to a table and removed the lid. Inside were the original drawings collected by Branfman and Nguen. Channapha showed me the battered blue photo album that had housed them for so long. They are now carefully catalogued and stored in archival sleeves. I find a drawing of a burning building, people falling from the windows as bombs explode around them. A type-written slip of paper accompanies it with the following caption from the sixteen-year-old boy who drew it: 'The school was hit and burned. There were many people in the school who died. But I didn't know who because I wasn't courageous enough to go look. I was afraid that the airplanes would shoot me.'

A timeline was taped to the office wall, outlining key moments in Legacies of War's history. The first preview of the travelling exhibition premiered in Seattle in September 2006. Only a month earlier, in its war against Hezbollah, Israel had pounded Lebanon with some 4 million cluster submunitions, launched from rockets, fired from helicopters and dropped from planes.[109] Media attention jump-started a nascent international advocacy campaign calling for a ban on cluster munitions. Legacies of War joined this Cluster Munition Coalition, as did MAG, MCC, several Quaker groups and many other NGOs. The US campaign was run out of Eaton and Batson's offices in Takoma Park. Stymied in the CCW by the big military powers – the United States, Russia and China were all major producers and exporters of cluster munitions – supportive governments decided to move forward on their own. Led by Norway, most of the world's countries negotiated a global treaty banning the production, stockpiling, trade and use of cluster munitions. This Convention on Cluster Munitions also obligated support for cluster munition clearance, survivor assistance and risk education.[110] Laos and Lebanon were among the first countries to sign the new convention on 3 December 2008. Participating in the Coalition helped Legacies of War gain 'partners and allies', said Channapha, as well as 'inspiration that so many other people were working' on the same issue. 'I remember a sense of such optimism,' she recalled, of the negotiation conferences she attended in Ireland and Chile.

By 2019, the treaty had 107 member states; the United States, however, is not among them. Channapha wanted Americans to better understand the ongoing impact of the aerial bombardment in Southeast Asia and so organized a speaking tour around the United States by cluster munition survivors. Though unable to get much traction on persuading the United States to join the treaty, Legacies of War found that elected officials were open to increasing funding for clearance and survivor assistance. In 2010, Channapha testified before Congress, calling for a tripling of US funding for addressing the threat of bombies that have 'been allowed to persist far too long … Too many innocent lives have been lost. … But it is not too late to stop this senseless suffering.'[111]

In its advocacy, Legacies of War struggled against widespread ignorance of Laos and the impact of the secret war. 'We had to invest in education', to raise awareness – not only of politicians but also among the Lao diaspora itself – of the human costs of the bombies. But this investment has paid off. By 2016, the United States had increased its appropriation for cluster munition clearance in Laos to $19.5 million and committed to $90 million over three years.[112] 'It's about settling history's account and meeting our responsibility,' said Obama's deputy national security adviser Ben Rhodes.[113] According to Sam Perez, then deputy assistant secretary of state, Channapha was 'a driving force' behind getting the United States to reengage with bombie clearance in Laos.[114] Increased funding has sped up the rate of bombie destruction in Laos: from 69,596 in 2010 to 100,022 in 2015.[115] President Barack Obama visited Laos that year and was photographed at the COPE visitor's centre in Vientiane, plaster bombies cascading around him.[116] 'The remnants of war continue to shatter lives here in Laos,' he said. 'The wounds, a missing leg or arm, last a lifetime. That's why I've dramatically increased or funding to remove these unexploded bombs.'[117] The incoming Trump White House threatened to slash the last two instalments of the $90 million commitment. However, Legacies of War was able to mobilize bipartisan support in Congress to defend it. At the time of writing, the newly elevated funding levels had broad political backing.

Legacies of War's lobbying on Capitol Hill has had an impact far beyond Laos. The United States has not used cluster munitions since 2009 and has destroyed 3.7 million cluster munitions (comprising almost 407 million bomblets) and removed from its active inventory a similar quantity of 'additional excess and obsolete' stocks.[118] Reports of extensive cluster bombing (including BLU-63s) by the Saudi air force of civilian areas in Yemen prompted the Obama White House to block further transfers of cluster bombs to Saudi Arabia. And in 2016, following a lengthy campaign by human rights advocates and peace activists, Textron, the last American manufacturer of cluster munitions, halted production indefinitely.[119] 'There are many, many problems in this world that might not be able to be solved in a lifetime,' said Channapha. 'But this is one that can be fixed. Given that it was ignored for so long, we need to redouble our efforts and finish the job.'[120]

In December 2017, the Trump administration reopened the door for US commanders to authorize use of cluster munition stocks, drawing condemnation from cluster munition campaigners and human rights groups.[121] Sharing coffee at a café in a converted horse stable around the corner from her office, Channapha and I reflected on what could be learned from the campaign to clear Laos's bombies to address the challenges of the current moment. She told me she had learned that individuals could 'shift and change history' by refusing to accept the political constraints of the time. But she also found in the drawings collected by Branfman a metaphorical counterpoint to the bombie. They too were 'tangible artefacts' that had lain hidden, 'a history that had been lost' and forgotten by most of the world, until they were unearthed, bearing testimony to a past not yet healed. She told me that for Branfman, just before his death, 'to see a younger generation pick this up for him was very redeeming'. The growth of Legacies of War, and US recognition of its responsibility to Laos, 'is almost a memorial to his work'.

Chapter 3

PERFECT SOLDIERS
PROXY WAR, CAMBODIA

Landmines were the 'weapon of choice' in Cambodia's proxy war of the 1980s.[1] Pol Pot, leader of the murderous Khmer Rouge party, called landmines the 'perfect soldiers' – they lie in ambush forever, never sleeping, never complaining, never needing to eat, never showing a modicum of humanity to the unlucky victim.[2] The Chinese Type 72A anti-personnel landmine was a Khmer Rouge favourite: a small, cheap, green plastic contraption, which now frustrates deminers trying to locate them with metal detector.[3] In 1991, the UK government admitted that its Special Air Service (SAS) commandos had been teaching the Khmer Rouge in secret bases in Thailand. 'We trained the KR in a lot of technical stuff – a lot about mines,' a British solider told the *New Statesman*. 'We used mines that came originally from Royal Ordnance in Britain, which we got by way of Egypt with marking changed.'[4] A later report by Human Rights Watch (HRW) alleged that the SAS had taught the Khmer Rouge 'the use of improvised explosive devices, booby traps and the manufacture and use of time-delay devices'.[5] Khmer Rouge used this training to fight the Vietnamese-backed government in Phnom Penh, but they also deployed landmines as a tactic 'of terror for social and economic control over the civilian population'.[6]

Responding to the perceived growth of Soviet power in the 'Third World', the 1980s Reagan administration adopted an aggressive 'forward policy', aimed at 'rolling back' Soviet expansionism. Breaking with the consensus of several decades, this new hawkish stance wanted to abandon 'Containment' as the guiding principle of US foreign policy, and combat communism, not merely restrain it within a bloc. That said, the United States did not want to clash with the Soviet Union directly – it was afraid of nuclear war. In what became known as the 'Reagan Doctrine', the United States supported anti-government insurgencies in socialist countries outside Europe, but limited American engagement to sustaining rebel forces through moral support, diplomacy, 'humanitarian assistance' and covert operations. These proxy wars militarized the borderlands between Soviet-sponsored governments and their non-communist neighbours. Between Honduras and Nicaragua; South Africa and Angola and Mozambique; Thailand and Cambodia, refugees flowed one way and CIA-backed rebels flowed the other. Landmines clogged the pathways they travelled.[7]

In Cambodia, the United States – along with its bloc allies and China (having broken with the USSR) – supported a loose coalition of resistance groups based in Thailand who were fighting the Vietnamese client regime. The rebels used both improvised and imported mines to harass the government's troops and protect 'liberated areas'.[8] The rebels included royalist and democratic groups, but was dominated by the Khmer Rouge, the extreme Maoist party that had ruled through mass death, killing 1.7 million people:[9] 'To keep you is no profit, to destroy you is no loss', went their chilling slogan.[10] The Khmer Rouge had invaded their neighbour, Vietnam, which unseated them in 1979. US assistance to the Cambodian insurgency, in the form of 'non-lethal' and 'humanitarian' aid, was supposedly limited to the so-called 'Non-Communist Resistance', including monarchist and republican factions. However, the Khmer Rouge had significantly more troops than the other parties and carried out most of the resistance's military operations against the Vietnamese. Reality was therefore more ambiguous. There is significant evidence suggesting that the Khmer Rouge benefited from US aid.[11] The United States also encouraged other governments – such as Thailand, the United Kingdom and China, which were more directly implicated. As Fiona Terry put it in her history of refugee aid, 'Superpower politics and regional realignments overshadowed the widespread and massive human rights abuses and crimes against humanity.'[12]

As the Vietnamese and their Cambodian proxies pushed the Khmer Rouge towards the Thai border in 1979, thousands of civilians tried to flee. Thailand sealed the border, forcing 45,000 refugees back over minefields at the Preah Vihear temple. Following international condemnation, the Thai government opened camps to accommodate thousands of refugees, but began supporting the Cambodian rebels (including the Khmer Rouge).[13] The Thai military saw the refugee population, says Terry, as a kind of 'buffer against the Vietnamese forces' and a source of proxy fighters to send back over the border.[14]

In all of the proxy wars, the cross-border pathways represented the lifeblood of the anti-communist insurgencies. Mimicking the McNamara Line that had so failed the US intervention in Indochina,

Vietnam conceived of a 'Bamboo Wall' between Thailand and Cambodia – codenamed 'K5' – aiming to block every possible rebel infiltration route. Not always sure of the precise border, K5 units mined large portions of Thai territory.[15] 'K5 was one of the world's largest mine belts', an expatriate landmine clearance expert told me. 'It had 2 million mines – many of them Soviet PMN and PMN-2s.' Dressed in a blue polo and khaki jeans, a Fit Bit on his left arm, he pointed to his PowerPoint projection with a stick normally used for demarcating minefields. We were in a room displaying a vast collection of landmines and ordnance found by deminers in Cambodia. He explained that 'the Vietnamese conscripted hundreds of thousands of people as forced labor from all over the country' to build K5. Terry alleges that 'exacerbated by lack of food and physical exhaustion, malaria was estimated to have killed … 50,000 of the one million peasants who were forced to participate [in building K5] in the first two years'.[16] Swaths of the jungle were clear-cut – an ecological calamity – to make way for the minefield. The minefields did little to prevent infiltration by the Khmer Rouge and other rebel units. While K5 lacked 'any real strategic value', argues Terry, 'the project succeeded in keeping the population in a permanent state of mobilization and under tight government control'.[17]

Following the October 1991 Paris Peace Accords that nominally ended the war, the UN established a quasi-trusteeship over the country until 1993, called the Transitional Authority in Cambodia (UNTAC). As UN peacekeeping troops and humanitarian agencies deployed, they realized the threat landmines posed to both their nation-building project and the repatriation of refugees. As a result, the Norwegian government asked the NGO Norwegian People's Aid (NPA) to support UNTAC by recruiting former military ordnance experts to provide technical assistance to the Cambodian government's mine action centre (CMAC).[18] The United States sent army psychological operations soldiers to develop mine awareness materials and Special Forces trained Cambodia's military deminers.[19] MAG also started its Cambodia demining programme in 1992. The Khmer Rouge continued to wreak havoc in Cambodia following the peace agreement. Humanitarian deminers were often targets.[20]

Another major British landmine clearance charity, the HALO Trust, started work in Cambodia in 1991, supporting the internationally sponsored repatriation effort, demining reception areas for returning refugees and conducting surveys of suspected hazardous areas. During the early 1990s, HALO's Cambodia programme remained small, with about 200 deminers, recruited in a kind of 'informal demobilisation' from the various military factions. HALO often hire from the communities in which they work to contribute to local development. As they established themselves, HALO began demining for international development agencies. The Cambodia programme is now HALO's second largest programme in the world (after Afghanistan), with 1,100 staff.

The expatriate landmine expert tells me that as Cambodia's economy recovers and ancient Cambodian temples at Angkor Wat have become a stop on the global sight-seeing circuit, the price of land is inflating quickly. This is pushing people who are looking for agricultural land into riskier areas. 'The last remaining land in Cambodia is mined and along the border,' he said. 'Poverty is driving people' to farm the Bamboo Wall minefields. Relations with Thailand remain tense. There were clashes between Thai and Cambodian forces at the Preah Vihear temple complex (subject to a long-standing border dispute dating to rivalry between the French colonialists and the Siamese King) in 2008 and 2013.[21] As part of its military preparations, the Cambodian government is building a road network along the border. However, this is drawing people to settle 'previously remote minefields'. Showing me photographs, the demining expert exclaimed: 'houses are being built within 10 meters of K5!' Thailand's impressive growth attracts many undocumented Cambodian migrants, who, to avoid detection by increasingly aggressive border enforcement, risk crossing through the minefields. He says that demining agencies need to 'invest in the densest areas that are causing the most casualties'. However, the 'rumpus over Preah Vihear' means there is a 'strong military presence' in the K5 area and deminers are 'not really given full access to the border minefields. It is very politically sensitive and we have to get special permission.' The military are particularly 'concerned when demining agencies do demolitions' – blowing up mines that have been discovered during the clearance work.

But there is a less easily accommodated challenge. Even though Cambodia and Thailand have both signed the Anti-personnel Landmine Ban Treaty – prohibiting them from relying on landmines for defence and committing them to timely clearance – there are powerful people on both sides who remain convinced that the minefields offer them security. A definitive study commissioned by the ICRC, endorsed by more than fifty of the world's top mine warfare specialists and senior military commanders, has demonstrated that 'even when used on a massive scale, [landmines] had little or no effect on the outcome of hostilities', particularly when used in large defensive formations like K5.[22] Landmines are not the perfect soldiers they were touted to be. Militaries just find a way around defensive minefields or plough through them if they really want to get to the other side. Instead, mines mostly kill and maim civilians. However, mine action experts tell me that they worry that some 'older generals still see K5 as integral to Cambodian defense', and have the 'misperception that demining' the Bamboo Wall 'will weaken Cambodia'. Even after the end of the proxy wars, they continue to treat the lives of civilians in the borderlands – and the religious heritage of Preah Vihear – as means to an end.

Despite their rhetoric of charitable good works, the early days of Cambodia's UN and NGO demining operations were dominated by military personnel. In the 1990s, HALO epitomized this approach (less pronounced these days), perhaps the result of its early managers being drawn from what in Britain we call the Sandhurst Set – well-bred army officers – including Colin Mitchell, who was known as 'Mad Mitch of Aden' for commanding a bold colonial intervention in Oman that stretched the limits of his instructions.[23] HALO expressed contempt for landmine ban advocates 'distracted by involvement in campaigns and conferences'.[24] 'Getting mines out of the ground, now', was their mission, nothing more and nothing less.[25] This culture – hyper-masculine, technocratic, expeditionary and paramilitary – has persisted in many demining organizations, with a fetish for maps and coordinates, jargon and acronyms, khakis and combat boots. But there were others – people of faith, human rights activists, humanitarian aid workers and mine survivors – who were not content with a myopic focus on the explosive device. They believed landmines represented a deeper malaise, in which people are pulled into the political trap of recrimination, using other people as proxies for their own ends. They saw in the landmine and a struggle against it, a symbol for the human – even spiritual – condition.[26]

* * *

The Metta Karuna Reflection Center in Siem Reap is a verdant retreat, located just outside the city on Cambodia's National Road 6. Amid sculptures and topiary, it houses offices, conference spaces and a chapel for Jesuit Refugee Service (JRS), a Catholic NGO founded in 1981 to help refugees fleeing from Vietnam, Laos and Cambodia.[27] In January 2017, I met with Tun 'Reth' Channareth, in the Center's canteen, roofed with orange tile but open to breezes on all side. Through my years of researching landmines, I had heard about Reth, as one of the most photographed faces of the campaign that banned them. Clean shaven, he is wearing large, black wire glasses. His shoulders and biceps are well built, and he wears a tight blue T-shirt with the slogan 'Push for Progress', illustrated with figures in wheelchairs. In a wheelchair with a wooden seat, he pulls up to the table where I am sitting and we share tea. Behind him, outside the canteen, there is a flowering pergola.

Following the 1975 Khmer Rouge revolution, Reth and his family joined the forced exodus to the countryside, where the ruling ideology insisted that people must work in subsistence conditions to appreciate the superiority of the peasantry over urban, intellectual and dissident Cambodians. His father and younger sister died from ill health. When the Vietnamese military invaded, he fled, escaping to Thailand and joining the republican rebel faction. On 18 December 1982, he was doing sentry duty along the border when he stepped on a Soviet-made landmine, which blew off both his feet. 'The army laid mines without thinking about the impact on people', he told me. 'I saw my legs, bone broken; saw everything lost. I take my own gun and try to kill myself. I cannot do so. ... I try to find another AP mine but I cannot because both my legs are broken already. Then I saw my friend carry [an] axe. ... I beg him.'[28] But his fellow soldier refused to let him die and carried him 20 miles to the nearest emergency clinic.[29] 'When you are injured in a landmine explosions', he reflected in a coauthored article two decades later, 'it is easy to think that your life is over and that there is no hope for the future. How can you provide for your family? How can you live a normal life?'[30] His injury was not uncommon for those living and fighting in the borderlands of the proxy wars. By the early 1990s, the ICRC's medical division was reporting thousands of casualties from landmines – the majority being civilians – at its field hospitals and clinics, particularly those serving Afghans and Cambodians. The kind of injuries sustained by Reth, tragically widespread, were also expensive to treat, requiring amputation, blood transfusions and aggressive treatment to prevent sepsis, followed by lengthy rehabilitation. UN and NGO humanitarian agencies expressed alarm that mines were preventing them from accessing vulnerable populations and hindering people's livelihoods, including farming and trade.[31]

After the peace agreement, Reth returned to Phnom Penh. He had learned how to be a mechanic in the border camp. But he recollected that his life circumstances were 'very bad'. Survivors struggled to support themselves. 'I tried my best, but having lost both my legs, it was hard.' Humanitarian agencies were, at the time, among the few institutions with decent employment, and he 'asked every NGO for a job'. He had little success, but told me, 'I've been Catholic since birth and I kept praying.' He also felt 'thirsty for knowledge of the outside world, I wanted to stay alive long enough to see it, and finally contribute something of myself to it'.[32] In a stroke of serendipity, he met Sister Denise Coghlan, a nun working for JRS, and using his skills as a mechanic, he joined the staff at the organisation's wheelchair shop. Reth said Sister Denise's 'compassion really opens you up and makes you feel good' about yourself.

After finishing my interview with Reth, he took me to see Sister Denise, now the JRS Cambodia country director, who was finishing a meeting with a visiting delegation from the Japanese Campaign to Ban Landmines. They were sitting in another tile-roofed conference building, open on all sides. Mynah birds chattered and a butterfly floated in the eddies of a ceiling fan. In the background, I hear crickets, a rooster and a barking dog; the air smells of burning wood. I bow awkwardly in greeting, and I am surprised when Sister Denise jumps in to translate my introduction into Japanese. Sister Denise's affability is combined with a determined competence. She had short grey hair and glasses with pink frames and chuckled as she spoke with the savvy of someone used to engaging with the public sphere: 'Those people who say church people should stay in the sacristy are talking baloney – all our actions take place in a political context.'

As a young nun from Brisbane, Australia, Sister Denise spent ten years in Papua New Guinea. In 1988, she heard that her order, the Sisters of Mercy, was looking for someone to help in the refugee camps in Thailand, and she accepted the challenge. She was assigned to JRS, which was providing humanitarian assistance and job skills training, particularly to people with disabilities.[33] Enrique Figaredo Alvargonzalez, a young Spanish Jesuit priest (now Monsignor) also working with JRS,[34] recalled feeling overwhelmed by the context. 'I was very afraid', he said, but recounted meeting Heng Meth, a leading advocate for people with disabilities in the camps. 'Despite his disabilities' – one of his legs had been amputated and he only had one eye – 'he stood before me with dignity', wrote Figaredo. Heng Meth asked the young priest if he had come to help. Figaredo nodded, nervously, and Heng Meth responded, 'Don't worry, we will help you and you will know what we need.' For the JRS staff, this anecdote represented their ethos – to live in solidarity with those most affected by the war and be led by them. 'I never felt so welcomed in my life', said Figaredo. 'They would help me help them.'[35]

Nevertheless, Sister Denise, Figaredo and other JRS staff became increasingly uncomfortable with the political implications of their work. Sister Denise said she was 'helping people with their legs blown off and we kept saying we needed to do something about landmines'. She was disturbed by the realization that many refugees from the camps – just like the K5 units – were 'Cambodians laying mines against Cambodians' in the border region. 'The ideology of the refugee camps was about fighting the Vietnamese,' Denise told me. 'We were concerned that we were becoming only associated with one side' of the conflict. The camps were run by the Thai military and their residents did not receive official recognition as refugees. Khmer Rouge and other rebel groups were using the camps as bases for their attacks in Cambodia and misallocating humanitarian aid to feed and support their troops. According to Terry, this 'posed arguably the greatest challenge to the international humanitarian system of the Cold War period'.[36] JRS were disquieted by the notion that their aid efforts were becoming entwined with the war, in which refugees were being used as pieces in a Cold War game. 'Seemingly powerless to change the political context in which their work was embedded', observed Terry, 'aid agencies had to confront the probability that their aid was reviving one of the most brutal regimes in modern history, the Khmer Rouge.'[37]

But what could they do? JRS staff felt they needed to better understand the situation inside Cambodia. In 1988, Figaredo visited the AFSC team, which was already providing aid to people with disabilities in the country. Speaking with landmine victims, he found the experience 'shocking': 'The country was completely destroyed and yet very little humanitarian aid was coming in.'[38] Aid donors associated with the Western bloc were unwilling to support a Vietnamese-backed regime. Moreover, the government in Phnom Penh were wary of independent NGOs.[39] Sister Denise conducted another assessment mission in 1989. A heart-rending period of prayer and discernment followed, which split the JRS team. The political polarization made the decision especially fraught. Terry writes that 'the majority of aid organizations were forced to choose whether they would work along the border or inside Cambodia.'[40] Some staff even quit, feeling that JRS should have halted its aid altogether, to send a strong message that they would not participate in prolonging the war. Instead, JRS decided to work 'against the division', as Sister Denise put it. JRS would continue to aid people in the camps in Thailand but also establish a presence in Cambodia itself, a choice few aid agencies made. JRS would also work for peace and reconciliation, collaborating with Buddhist monks on both sides of the border. It was not enough to help those hurt by landmines, said Sister Denise, 'you have to work to address the structural issues'. Countering the prevailing ethos of the proxy wars and inspired by Catholic Social

Teaching, JRS worked for recognition of the 'human dignity of each person'. As Sister Denise put it, 'People shouldn't be used as pawns in political processes.'

Sister Denise and a small JRS team moved to Phnom Penh in early 1990. The government's Ministry of Social Action offered them a plot of land called *Banteay Prieb* (Khmer for 'fortress of the dove'; JRS prefers the less militaristic translation 'Center of the Dove'), which had been used as a communications centre for US military carrier pigeons during the American interventions in Indochina. Later, it was a Khmer Rouge killing field and prison. The ground was sown with landmines and cluster munitions. There were several people with disabilities living near the grounds, including a landmine victim who was so traumatized that he could no longer speak. But JRS saw possibility in this seemingly undesirable and tragic site. They decided to keep the name Banteay Prieb, but imbue it with new meaning, as a centre for peace and reconciliation. In September 1991, just before the signing of the peace agreement, they enrolled their first class of students in a new Banteay Prieb Vocational Training Center. They planned to bring people with disabilities from across Cambodia's political and religious divides together, while also teaching them useful skills. This was the centre that welcomed Reth. JRS set up a workshop producing mobility aides – called the Mekong Wheelchair – that were designed specifically for the Cambodian context. Reth helped in its iterative design; by 2015, the workshop had produced more than 20,000 wheelchairs for Cambodians with disabilities.[41] Figaredo joined the Cambodia team in 1993 and rather than staying in the relative calm of Banteay Prieb, he decided he should 'go out, to meet the people and bring their needs' back to the JRS team. He would travel around the country with Cambodian JRS staff, bringing wheelchairs to people with disabilities in the villages and towns, far beyond where most aid agencies dared to venture. Figaredo described his work as administering the 'Sacrament of the Wheelchair', saying that for people with disabilities 'to receive a wheelchair supposes an authentic revolution' in their life, a 'visible sign' of 'grace' that ushers in a 'profound change in [their] way of seeing the world'.[42]

JRS combined their social service activities with public advocacy for reconciliation and human rights in Cambodia. They began participating in the Cambodian *Dhammayietra* peace movement, led by Samdech Preah Maha Ghosananda, a Cambodian Buddhist monk nicknamed the 'Buddha of the Battlefield' by the press.[43] The Khmer Rouge regime had tried to eradicate religious institutions in Cambodia, viewing them as parasitical on the peasantry and a competing source of authority. Of the 65,000 monks in Cambodia before the revolution, only 3,000 survived the Khmer Rouge massacres that also destroyed almost all of Cambodia's 3,600 active temples and monasteries, turning some of them into killing fields.[44] Ghosananda had escaped the massacres but his parents and sixteen siblings had not. He had left the country in 1953 to study in India for fifteen years, under the tutelage of Nichidatsu Fujii, a Japanese Buddhist monk who had been an acolyte of Mahatma Gandhi. Nichidatsu had preached against Japanese aggression in the Second World War. After the war, he became a prominent voice for disarmament, asserting that 'civilization' is not found in 'science and technology' – which produced the 'great disgrace' of nuclear weapons – but rather in 'humanity', the ability to 'hold out all respect and affection for one another'.[45] Nichidatsu taught Ghosananda the spiritual practice of 'walking among the people every day'. Nichidatsu saw this as an implicit rejection of technology, but also as a way to encounter humanity. 'The true monk', said Nichidatsu, 'does not stay in one place.'[46] In 1972, Ghosananda moved to a monastery in Thailand. When Cambodians began crossing the border following the Vietnamese invasion in 1978, he began distributing pamphlets to refugees on the Buddha's teachings of loving kindness: 'Hatred can never overcome hatred; only love can overcome hatred.' His humble charisma drew people longing for reconnection with their past and for spiritual transformation: 'Crowds of people sometimes burst into tears of emotion at the sight of him,' recalled an American Buddhist monk who knew him. 'All other activities came to a standstill, and all eyes would be riveted on him.'[47] Discerning a vocation to revive Buddhist values, Ghosananda established simple 'shack temples' in the camps, even those controlled by the Khmer Rouge, and offered sanctuary to refugees resisting rebel conscription. In 1987, he participated, along with other monks, in the peace talks in Jakarta, Indonesia, that led to the eventual Paris Peace Accord in 1991. It was there that Ghosananda met Bob Maat, a Jesuit priest with JRS, and challenged him to get JRS more engaged with peacemaking inside Cambodia. Ghosananda was elected Cambodian Buddhism's Supreme Patriarch in 1988.

In April 1992, Ghosananda led the first Dhammayietra for Peace and Reconciliation, walking for a month from the Thai border to Phnom Penh, with a crowd that grew from a hundred to a thousand people, including monks, refugees, local residents and international peace and human rights activists.[48] JRS staff and friends were among them, including Liz Bernstein, who would later become the coordinator of the International Campaign to Ban Landmines (ICBL) from 1998 to 2004.

The Dhammayietras, modelled on a story of the Buddha walking into a battlefield to halt hostilities, were more than a demonstration or political march. *Dhammayietra* literally means 'truth pilgrimage' and the walks were intended to revive in Cambodians a sense of loving kindness and compassion for each other. Ghosananda wanted to challenge religious leaders to encounter the human cost of the war, to make 'the battlefields ... our temples'.[49] Ghosananda's slogan was 'Peace is Possible', which in the midst of the lingering instability seemed absurd. But his courage and determination 'was very important', said Sister Denise, 'in making people believe that it was indeed possible'. Dith Pran, subject of the 1984 Oscar-winning film *The Killing Fields*, called Ghosananda the 'dreamkeeper of Cambodia'.[50] Thousands of people joined the annual Dhammayietras that followed. The walks were organized to bring people to areas where they would not have normally gone, learning about the struggles faced by people in parts of the country that the walkers may not have visited. But they also had an external dimension, drawing media attention. Pilgrims braved minefields, battlefields, banditry and government harassment; several people were killed and injured. But Ghosananda led by example, declaring that the Dhammayietras could form an 'army of peace' of so 'much courage that we will turn away from violence': 'We will shoot people with bullets of loving kindness. ... Mindfulness will be our armor. ... Our goal will be to bring an end to suffering'.[51] For Ghosananda, the perfect solider was not the landmine, but the non-violent activist, grounded in spiritual discipline.

Ghosananda and the JRS priests, nuns and lay workers saw landmines as a symbol of the war's disregard for the preciousness of human life. As a result, when the JRS team learned of launch of the ICBL in 1992, they knew they had to be involved.[52] Sister Denise was invited to the ICBL's second international conference in Geneva in May 1994 and later joined the Campaign's Executive Committee. The global grassroots movement to ban anti-personnel landmines grew out of a sense of moral outrage at the humanitarian impact in the proxy wars, particularly in Afghanistan and Cambodia. The first ever call for a ban was voiced by Anne Goldfeld of the Women's Commission for Refugee Women and Children in April 1991, during a US Senate hearing, in which she testified about her work providing medical care to Cambodians in the camps in Thailand.[53] In September 1991, Human Rights Watch (HRW) and Physicians for Human Rights (PHR) published a seminal report on landmines in Cambodia, entitled *Coward's War*. Analysing medical data, they found that in 1990 alone, 6,000 Cambodians had received amputations. The country had 'the highest percentage of physically disabled inhabitants of any country in the world' and its conflict 'may be the first ... in history in which landmines have claimed more victims – combatants and noncombatants alike – than any other weapon'. The report concluded with a call for an 'unconditional' global ban on victim-activated landmines.[54] In a later report, HRW and PHR called the landmine 'a weapon of mass destruction in slow motion'.[55] After reading *Coward's War*, Cambodia's king Sihanouk called for a ban on anti-personnel landmines in an October 1991 speech at the UN, becoming the world's first monarch to do so.[56]

Meanwhile, Vietnam Veterans of America Foundation (VVAF) and Medico International, which had opened a joint prosthetics clinic in Cambodia in mid-1991, hired an American peace activist, Jody Williams, to establish an international campaign. The ICBL was officially launched in New York in October 1992, by six NGOs: Handicap International (now Humanity and Inclusion, or HI), HRW, MAG, Medico, PHR and VVAF. The Campaign had some early successes. Patrick Leahy, the US senator, had been moved to address the humanitarian costs of landmines when he met a young Nicaraguan survivor in Honduras in 1985. At the urging of the ICBL, Leahy sponsored legislation placing a renewable moratorium on US landmine exports in 1993. He also lobbied the newly elected president Bill Clinton to call for the 'eventual elimination of antipersonnel landmines' at the UN General Assembly in 1994. In France and Belgium, HI – which had been assisting landmine victims in clinics on the Thai–Cambodian border – leveraged a 1992 translation of *Coward's War* to start their campaign for a ban, called 'Stop the Coward's War'. During a February 1993 visit to Cambodia, French president Francois Mitterrand announced the establishment of a 'voluntary abstention' from exporting mines. Following recommendations in *Coward's War*, campaigners successfully pushed France to sponsor a resolution at the General Assembly later that year, calling for a review of the Convention on Certain Conventional Weapons (CCW). While the 1981 CCW had established nascent regulations in its Landmines Protocol, and included the world's major suppliers, its loophole-ridden restrictions did nothing to stop the massive landmine contamination crisis during the proxy wars. By the early 1990s, it had only been ratified by forty-four states and its regulations did not apply in civil wars (only international armed conflict). The indiscriminate aerial mining of Afghanistan by the USSR, a CCW signatory, was emblematic of the CCW's failures. It had little normative impact. The researchers of *Coward's War* found that almost no one in Cambodia had heard of the Landmines Protocol.[57] Nevertheless, the ICBL saw the review of the

CCW, which was scheduled for 1995, as an opportunity to push for a legally binding global ban. The CCW is a framework convention, which allows states parties to add additional protocols addressing weapons 'deemed to be excessively injurious or to have indiscriminate effects'. Reading *Coward's War* also inspired Belgian parliamentarians to pass the first national comprehensive ban in March 1995.[58]

When Sister Denise returned to Phnom Penh following the ICBL Geneva conference, JRS started the Cambodia Campaign to Ban Landmines (CCBL) in 1994 with MAG, HI, the Dhammayietra Movement and the Cambodian NGO Forum, an umbrella organization for many civil society organizations in the country. The Red Cross also agreed to coordinate its public outreach with the campaign. The CCBL 'quickly became a strong and important national campaign' for the ICBL, according to Jody Williams.[59] For Sister Denise, the CCBL was an obvious step: 'If you are working on an issue such as helping the people who have been injured by landmines, justice demands that you also advocate that the cause of the suffering be stopped.'[60] She asked Reth if he would be interested in joining the nascent campaign. From the very beginnings of the Cambodian campaign, Sister Denise told me, 'we were focused on hearing the voices of survivors'. Meeting him, I could see how she saw his potential. Reth is extroverted and expressive, talking with his hands and a booming voice. He laughs often, infectiously. At first, though, he was scared. 'There were guns and grenades everywhere' in Phnom Penh and 'the government didn't like people who spoke up'. Even though the Paris Accords purportedly ended the war in 1991, the Khmer Rouge had boycotted and condemned the deal. The government was often intolerant of dissent. But Reth found in himself an unexpected courage. He told me he felt God was calling him to 'share my testimony' and help achieve a global ban on landmines: 'I am a servant of God. While I am on this earth I must work for him. God uses me to help other people.' Reth agreed to co-author the following open letter with three other Cambodian landmine survivors, Hem Phang, Klieng Vann and Suon Chreuk:

We are amputees.
Before we were soldiers,
members of different armies,
that laid mines that blew the legs,
arms and eyes off one another.

Now we teach and learn together at the Centre of the Dove.

We beg the world to stop making mines.
We beg the world to stop laying mines.
We beg for funds for clearing mines so that we can rebuild
our families, our villages and our country again.

The CCBL printed the letter on petitions calling for an international ban on landmines and Reth began collecting signatures. Reth's irrepressible sense of humour made it difficult for people to refuse his pitch. Reth got an audience with Cambodia's king Norodom Sihanouk and persuaded him to sign the petition and back the campaign. Sihanouk listed his job title as 'King of Cambodia' and address as 'Royal Palace, Phnom Penh' on the petition. 'He really supported us – he understood the impact of landmines on his nation,' said Reth. Soon they had collected 30,000 signatures. Even Hun Sen, the co-prime minister who was sceptical of the Campaign, was among them.

Maha Ghosananda dedicated the May 1995 Dhammayietra to highlighting the impact of landmines. Marchers gathered 20,000 signatures for the CCBL petition along the way, as they traversed Cambodia from the Thai to the Vietnamese borders. The Landmines Dhammayietra was timed to link up with the Interfaith Pilgrimage for Peace, whose participants were walking from Auschwitz to Hiroshima. As they set off from Poipet, a Khmer Rouge stronghold, the pilgrims could hear artillery in the distance, as government troops clashed with the recalcitrant rebels. Landmines remained a common theme during future Dhammayietras.[61] Ghosananda told villagers alongside one march that they must 'remove the landmines in our heart', such as 'greed, hatred and delusion' that 'prevent us from making peace'. To address the landmines, both external and internal, we must 'listen with compassion, not pity' to those 'disabled by mines'; we must extend 'great gratitude to the deminers' and imitate the 'mindfulness' it takes to do their work. Finally, he said, we must reject the artificial divisions between human beings, seeing all people as 'our brothers and sisters in Afghanistan, Rwanda, former Yugoslavia and every country throughout the world'.[62]

Impressed by the Cambodia Campaign, the ICBL decided to hold its third major international conference in Phnom Penh, from 2 to 4 June 1995. Some 400 NGO, UN, Red Cross and government participants from forty countries participated, focusing on landmines' 'human and socio-economic impact'.[63] It was the first ICBL meeting held in a mine-affected country, and it developed a model, dubbed the 'Phnom Penh formula', which intentionally replicated elements of the

Dhammayietras. Firstly, CCBL infused the discussions with attention to the 'ethical dimensions' of landmines, rather than technical wonkery. The conference featured Buddhist, Christian, Jewish and Muslim religious voices declaring that landmines' violence 'against civilians long after war had ended could not be accepted by their faith traditions'.[64] Maha Ghosananda addressed the conference, urging participants to 'ban the landmines of the heart as well as in the earth'. This framing shaped how CCBL advocates, particularly Reth, spoke about landmines as they later travelled around the world.[65] Secondly, CCBL wanted attendees to see the realities of mine-affected communities outside the conference rooms, by visiting victim assistance, risk education and demining teams in the field. The testimony of survivors, including Reth, was also privileged in the programme. Impressed, ICBL coordinator Jody Williams personally requested Reth to get more involved in the campaign. She wanted to raise the profile of those most affected by landmines in a global coalition that had thus far been dominated by voices from the Global North. Thirdly, like the Dhammayietras, the CCBL framed the conference as an advocacy event, drawing media publicity and political attention. Sister Denise and other conference organizers sent a message to the Khmer Rouge leadership, pleading with them to 'make the first step [towards peace] today ... and stop laying mines'.[66] The final factor in the 'Phnom Penh formula' was an effort to replicate the success of the CCBL, through developing vibrant national-level campaigns, particularly in mine-affected countries and the Global South. A scholarly history of the Campaign states that 'the Cambodia conference was important because it was a major catalyst for broadening and expanding the ICBL membership ... [which] truly helped create a global movement'.[67] The Phnom Penh conference, writes Jody Williams, was also 'the first to push us to use email' – a much cheaper and reliable alternative to mail in Cambodia – as the primary means of communication.[68] Several scholars have observed that the ICBL's early adoption of email as a campaign tool enabled it to build a transnational advocacy network faster than had previously been achieved.[69]

Sister Denise explained that the ICBL was 'very decentralized' and that Jody Williams 'allowed national campaigns to do their own thing' at the national level as long as they backed a ban on anti-personnel landmines. Following the conference, the CCBL stepped up its petition drives – eventually collecting 310,000 signatures – as well as a disinvestment campaign, targeting a food aid contractor that was investing in landmine manufacture. They persuaded journalists to file reports and make documentaries about the landmine crisis in Cambodia. But JRS also realized that they could make important contributions to the international campaign, by 'ensuring victims are heard and assisted,' said Sister Denise. She was concerned that people with disabilities were 'often depicted as abject, but that is not true. They have to be subjects of their own future.' JRS also channelled 'moral and ethical arguments' into advocacy with diplomats, working through interfaith networks. Sister Denise said that interfaith rituals helped to draw 'ordinary people from the parishes' into the campaign.

CCBL sent twelve campaigners to Vienna for the CCW Review Conference, 25 September to 23 October 1995. NGOs and activists had been largely excluded from preparatory meetings in Geneva, but the chair of the Vienna conference, Swedish diplomat Johan Molander, was sympathetic to ICBL's assertion that diplomats needed to hear the voices of those affected by mines. Reth and other landmine survivors from Afghanistan, Cambodia, Mozambique and the United States presented to Molander the petition – now with 1.7 million signatures from fifty-three countries.[70] Reth and Song Kosal, an eleven-year-old Cambodian landmine survivor, delivered impassioned pleas to the delegates for a ban on mines, accelerated humanitarian demining and support for people with disabilities. However, the CCW operates on rules of consensus, which the more powerful states wielded as a de facto veto. Strong proposals from pro-ban governments were repeatedly watered down, to the chagrin of ICBL campaigners. Governments failed to reach a settlement, merely agreeing to continue negotiations on an Amended Landmines Protocol over two meetings in Geneva (in January and May 1996). As the conference ended, Reth's article on the front page of the ICBL conference newsletter said that he and other landmine survivors were to 'leave Vienna very sad. We came with such high hopes ... to speak to you all and ask for a total ban on landmines, which hurt the poor. But you did not listen to us. ... Please think again.'[71]

After Vienna, the ICBL decided it could not be held captive to a moribund diplomatic process. They took their case directly to the public, getting on the evening news, badgering political leaders and winning celebrity endorsements. JRS sent Reth, Kosal and Figaredo on a speaking tour around the world. They met with President Mary Robinson of Ireland, the king and queen of Spain, the English actress Glenda Jackson and, in one of Reth's favourite moments of the Campaign, the Holy Father in the Vatican: 'I still remember the bells ringing in Rome when he called for a ban.'[72] I asked Reth what it was like to meet Pope John Paul II. 'It was very funny! I showed him an antipersonnel landmine and people were shocked. I told him it did this to me,' he laughs, slapping his knee; his right leg is amputated just below it. 'I told him about the situation in Cambodia and asked him to support the Campaign.' Reth often carried models of landmines with him – certified Free From Explosives, he reassured me – to show people what caused his disabilities. He guffaws, saying that once had told UN guards that his defused mine was a plastic tobacco box to get it through security. Reth used Maha Ghosananda's 'landmines of the heart' line wherever he travelled and used it on me too: 'Landmines start in your heart, when you hate someone or want something from them and resent them.' To remove them, 'we must grow love and justice'.

Reth was not able to make it to the January 1996 CCW meeting. But in a message he, Kosal and four other Cambodian landmine survivors wrote to the conference delegates, they lamented that in Vienna, the world's governments 'had let military desires and business interests prevail over humanitarian needs'. They acknowledged that they were 'little people in a small, poor, mine ravaged country', but claimed that they too have a kind of power, one that 'does not come from money or position'. Rather, it derives from 'our suffering, caused by mines'. They had 'faith in the ultimate goodness of other human beings ... because we experience deep within our bodies the inner courage and resilience to begin life again, maimed and poor as we might seem to you'. This gave them an advantage over the delegates:

> If you fail to outlaw landmines you will not extinguish our hope ... .
> But you will be less human for your decision. You will go home
> knowing that you had it in your power to alleviate the suffering of
> many and you will also know that you did not have the courage to
> break free from old thinking and out of date ideology.[73]

When governments reconvened at the UN in Geneva in May, CCBL sent a large delegation, including Reth, Kosal, Sister Denise, Ghosananda, Figaredo and Bernstein. They set up a 'Wall of Remembrance' outside the negotiation room, displaying photographs of the 230 people hurt by landmines in Cambodia's Battambang province since the CCW Review Conference. Above it, they placed a digital counter showing the global number of mine victims since the Vienna meeting, which continued to increase at the estimated rate of one new victim every 22 minutes. Several observers recalled how chilling it was to watch the number tick upwards throughout the conference. Reth told assembled delegates that 'if it were their children being blown up', they would have already banned landmines.[74] But pro-ban diplomats again struggled with the CCW's constraints. They were unable to prevent the major military powers – the United States, Russia, China, India and Pakistan – some of the biggest producers of landmines, from using consensus to water down proposed new regulations. In despair, Reth and other landmine survivors protested outside the gates of the UN, stopping diplomats' cars to hand them ICBL literature. Reth was particularly pleased to impede the entry of the Russian ambassador, having lost a leg to a Soviet mine. Nearby, HI had built a 'mountain of shoes' to represent all the landmine survivors who would no longer need footwear. Reth and others were blocked from entering the UN for several hours after their demonstration; one recalled that 'the delegates did not disguise their contempt for being put in an uncomfortable position'.[75]

The conference concluded with the adoption of the CCW's Amended Landmines Protocol, whose convoluted provisions would do little to address the humanitarian crisis in places such as Afghanistan and Cambodia. Indeed, it allowed states to continue using mines as long as they were detectable and self-destructed within thirty days, 90 per cent of the time. The ICRC expressed disappointment and the ICBL condemned the result outright, saying that it had weakened provisions of the original instrument, since it could encourage states to develop new types of high-tech mines. The ICBL argued that self-destructing mines were still indiscriminate while they were active and, given the failure rate, all of them would have to be treated as potentially dangerous by deminers.[76]

As the CCW conference drew to a close, Reth told me he was unable to hold back tears as he addressed the delegates. He pleaded, 'We want you to see us', the survivors who had come to the conference from 'Afghanistan, Mozambique and Cambodia ... to put a human face on the mass suffering caused by landmines'. He said that it was 'easy to legalize new war toys ... from inside big buildings where you do not see the hospitals and killing fields of our country', but he demanded that delegates look at him and his fellow survivors: 'We are living reminders of what the power of hate can do to our legs and arms and eyes'. Drawing on Ghosananda's wisdom, he told the gathered officials that they needed to remove the landmines of their hearts that left them 'trapped by fear and mistrust'. He finished on a defiant note: 'Because we believe that the power of love and kindness is much stronger than the power of hate. ... We will win! Landmines will be banned'.[77] His optimistic tone seemed out of touch with the conference's failure, but there was reason for hope. A small group of pro-ban states, along with the ICBL and ICRC, had been holding discreet meetings at the Quaker UN Office in Geneva to strategize a way forward outside the CCW. At the end of the conference, the Canadian delegation announced that it would host a meeting in October for those governments that were dissatisfied with the new protocol and wanted to explore alternatives.

The meeting, held in Ottawa, was organized in a radically different fashion from the CCW conferences. The Canadian government worked with ICBL campaigners, who advised them to use the 'Phnom Penh formula', putting ethical and humanitarian – rather than military – concerns at the centre of the conversation.[78] To participate fully in the conference, states were required to sign a declaration committing to pursue a ban on anti-personnel landmines (detractors could attend as observers). The Ottawa meeting prioritized the voices of survivors, aid organizations and advocacy groups, allowing the ICRC, ICBL and other civil society organizations not only the right to sit in the room, but to intervene actively in the debate. The meeting was also framed as a public event – not just a diplomatic negotiation – drawing media and political attention. In what was expected to be a formulaic farewell speech (several key diplomats, including the head of the US delegation, had already left), Canada's foreign minister Lloyd Axworthy delivered a surprise announcement. He declared that Canada itself would sponsor the negotiation of a ban outside traditional channels. Next December – just fourteen months away – he would reconvene another meeting in Ottawa in order to sign a completed treaty, even if only one other country was there to join them. ICBL campaigners leapt to their feet in applause that drowned out the rest of Axworthy's speech. Before sceptical states could object, the ICBL and ICRC were given the opportunity to welcome Canada's proposal (they had been told about the plan only 90 minutes before) and the conference was gavelled closed. Canada's gamble infuriated many diplomats. The Americans, who had been caught off guard, expected closer consultations with their neighbour.

The ICBL, ICRC and key supportive states – Austria, Belgium, Canada, Denmark, Ireland, Mexico, Norway, South Africa and Switzerland – realized that the 'Ottawa Process' would only succeed if it conveyed overwhelming momentum towards a ban. Working closely together, they generated an unprecedented global public outcry against a conventional weapon. Many notable moral authorities joined the call, such as Nelson Mandela and Archbishop Desmond Tutu. Princess Diana expressed her support for a ban, visiting demining programmes and survivor support projects in Angola and, shortly before she died, Bosnia. CCBL campaigners continued travelling. In 1997 alone, Reth spoke in Japan, New Zealand, Australia, France, Belgium, Ireland, Spain, Italy, the UK, Norway, Switzerland, Austria and Germany.[79]

Unlike the CCW process, the emerging draft text of the 'Ottawa Convention' strengthened over the course of negotiations in Vienna, Brussels and Oslo, chaired by the no-nonsense South African diplomat Jacob Selebi. Landmine survivors objected to the lack of provisions for victim assistance and fought successfully (even over objections from some ICBL members) for its inclusion.[80] This was the first time an arms control or disarmament treaty had included help for those hurt by a weapon. Two-thirds majority voting, rather than consensus rules, meant that one government's vested military interests could not derail the text. Embedding civil society in the process, rather than keeping them outside the room, also prevented delegations from straying from the treaty's humanitarian imperative. As a result, the United States failed to strong-arm other governments into including exceptions for the Korean peninsula and American mines, as well as a delayed entry into force of the treaty. Campaigners provided diplomats with talking points and pep-talks for their meetings with the United States and publicly shamed delegations – even Canada at one point – that seemed to waver in their commitment to a categorical prohibition. 'No exceptions, no reservations and no loopholes' was the ICBL rallying cry.

When 122 states reconvened in Ottawa in early December 1997 – just ten years after aid agencies began experimenting with mine clearance in Afghanistan – they signed a complete ban on the manufacture, trade, use and stockpiling of victim-activated anti-personnel landmines. The new treaty, rooted in international humanitarian law, also including provisions committing governments to the clearance of all minefields, as well as ramping up aid for mine risk education and 'the care and rehabilitation, and social and economic reintegration, of mine victims' (Article 6(3)). 'It was a miracle,' Sister Denise told me. What had been unthinkable just a decade earlier – a disarmament treaty championed and drafted by non-superpowers and NGOs – had sped through negotiations in one year. Small states, drawing confidence from the end of the Cold War, had forged an independent path, refusing to be superpower proxies.

One week after the treaty signing, the ICBL and Jody Williams, as its coordinator, were jointly awarded the Nobel Peace Prize in Oslo. There was a poetic justice in the award, since the Nobel family made their initial fortune selling mines to Russia during the Crimean War. Alongside Jody, Reth accepted the Prize on behalf of the Campaign and

Rae McGrath, founder of MAG, delivered the Campaign's lecture. To the blast of trumpets, they entered Oslo's city hall, processing through an audience of campaigners, dignitaries and the Norwegian king and queen. With a wide smile, Sister Denise said that watching Reth receive the medal, in his Mekong wheelchair, triumphant arm raised, 'was the best moment' and it 'brought everyone to their feet'. As one observer put it, 'Channareth became a symbol of a global movement; if he could transform his suffering and pain into a single-minded drive to ban mines, could not a world movement transform the private loss of all victims and survivors of [antipersonnel] mines into a public problem that demanded a solution?'[81]

In her Nobel Lecture, Williams celebrated that smaller states 'can work together with civil society and address humanitarian concerns with breathtaking speed. It shows that such a partnership is a new kind of "superpower" in the post-Cold War world.'[82] For Williams, collective action, guided by the principles of humanity, offered a way out of the explosive traps of modern warfare. Many campaigners believed the landmine ban would be, as one activist put it to me, a 'seismic shift' in international relations, a new dispensation in which 'the little guys' could shape global institutions, resource flows and even how militaries used violence. In its article on the ban's signing ceremony, the *Ottawa Citizen* quoted Reth heralding 'a new dawn of peace and kindness'.[83]

Sceptics were less sanguine. They expressed doubts that the new Anti-personnel Landmine Ban Treaty would constrain those most committed to violence. The treaty has few monitoring measures or punitive sanctions – instead relying on a non-governmental project, the ICBL's *Landmine Monitor* as its de facto verification regime. Few of the major military powers have joined the treaty. Moreover, the treaty can only be signed by internationally recognized governments. How likely is it to have any impact on the behaviour of the world's quasi-states, rebel groups, armed gangs and terrorist networks?

But the treaty has had a more profound normative impact than the cynics would have expected. All of the major landmine-producing states now have export bans or moratoria (including the United States, Russia and China). Many states that have remained outside the Ottawa Convention have slowly drawn closer to its standards. Few continue to manufacture, stockpile, use or transfer anti-personnel landmines. The United States has become the biggest donor of foreign aid to mine action projects around the world. And campaigners have persuaded at least some non-state armed groups to comply with the prohibition on anti-personnel mines and facilitate the work of deminers, mine risk education and victim assistance.[84] In early 2020, Trump abandoned joining the landmine ban as the eventual goal of US policy. But he seemed motivated more by animus toward his predecessor than any pressure from the American military, which has largely recognised the norms against landmines.[85] A former Pentagon official with responsibility for landmine policy acknowledged that the ban treaty, 'has undeniably had an incredible effect on tamping down the use of APLs [anti-personnel landmines] globally. Even the casual or jaded observer would have to admit that the chill in manufacturing, transfer and use of APLs is directly or indirectly attributable to the Ottawa Treaty.'[86]

Sister Denise says that 'part of the success of the treaty' comes from the fact that the campaign 'stuck together' to monitor and advocate for robust implementation. In 2011, Reth, Sister Denise and the rest of the CCBL team were able to welcome the international mine action community back to Phnom Penh for the 11th Meeting of States Parties of the ban treaty. Reth continues to campaign at the international, regional and national level to reinforce the stigma against mines and similar devices. He and Kosal played an important role as advocates for the Cluster Munition Coalition, and Reth told me he has joined efforts calling for a ban on killer robots. In Cambodia, Reth works with a programme providing education, housing, wheelchairs, toilets and wells to landmine survivors and fights for the rights of people with disabilities. He says, 'Finding ways to earn a living is still the number one priority for survivors in mine-affected communities.'[87]

*   *   *

When I ran out of interview questions, Sister Denise offered to guide me around the Metta Karuna Center's grounds. JRS built the Center in the hope that people would come to Cambodia and stay with JRS. Sister Denise said they anticipated visitors would 'see the situation of the poor from an interfaith perspective, to see the underside of history'. JRS also use the facilities as a base for their aid to people with disabilities. 'It is supposed to be a place of reflection and hopefully action,' Sister Denise told me. Near the entrance to the property was a striking sculpture of a kneeling Jesus in white stone, prostrate before a young man, with the familiar cloth and bowl of the foot washing in the Upper Room. But the young man's lower limbs have been amputated. A sign offers a caption: 'I have no foot to wash.' The artist, a former teacher at Banteay Prieb, Chay Soran, lost his leg to a mine. As we walk down a path winding through the compound, Sister Denise tells me that 'when they dug up the back of this place they found a mine'. Ambling by fruit trees, pots filled with water and floating lotuses, orchids in hanging baskets, we pass under a styrofoam mobile, fashioned by Reth, representing an airplane dropping cluster bombs over our heads. 'It needs a few more bombs,' Sister Denise chuckles. 'A few of them have fallen off'. We round a pond; local people told Sister Denise that the crater, now filled with water, was made by a cluster munition strike. Sister Denise then introduces me to white stone statues, also made by Chay Soran, of King Jayavarman VII, who is depicted with no arms, and Queen Indradevi, remembered in Cambodian lore as wise rulers of the Khmer Empire from 1125 to 1215. Jayavarman is known as the 'The Leper King', as legend has it that he suffered from the disease. Converted to Buddhism by his spouse, Jayavarman was moved to compassion for his less fortunate subjects, establishing hospitals for the sick, caring for the poor and welcoming strangers.

Next we come upon a large wall with a bas-relief depicting a Dhammayietra in the style of the Khmer temples in the Angkor complex. The figures – Buddhist monks, Catholic priests and nuns, farmers, people in wheelchairs and soldiers – are modelled on actual people. Sister Denise points out Maha Ghosananda and Msgr. Figaredo. We end our tour with the chapel. On the wall is an abstract representation of the crucifixion, in wire. Jesus's head, a simple metal oval, leans slightly to the left, hinting at his agony. I realize I recognize the piece. Sister Denise has been wearing a smaller version around her neck. But she points out something I had not noticed, the right leg is significantly shorter than the left. Figaredo found this representation in a Jesuit retreat centre in Portugal. Though he could never locate the artist, he has adopted it as the symbol of the Catholic mission in Cambodia.[88] He calls it the Disabled Christ. For Figaredo, Sister Denise, Reth and their colleagues at JRS, it symbolises finding the spirit of Christ among the people with disabilities with whom they work. When a landmine maims a person, the incarnated God is also mutilated and suffers. We are commanded to love our neighbour, not use them as a proxy for our own ends. To ban landmines rebukes those who take the limbs and lives of people who are made in the image of God. When we serve the landmine survivor, Sister Denise asserts, we serve God.[89]

Chapter 4

FRAGMENTATION
NEW WAR, BOSNIA AND HERZEGOVINA

On a summer day in the late 1990s, a commercial demining team was clearing a minefield near a body of water in Bosnia and Herzegovina. The internationally funded contract, which they had been working on for just over three weeks, required them to clear an overgrown patch of land on the south bank of the water, not far from a war-damaged coffee shop under reconstruction. The boundaries of the minefield had been well marked by the Bosnian government, with signage warning people to stay away. That morning, the team of six deminers, a paramedic, drivers and a team leader, had arrived on site at dawn. It was sunny and clear that day and the ground was soft with moisture from the river, making it easier for deminers to prod the ground in their search for landmines, though thick vegetation complicated their work. Following a safety briefing and verification of their equipment, the deminers worked in the minefield for an hour and a half. The deminers exited the hazardous area, removed their protective equipment and took a 15-minute coffee break.

They had only just returned to work when a PROM-1 bounding fragmentation landmine – which had been completely covered by the silty soil at the water's edge – exploded into the air. A Yugoslav-made mine, the PROM-1 is a variation of the German Nazi-era S-mine that Allied soldiers nicknamed the 'Bouncing Betty'. It has a small charge that when set off by the victim, launches the device into the air before a secondary explosion sprays deadly shrapnel up to 100 metres away. The PROM-1 was one of the nastiest pieces of ordnance deployed during the violent break-up of the former Yugoslavia. It is a deminer's nightmare. It has caused a disproportionate number of casualties in Bosnia after the war. 'Victim No. 1', as the scrubbed government's accident report calls him, 'took the full blast of the PROM1 mine on his face and died on the spot'. Fragmentation from the mine hit a second deminer – 'Victim No. 2'– in the throat and, bleeding heavily, he died on the way to the hospital. The team leader was injured in the back but survived after two days of treatment in a nearby hospital. The government's report praises the paramedic who performed his duties 'very effectively immediately following the accident'.

When investigators from the government's Bosnia and Herzegovina Mine Action Center (BHMAC) visited the accident site mid-afternoon, they found that 'Victim No. 2' had failed to find the PROM-1 mine, despite an earlier admonition from the team leader to carefully excavate anything that set off his metal detector. They also discovered that the two victims had been working much too closely to each other, which the accident investigation described as a 'flagrant disregard of such a fundamental and commonsensical procedural regulation'. The regulations required deminers to be spaced 50 metres from each other in the minefield to limit casualties in the event of an accident. Commercial demining companies sometimes balk at such regulations that slow their work down, limiting the number of deminers who can work in a minefield at the same time. BHMAC found that two of the deminers on this site had only been 8 metres from each other. They had also not been wearing protective equipment, because they had been in an area that was 'presumed "cleared"' already. However, there were signs that the 'site had been tampered with prior to the' arrival of the investigators. This was not the only sign of potential problems on the site. Five days earlier, a government inspector had raised concerns about the methods being used to clear vegetation on the site, and the accident investigation found that the team had been clearing a rate faster than normal for such a densely overgrown area. 'It would appear', suggested the investigation, that the 'rate of productivity was too high under the circumstances' and that there was 'evidence that several actions contrary to normal and safe procedures were permitted to take place'.[1]

* * *

The 1992–5 war in Bosnia divided a land associated with cosmopolitan coexistence into 'ethnically cleansed' fragments. It was one of several post-Cold War conflicts that were described by the scholar Mary Kaldor as 'New Wars', characterized by a disintegration in state authority, dominance by political–criminal networks and ethno-nationalist violence.[2] Since the former Yugoslavia had been a major manufacturer of landmines such as the PROM-1, armed groups – particularly those associated with the breakaway 'Serb Republic' – had used them extensively to create new explosive boundaries between communities.

During the war, according to security scholar Mats Berdal, many 'participants became preoccupied primarily with economic gain', fuelling a 'process of fragmentation' that transformed the marketplace into 'a criminalized war economy'.[3] Concerned about becoming complicit in corruption, foreign donor governments and international institutions such as the World Bank wanted post-war demining in Bosnia to be privatized, contracted out to companies and NGOs. According to the political orthodoxy of the time, private actors were seen as less likely to be tainted than government agencies. But this approach actually entrenched the splintering of the political system, empowering those with vested interests in militant nationalism and criminality.[4] While privatization of public services was intended to undermine graft, in Bosnia it did the opposite – allowing the criminal networks to capture reconstruction programmes. When aid donors showed up after the war, offering millions of dollars to address the landmine hazard, former officers from the local military factions hastily set up local demining firms. Some of these people had been implicated in the horrors of the war; some had rumoured links to organized crime.[5] There were 'numerous allegations of corruption, including clearance tasks undertaken to benefit specific individuals ... kickbacks for the award of contracts ... burying meat on test sites for explosives detection dogs to distract competitor's dogs during accreditation trials, and re-laying landmines on sites cleared by competitors'.[6] These problems are not unique to mine action. Aid workers in conflicted contexts often find themselves drawn into the politics of the war and its aftermath. As Mary Anderson wrote in her study *Do No Harm: How Aid Can Support Peace – Or War*, 'Aid too often ... feeds into, reinforces, and prolongs conflicts. Again and again aid workers tell how their aid is distorted by local politics and is misappropriated.'[7]

The World Bank was the first major contributor to raise concerns, terminating their Bosnian demining funding in 1999. An internal evaluation deemed the programme, which was contracted out to a variety of local and international companies, 'Highly Unsatisfactory'.[8] Their decisive move reflected a broader shift in mood. By the end of the 1990s, international officials granted the powers to govern Bosnia by the peace process began to exert their authority against the local structures that they believed were hindering the implementation of the peace treaty. In 1999, the High Representative representing the international community imposed ninety decisions on the country, compared with thirty in the previous three years combined. The High Representative removed mayors, civil servants and elected officials, even the president of Bosnia's Serb entity.

In August 1999, Wolfgang Petritsch took over as High Representative and continued his predecessor's robust approach. Petritsch, an Austrian of ethnic Slovenian descent, was a respected international diplomat and scholar who had a PhD in south-eastern European history. By late 2000, he became alarmed by reports of corruption in the demining sector, which he saw as crucial for Bosnia's post-conflict recovery. He later told me that he had a 'military cell' within his office – a group of NATO officers assigned to advise him. Demining fell within their remit and as the depth of problems within the mine action sector became clear, they relayed information of an 'ongoing fraud scheme' to Petritsch. That summer, Bosnia's Financial Police raided the offices of several demining organizations, and by October, Petritsch had had enough. 'It is unacceptable', said Petritsch, that Bosnians and international donors 'should be left with just cause to doubt the integrity and commitment of those ... entrusted with the essential task of demining'. He felt 'obliged therefore to take upon myself the responsibility of preventing further harm from being done'. He removed the government's Demining Commissioners, citing 'misuse of office', 'breach of public trust' and 'widespread conflict of interest'.[9] All three were also banned from holding public office. This was lifted in 2006 for two of them, though the Office of the High Representative insisted that this 'does not call into question the validity of the 2000 Decision'.[10] The third, Berislav 'Berko' Pusic, remained banned and was later convicted by the international war crimes tribunal at The Hague of playing 'a major role in organizing' the effort 'to expel the Muslim population' in the breakaway Croat region of Bosnia during the war.[11] Petritsch handed his files over to the Financial Police but told me, 'I don't think anything ever came out of it, that is of course due to the weakness of the judicial system there'. He believed the 'decisive flaw' in the structure of the Bosnia demining sector was that it was divided along ethnic lines, allowing Commissioners to set up ethnic patronage networks. As a result, Petritsch decided to 'take away' demining from the ethnic entity level and 'elevate mine action issues to state level'. This made the newly reorganized demining programme one of the first centrally shared public services in Bosnia's post-war era.

Nevertheless, as it reeled from the resulting fallout and scandal, the demining sector took several years to regroup. Funding dropped and additional problems emerged. Shortly after I began the demining project in Brcko, NATO intelligence services found credible evidence that certain demining companies might be fronts helping fugitive war criminals evade capture. We were ordered by our funder to change our choice of contractors on our project. Elsewhere, NATO troops conducted raids, arrested demining managers and an international prosecutor opened a case on demining corruption (it was eventually dropped).[12] It took time for the implications of this information to filter out of the demining sector, but as it was leaked to the press and advocacy organizations, government aid donors blacklisted certain local companies and conducted a thorough review of the sector.[13] A US diplomatic cable titled 'Demining: Allegations of Fraud and Malfeasance in USG [US Government] Programs' (made public by WikiLeaks) summarized the results of a week-long investigation by State Department officials in Bosnia. 'At all locations' they visited, the cable's authors reported hearing 'allegations of systematic and pervasive fraud throughout the demining process'.

> [Demining] inspectors told us that they have been instructed by superiors to falsely declare clean areas as 'mined' in order to award fraudulent demining contracts. Even more troubling, they report pressure to falsely declare areas free of mines after shoddy work by ... contractors.[14]

According to two additional cables the following year, the US Embassy in Sarajevo requested Bosnian police to open a 'full investigation' of all demining programmes with American funding. The cables went into more depth about the allegations, providing evidence of 'a practice approving annexes to contracts long after the work was completed', which 'often resulted in thousands more dollars being given to the contractor without due diligence being performed on services provided'.[15] The cable notes with concern that 'in the near term, we expect to deal with the fall-out as word ... circulates throughout the demining community'.[16]

Around the same time of the State Department-sponsored investigation, the director of BHMAC, Dusan Gavran, told me that he was 'very sad' to read reports of corruption in Bosnian demining. He wanted me to know that early on in mine action 'it was, as you say, a bit difficult here'. But, 'now', he said, 'everything is solved'. Back then, he told me, the country didn't have sufficient 'regulations and procedures'; 'now we do. ... We have a good system ... so everything needs to go by the rules.' He told me, 'I've been involved with mines all my life', emphasizing that his technical credentials were 'untouchable'. He had studied mines and military engineering in Belgrade with the Yugoslav National Army, later lecturing on mine warfare at its Tito Barracks in Sarajevo. During the Bosnian war, he was an officer in the army of the breakaway Serb Republic. Afterwards, as a lieutenant colonel, he was part of Bosnia's national-level Standing Committee on Military Matters. He joined BHMAC in 2002 and came to it with extensive leadership experience: 'I was an officer and I've always worked in state institutions. … I was always at the top, as a commander, director. That's why I survived here.' As a result, he said, 'I can talk to you and look you in the eyes' and 'I can say firmly that I'm not involved in any kind of criminal activity'.

Petritsch was insistent that corruption within the Bosnian demining sector should not be depicted simply as a 'local' problem. He believed it was at least partially 'of our own making' – 'our' being the international community – for not advocating for an integrated, rather than ethnically divided, system. Similarly, Mary Anderson has argued that if it is not politically aware, 'international assistance … can feed intergroup tensions' and entrench problematic social structures.[17] Petritsch said that a combination of 'ignorance and not really wanting to get involved' meant that the international community bore some responsibility for the problems that arose. Petritsch said he was caught off guard when certain Western diplomats were 'not very enthusiastic' about his assertive response to the demining sector. Petritsch suspected there were some expatriates and international companies who were benefiting commercially from the status quo. 'Corruption', Petritsch mused to me, 'is not always the "Others", the locals.'

The expatriate manager of one international company – a subsidiary of an arms manufacturer that had once designed landmines – had served in some of the most feared institutions in South Africa's apartheid security apparatus. According to the Truth and Reconciliation Commission, he had been involved in the torture and extrajudicial killing of black activists.[18] I met other expatriate demining professionals who had spent their lives as soldiers, police and mercenaries in the shadows of the Cold War's uglier episodes. In competing for demining tenders, several international companies had profited from the weak rule of law in the post-war environment and from partnerships with the local ethnicized patronage system. International companies formed the funnel through which lucrative contracts with foreign government donors flowed to the local level. For a time, enough people benefited from this arrangement that few raised much fuss.

The 1990s boom in the demining market in Bosnia coincided with a global privatization of security services. The failure of security in states once propped up by Cold War aid, exacerbated by a glut of ex-Soviet weaponry pouring into conflict zones, created a demand for private protection for multinational corporations, VIPs, aid agencies and diplomatic personnel. This was met by an unprecedented supply of military personnel, knowledge and equipment being released into the private sector, as countries around the world cut their military budgets and retrenched their armies in anticipation of a post-Cold War peace dividend. At the leading edge of this burgeoning industry were South African firms, stocked with highly trained white officers laid off or alienated in the transition from white rule. Enterprising former soldiers and police officers set up new corporations dedicated to offering security, military training and even combat operations for hire.

Many of these private military companies, joined by large weapons manufacturers, saw demining as an opportunity to diversify their corporate profiles, drawing on the same human resources pool of former military personnel while appearing to do something 'worthy'. A telling symbol was the ubiquitous use by commercial demining firms of South African Casspir mine-resistant armoured vehicles, once a frightening symbol of the apartheid's militarized regulation of township life, now retooled for 'humanitarian' purposes. In the aftermath of the 1991 Persian Gulf War, Kuwait ploughed $800 million into frenetic demining contracts, mostly with weapons manufacturers. Within the demining community, the Kuwait programme has become a watchword for money-driven carelessness and sloppiness – 84 people were killed and 200 injured. Some areas had to be 'recleared' years later.[19] Some of these firms had previously been linked to the development of mines and cluster munitions, spurring cries of 'double dipping' – making money from both selling and clearing mines – from anti-landmine campaigners.

I once asked a former international demining contractor if he felt uncomfortable with some of the people he did business with in Bosnia. He dismissed such concerns as 'an absolute waste of time. They were thugs. But the fact was we were able to get some demining done through these thugs. You wanna start a demining program or do you want to sit on your hands and twiddle your thumbs at the same time?' I found similar attitudes among many of the international aid officials bankrolling the Bosnian demining programme. Parroting the fashionable rhetoric of privatization, they argued that commercial companies brought 'a more business-like response to mine action' than the UN, military or NGOs.

The rigours of competitive contracting, they claimed, would bring cost-savings, higher productivity and increased effectiveness.[20] In private, NGO professionals would speculate to me that some of the government donors preferred hiring commercial firms because they made less noise and didn't join the global campaign for a landmine ban.

*   *   *

To squeals of derision, two green puppets with sharp teeth and gruff voices pleaded their innocence to an incredulous Judge. The Judge, a professional actor with gavel, robes and elastically expressive face, asked the 'Jury' – an audience of five- to eleven-year-olds – if they found the two scruffy marionettes, representing an anti-tank mine and a grenade, guilty of hiding in the ground and hurting people. The anti-tank mine had long arms, angry eyebrows and an unruly tuft of brown hair. The grenade had jaundiced eyes and a Green Man laurel resting on his forehead. Having heard witness testimony from a floppy yellow rabbit, a grey mouse wearing a red tie and an enormous bumblebee, the children chorused their verdict, *Da!*, in unison and a Deminer, in blue boiler suit and Kevlar jacket, came to take the offending ordnance away, to the jeers of the classroom. Following this 'Strange Trial', a puppet show put on by a local NGO named Genesis Project, the Judge and Deminer quizzed the children on the lessons of the performance. The kids bounced in their chairs and strained their hands in the air to answer: 'Do not pick up or touch unknown objects', 'Do not let your friends play with dangerous objects', 'Never go alone into unknown areas'.

After hanging around the paramilitary culture of demining organizations, I found my first interactions with the Genesis Project rather comical. Rather than the macho and hierarchical environment of a demining team, the Genesis Project resembled a travelling band of players. Actors, artists, educators and foam puppets touring Bosnia's primary schools seemed somehow less, well, badass, than ex-soldiers harrumphing around minefields. Even the man playing The Deminer in 'The Strange Trial' seemed too nice, too kind, too kid-friendly.

When she first heard about puppet shows raising children's awareness of landmines, the vice-principal of a village school in Lopare, north-eastern Bosnia, was rather sceptical. How could such important topics be taught by funny-looking toys? However, as she later recalled in tears to Genesis Project staff, her mind was changed when she experienced the impact the puppets could have. A few months after the performance, the vice-principal's own children (who attended her school) had snuck away. Without permission, they visited the home from which the family had been driven during the war. Exploring the now-destroyed house, the two youngsters spotted a landmine. Freezing in her tracks, the daughter told her younger brother everything she had heard in the Genesis Project presentation. They then acted exactly as the characters in the puppet show had instructed them to do. No one was hurt. Floppy rabbit puppets might look childish, but they could save lives.

In collaboration with the UNICEF office in Sarajevo, the Genesis Project developed the puppet shows to deal with the pedagogical challenge posed by landmines and UXO. How do you talk to small children about serious, life-threatening topics without frightening them? How do you deal with the fact that some of their parents may have in fact laid the landmines in their community? Traditional landmine awareness education was adapted from military briefings: heavy on the swagger sticks and featuring gruesome photographs. At best, such presentations were too dull for squirming six-year-olds. At worst, they were terrifying, leaving a child anxious, rather than equipped with survival skills. UNICEF and the Genesis Project found that children were less scared by disturbing messages when they came from the mouths of puppets, rather than directly from an adult. Rather than shutting down discussion, in which a child would feel unable to question the 'expert' briefer, the puppet plays engaged children's imagination and creativity, evidenced by this delightful sample from one of their scripts:

PECURKO: (WHISPERING)
Let's call forest wizard to ask him what mines are.
(Sound effect. Worm appears at the window of the log cabin)
WORM:
Scientist ... you should call a scientist!
BIRD:
Scientist! (short break) I will call a scientist.
(Sound effect and bird flies away to get scientists)
(Music)
SCIENTIST: (HE PUTS ON HIS GLASSES AND LOOKS LIKE HE IS
    PREPARING A LECTURE)
(HE STARTS TALKING SERIOUSLY AND WITH AUTHORITY)
(MUSIC STOPS)
You asked what mines are?! A mine is a device ... (THINKS)
WORM: (LOUDLY)
... is an explosive device. BOOM. BOOM. BOOM.

By June 2005, when I visited, almost 100,000 children had seen performances in their primary schools of at least one of the three Genesis Project puppet plays – 'The Strange Trial' being the latest. UNICEF financed moving the adventures of the Genesis Project puppets from the stage to the screen. After broadcasting the shows on nine Bosnian TV stations, the Genesis Project distributed videotapes of the productions, along with resource packs to schools throughout the country.

UNICEF's mine action at the time was supervised by Nathalie Prevost. Full disclosure – I worked for her on this project for a couple years and she was one of the best bosses I have had. Exhibiting a wry Gallic sense of humour, she had always had a self-deprecating smile below fashionable spectacles that betrayed her earlier career: a decade as an art director at the French public relations giant, Publicis. At some point, she decided that she wanted more from life than a career in advertising and parlayed her skills in communication into mine risk education, working for Handicap International (now Humanity and Inclusion), MAG, UNICEF and the Red Cross in a wide swath of the mine-contaminated world, including Angola, Mozambique, Cambodia, Ethiopia, Palestine and, by the time I met her, Bosnia.

Nathalie was not taken in by the masculinity fest of mine action and yet remained widely respected. 'I just do children's coloring books', she would say with a laugh when the testosterone level in a mine action meeting rose too high, 'I just fund puppet-shows'. Around her office were funny crayon drawings by her daughter, to whom she was a dedicated mother. This feminine persona regularly led people to underestimate the influence she had in the slow transformation of Bosnian mine action. She supported the local people who were trying to move mine action away from a paramilitary affair led by those who had perpetrated the conflict, into something more developmental, peacebuilding and humanitarian. Her programme didn't have much money, compared to the millions sloshed around by other donor agencies, but she used it thoughtfully. She made sure grants went to organizations such as the Genesis Project and helped mould policies that were more gender-equitable and aware of the human rights of landmine and UXO survivors. And she encouraged the involvement of a broad cross section of Bosnian society in the decisions about demining priorities.

At Nathalie's request, I once went out into the field with Bosnian Army officers, who were planning demining efforts in a rural village. Meeting in a farmer's back garden, under the shade of a grape vine pergola, the officers met with local leaders, calmly listening to their concerns and incorporating them into the planning process. They were using the methodology of community engagement that Nathalie had helped develop, a stark contrast to the way the military had treated the civilian population during the war. Nathalie and her network of unlikely mine action personnel – artists, actors, academics and social workers – were even influencing the way the Army was interacting with its people. Nathalie saw landmines as an expression of wider divisions in society. As a result, rather than seeing her work as simply about mines, she thought about it holistically as an effort to build links between people torn apart by war. She saw UNICEF's role as a low-key effort to make Bosnian demining more civilian, gender-sensitive, aware of the needs of children and shaped by local community participation.

Nathalie sent me to the Genesis Project's headquarters in Banja Luka, capital of Bosnia's Serb entity. As much as I admired their work, I was not excited about going. Nationalist forces drove non-Serbs out of the city during the war and flattened all sixteen of the city's mosques. I had always found visiting Banja Luka an unpleasant experience. It seemed hostile to foreigners. I felt queasy when I thought of the violence of the not-too-distant past and unsettled by the chauvinistic graffiti, t-shirts and posters all around me. Banja Luka had a grey, martial character and the large government buildings in the downtown area appeared creepy to me. However, in meeting the staff and volunteers, I realized that I had missed an entire dimension to Banja Luka on my previous visits. There were people who, in small but significant ways, were trying to humanize the place, to resist the spooky crypto-nationalism through art, education and a sunny optimism that things could get better. Unlike the demining organizations, which were run and staffed by men who had prosecuted the war, the Genesis Project aimed to foster creative, artistic and life-affirming responses to conflict. Like their manager, Dijana, the staff and volunteers were vivacious and good humoured. They challenged my stereotypes of Serbs. Even the name of their organization was whimsical.

The genesis of the Genesis Project was in June 1996, shortly after the end of the Bosnian war. It was started by Dijana Pejic, from Banja Luka, and Atila Kuchar, from London, who had worked together for the American Refugee Committee (ARC). After the end of hostilities, ARC withdrew from Bosnia, but Dijana and Atila wanted to continue their good work. They decided to start their own organization to solve social problems arising during the transition to peace. 'What's with the name "Genesis Project"?' I asked Dijana, when I had a chance. Since I had seen International Orthodox Christian Charities on their list of donors, I figured it had some theological meaning. Her answer was a surprise: 'It's from Star Trek.' In addition to a shared commitment to humanitarian endeavours, Dijana and Atila were both passionate Trekkies. Apparently, the original 'Project Genesis', depicted in the 1982 film *Star Trek II: The Wrath of Khan*, aimed to generate new civilisations on uninhabitable planets. 'Put simply', the character Dr Carol Marcus explains in the movie, 'Genesis is life from lifelessness. ... Instead of a dead moon, a living, breathing planet.'[21] Dijana and Atila felt it was a good metaphor: a new hope for a country emerging from the devastation of war.

With funding from UNHCR, the Genesis Project's first projects tried to reconnect people living in displacement camps with art and culture. They had a mobile library and cinema – 4,000 books and a video projector housed in a Mercedes van. A troupe of out-of-work actors, artists and writers, their staff began staging itinerant puppet plays about tolerance and human rights. They soon learned that the puppets were a powerful tool for helping children to deal with frightening topics, such as war-related trauma. When the Genesis Project staff observed the mortal risk landmines and UXO posed to children in the camps, they wrote new plays to convey the dangers.[22] As the puppet shows became a popular fixture, the Genesis Project used them as an opportunity to build deeper relationships with schools. They found that most pupils were receiving only one 45-minute class session on mine risk education each academic year, often from ill-informed teachers. In response, Genesis Project staff trained child peer educators, produced lesson plans and class materials and worked with teachers to brainstorm ways to mainstream mine risk education into a variety of disciplines.[23]

Near the beginning of her interminable 1940 travelogue, *Black Lamb and Grey Falcon*, Rebecca West sniffily satirizes 'English persons ... of humanitarian and reformist disposition' who march out to the Balkans 'to see who was ill-treating whom'. With a 'perfectionist faith unable to accept the horrid hypothesis that everybody was ill-treating everybody else', these do-gooders 'all came back with a pet Balkan people established in their hearts as the suffering and innocent, eternally the massacree and never the massacrer.'[24] In cynical moments, I wondered whether aid donors' enthusiasm for the Genesis Project displayed a similar tendency, 'collecting' a pet project, one that seemed endearing, 'innocent' – even infantile. Were their puppets non-threatening and apolitical marionettes that merely entertained my 'humanitarian and reformist disposition'?

Possibly. But the Genesis Project was also part of a system developing quietly in the marginal spaces of the Bosnian mine action sector. In contrast with the hyper-masculine, military–commercial complex that dominated demining, alternatives were germinating in the more 'feminine' programmes of mine risk education, community liaison and survivor support. As with the commercial demining sector, the line between 'local' and 'international' was blurry, it involved people and organizations from both Bosnia and elsewhere. But it had a different set of global linkages. Rather than multinational private security firms and military institutions, groups such as the Genesis Project built relationships of solidarity with people in UN agencies, advocacy groups and a network of charities.

One such international partner was Norwegian People's Aid (NPA), which worked closely with both the Genesis Project and UNICEF in developing an approach to mine action driven by humanitarian priorities. The Genesis Project would often provide landmine risk education in the communities where NPA, one of the largest agencies involved in Bosnian demining, cleared minefields. Together, they collaborated with UNICEF to develop methods of engaging with communities about the landmine hazards in an inclusive and participatory way.

I first encountered NPA in winter 2003 when I was working in Brcko and first learning about mine action. I set up a meeting with NPA's country programme manager, a trim, blond-haired man named Per. It took me forever to find his office, which at the time, was located in a bare, hard-scrabble camp on the outskirts of Sarajevo. I had trouble communicating with the taxi driver and he had never heard of NPA, so we drove up and down the same stretch of road several times, asking every person on the street before finding our way to their wire-fenced compound. It was a grim, freezing day, and I was surprised to find Per's office in a converted shipping container. Minefield maps plastered the thin metal walls of the office, a space heater whirred in the corner and Per sat relaxed behind his desk in one of those enormous woollen sweaters that every Norwegian seems to own. An employee poked her head around the door, asked a question and Per responded in fluent local language.

In contrast to the mercenistic edge of commercial demining managers, who smelled the potential for funding when I spoke to them, Per was interested in our idea of an agricultural demining project in Brcko, but wasn't eager to cash in on it. Instead, he took the strategic long view. In a year, he told me, once they had the worst landmine contamination in Sarajevo under control, they would concentrate their personnel and assets in the Brcko area. They wanted to support the peacebuilding and agricultural development efforts in that important, though severely landmine-affected, municipality. But he wanted to finish the job in Sarajevo before moving on to the next thing. He said that their long-term commitment to Bosnia, steady funding from the Norwegian government and humanitarian mission meant they could focus their programme on areas where demining was needed most rather than those areas that would offer the most profit.

NPA was the favoured conduit of Norwegian government funding for demining, which is allocated differently than the commercial tendering model preferred by the United States and much of the UN. In contrast to donor countries that prioritize demining projects advancing their immediate national interest, Norway focused the majority of its demining funds on areas 'worst affected by mines', particularly those which 'constitute unacceptable threats to the lives and livelihoods of civilians'.[25] Of course, there was some element of self-interest too. A Norwegian diplomat in Sarajevo admitted to me that 'it's easier to explain to the Norwegian parliament that we're providing all this money for mine clearing if it's a Norwegian entity involved'. However, they do not give their money just to any Norwegian entity. The Norwegian Ministry of Foreign Affairs makes long-term, close partnerships with international NGOs. This builds a degree of trust that enables such groups to spend more on paying their local staff a living wage and generous health and pension benefits, provide ongoing training, invest in research and development and concentrate on activities that are needed, but are not necessarily profitable. The diplomat explained to me:

> We don't like to provide [demining] assistance money to commercial companies … they are there to make money and for them making money means that they will try to provide the least amount of service in order to maximize their profit. … We think that NGOs have a tendency to work somewhat differently, that there's a stronger sense of idealism, that they're more committed to the task at hand, rather than being committed to the bottom line and the statement of accounts and shareholder responsibilities.

NPA was born out of the Norwegian labour movement and its early roots lie in Norwegian leftist support to the Republicans during the Spanish Civil War. It has retained its radical edge (and close relationship to the Norwegian Labour Party) ever since, declaring 'Solidarity' with the poor and oppressed its primary mission. This has placed it at the centre of controversy on numerous occasions, given its unabashed support for anti-colonial 'liberation movements', including the PLO, the Sudan People's Liberation Army and the Sandinistas. Prompted by the Norwegian government to support the UN peacebuilding efforts in Cambodia, Angola and Mozambique, NPA was an early innovator of humanitarian demining, seeing it as a way to express solidarity with civilians in conflict. Initially, the mine action programme was developed at an arms-length from the rest of the institution. One former NPA demining manager told me, 'For a long time most of the people working for NPA were not aware that they had a demining program, at all.' Then a few years down the line the problems occurred, because suddenly now you have a style of program which is not integrated into the rest of the NPA portfolio – a completely different culture.' He told me that 'NPA used to be mainly powered by anti-militarist, anti-war, pacifist people', typically trained in the human and social sciences, such as sociology and anthropology. Into this mix, another mine action manager told me, 'this bunch of army guys comes crashing in'. The demining staff were mostly former Norwegian military officers, usually men, and tended to be more conservative than the rest of the organization. They dismissed NPA's other staff as 'batik skirts' and 'hippies'. Over time, though, mine action has been integrated into the core of the organization, which has tried to ensure that its demining programmes are 'implemented according to our ideological foundation and principles' of 'human dignity, equality, solidarity, unity, peace and freedom'. This political approach makes NPA unafraid of outspoken advocacy, and it was an important player in the campaigns to ban landmines, cluster munitions and, most recently, nuclear weapons.

NPA's more conservative demining managers are embarrassed by the leftist rhetoric and tend to downplay it in the field. However, the organization's ideological commitments have an observable impact on their programmes. The commercial companies' demining programmes in Bosnia (both international and local firms alike) started in response to the World Bank, US State Department and other donors' tendering processes. In contrast, NPA's involvement in Bosnian mine action grew out of its humanitarian assistance to displaced persons during the war. In keeping with their explicitly political approach, NPA had focused its efforts in and around the northern city of Tuzla, whose municipal leadership had worked hard to maintain the city's cosmopolitan character throughout the conflict. After the end of the war, NPA supported a variety of grassroots peacebuilding projects and tried to help refugees and displaced persons return to the Tuzla area by building over 5,600 homes. The demining programme started in 1996 to support the home reconstruction efforts and expanded to provide technical assistance to the UN Mine Action Center in Sarajevo.

From the beginning, both NPA and their donors in the Norwegian Foreign Ministry saw mine action as more than a technocratic activity – they sought to advance a progressive agenda to undermine the violent politics of those who perpetrated the war. The Norwegian diplomat in Sarajevo explained that a key focus of Norwegian-funded mine action in Bosnia has been 'to facilitate refugee return' and restore 'freedom of movement'. He said, 'The military forces in Bosnia-Herzegovina had a sad tendency to mine buildings in the hope of causing civilian casualties, or at least creating uncertainty and preventing return. If refugees were going to return to their homes, or what was left of them, there needed to be mine clearance.' Therefore, landmine clearance 'is not only humanitarian, it's also a political agenda' – Norway and NPA were determined that 'ethnic cleansing was not to be seen to succeed'. At the same time, supporting landmine clearance and refugee return in Bosnia demonstrated Norway's commitment to progressive international law – such as the landmine ban and Refugee Convention – which, the diplomat told me 'has always been a very strong motivating factor in Norwegian foreign policy'. To offer an alternative to the militarization of the Bosnian reconstruction process (USAID-funded commercial demining had focused on areas of priority for the US Army), the diplomat insisted that the Norwegian peacekeeping forces in Bosnia had no influence over NPA's demining priorities, which were 'clearly and unambiguously civilian'.

Not everyone in Bosnia liked NPA. There were powerful interests, both local and international, that preferred commercial demining. They saw NPA as expensive, slow, expatriate-heavy and self-righteous.[26] For many years, people linked to the commercial demining sector and their international donor champions had argued that competitive tendering of demining had reduced the cost of clearance in Bosnia. In 2003, commercial demining cost on average $1.61 a square metre, compared with $2.25 for NGOs and $2.82 for governmental agencies.[27] NPA was particularly expensive – almost $6.50. The data on speed was fuzzier, less clear, but it did seem like the local organisations and commercial companies cleared at a faster rate than the international NGOs, including NPA.

However, analyses of NGO and commercial cost and speed data had made a fundamental statistical error – assuming that all square metres of cleared minefields were broadly comparable. Digging deeper into the data, it becomes obvious that this was not true. The quality of NPA's work was better than that of the commercialized demining agencies. When government inspectors came to observe their work, NPA received far fewer citations for errors (such as using equipment properly, having a medic onsite and maintaining adequate distance between deminers) than demining groups funded through competitive tenders. This meant they had far fewer accidents. In the early days, some companies in Bosnia even paid deminers by the square metre, which encouraged deminers to rush their work, rather than use caution and care. The race to the bottom, in terms of cost, may also have provoked cutting corners in standards.

NPA's demining was also more expensive because they systematically selected more difficult work. Per explained to me that NPA deliberately focused on clearing complex but high-priority tasks such as apartment buildings in dense urban areas, rather than a flat open field far from human habitation. According to Ian Mansfield, a former UN mine action official in Bosnia, clearing buildings 'was the hardest task as the metal detector was rendered useless because of all the steel reinforcing bars in the concrete floors and wall. Often deminers were forced to remove rubble by hand and carefully prod their way through houses.'[28] From 1997 to 2004, NPA took the lead on the most daunting landmine clearance challenge in the country, Sarajevo, where minefields ran directly through residential and business districts in the centre of the capital city. Before beginning any demining task, NPA would deploy 'community liaison teams' to conduct an assessment of the potential socio-economic impact of clearance effort, the likelihood the land would be used productively in the future and how it would impact the local political economy – to 'make sure we're not demining the back gardens of politicians', as Per liked to put it. During the demining process, the team would also meet regularly with local authorities and local residents to listen to their concerns and educate them about the nature of the process and residual threat, often working in tandem with the Genesis Project. This investment into the human side of demining was one few commercial companies were willing to spend much of their profit margin doing.

Over time, many of the earlier problems with the competitive tendering system were ironed out. The worst offenders were disqualified from bidding for US funds, rule of law was stricter and the demining sector became more professionalized. But NPA still set the standard to beat. And the lesson was clear. In demining, as in most situations, you often get what you pay for. Data from Afghanistan and Sudan/South

Sudan display the same pattern: organizations that were competing for short-term tenders, though cheaper and faster, usually demined less relevant land, had more accidents and made more errors in the minefields and cared less about the human dimension of community liaison.[29]

There were less tangible, though no less important, differences between NPA and other demining groups in Bosnia. While commercial companies and local NGOs mostly hired short-term labour, NPA invested in their staff, providing long-term job security, training and decent compensation. While the companies and local NGOs were usually male-dominated mono-ethnic entities, NPA cultivated a multi-ethnic workforce that, though not completely gender-equitable, was more willing than most agencies to put women in positions of power. By hiring a diverse workforce, NPA was quietly trying to subvert the nationalistic, patriarchal order created by the war.

This extended into the work they chose to do. They provided landmine clearance support to the forensic scientists opening mass graves for the international war crimes tribunal and made a special effort to demine the Sarajevo Jewish cemetery, the second oldest in Europe, intending, as the Norwegian diplomat explained, to send the 'political and symbolic' message that Sarajevo was an 'interethnic city'. By contrast, the competitive tendering system faced persistent rumours in its early days that several tasks were done 'in pursuit of the chauvinist objectives of the nationalist parties'.[30] The voices of the commercial companies were also noticeably absent in the ICBL, whereas NPA tried to link its demining work on the ground to global advocacy efforts to curtail the use of landmines, cluster munitions and other indiscriminate weapons. In the last working week before her death, NPA hosted Princess Diana's visit to landmine survivors in Bosnia, raising awareness of the human costs of mines.

*   *   *

Over time, the world began to forget about Bosnia's minefields. Aid agencies slowly lost interest and political sclerosis in Sarajevo stalled what initiative remained. With authority fragmented, parliament could not pass a new demining law and consistently underfunded mine clearance – contributing less than a third of its planned budget for 2013 alone. When it joined the landmine ban treaty in 1999, Bosnia committed to finish clearing all mined areas as soon as possible, and no later than 2009. The deadline was pushed back to 2019, but, when I visited Bosnia in spring 2014, few believed they would meet it.

The Bosnian mine action sector was caught in the midst of another scandal. In April 2014, Dusan Gavran, director of BHMAC, was arrested by the police, who also searched his house and BHMAC premises. A spokesperson of the State Prosecutor's office said, Gavran was, 'under investigation for ... suspicions that he abused his official position and made illegal profits' in the demining contract tendering process.[31] Meanwhile, the Greek press broke news of alleged fraud and money laundering by a Greek NGO that had been involved in Bosnian mine action. The story travelled around the world, making the pages of the *Los Angeles Times* and *The Economist* – awful PR for the struggling demining effort.[32] A local demining professional told me he feared it was 'one of the most dangerous times for mine action in Bosnia'. A government official confessed, 'It's not good for BHMAC to be in the papers in that way', but remained stoic: 'in terms of operations, we are still going'.

Gavran was released from custody on 9 May 2014, but a new ordeal lay in wait. Four days later, a cyclone ripped across the Balkan peninsula, causing extensive flooding and a humanitarian crisis. People whose closest call with a minefield is the computer game 'Minesweeper' are often surprised to learn that mines do not always stay put. Landmines are laid within a dynamic ecosystem. They can shift positions as soil surrounding them freezes and unfreezes with the seasons. Soil erosion may expose a mine. Floods and landslides can dislodge and wash them into new places. When a landmine exploded on 21 May in Brcko – the town had experienced severe flooding – it exacerbated widespread fears that Bosnia's minefields might be on the move. Areas that had been confirmed safe might be life-threatening again.[33] Sensationalist reporting exaggerated the risks and heightened people's anxieties.

But, despite the absence of the BHMAC director – he was not welcomed back to the agency following his release from jail – the Bosnian mine action sector mobilized quickly. BHMAC, local civil protection agencies, local NGOs and NPA conducted emergency survey, clearance and demolitions. They alerted the public and the press to the dangers, pleading for a revitalized investment in mine action. The emergency clearance effort was later deemed 'extremely effective' by a European Union evaluation. To great relief, a joint NPA and BHMAC investigation found that 'migration of mines cannot be considered as massive and did not cause a significant increase of the mine problem' in Bosnia.[34]

But a top BHMAC official later admitted that the turmoil put the Bosnian mine action sector 'under pressure'; it felt like there was a

'dark cloud around us'. A local NGO representative told me, 'Things …
are not good. … [T]here's nobody to be the engine.' With no BHMAC
director, 'We lost the opportunity to put demining at the top of the
agenda' of aid donors and Bosnian parliamentarians. In a plea deal,
Gavran was later sentenced to ten months in prison 'for abuse of official
position or authority and falsification of an official document'.[35] Despite
the appointment of a new, widely respected director, and new policies
on contracting and whistleblowing, in 2016, BHMAC lamented that
Bosnian mine clearance was almost four years behind schedule and
starved for funds.[36] A 2016 evaluation by Bosnia's Audit Office found that
government 'institutions … have not undertaken all activities required
to ensure efficiency of the demining system' and that a 'conclusion can
be drawn that [Bosnia] is not committed to dealing seriously with the
demining problem'.[37] Meanwhile, increased flows of refugees through
south-eastern Europe raised concerns about the risks they faced from
mines as they crossed Bosnia on their way north.[38]

In the Oscar-winning film *No Man's Land*, released only six years
after the war's end, Bosnian director Danis Tanovic used a PROM-1
to represent his country's predicament. A wounded soldier awakes in
a trench between front lines to discover he is lying, booby-trapped,
on a bounding mine. If he moves, he will blow himself up, along with
two other soldiers – from opposing sides – who have found themselves
stuck in the trench. The men, engaged in a conversation that alternates
between camaraderie and murderous rage, fail to solve the deadly puzzle.
Outsiders soon get involved – international press, UN peacekeepers
and hotshot diplomats – but despite sensational coverage and righteous
bloviating, they also fail. Good intentions come to naught, as the
political minefields entrap all those who try – or pretend to try – to save
the man on the mine.

Nevertheless, in contrast to Tanovic's despair, the Genesis Project's
puppets still entertain students around the country, educating them
about avoiding mines, preventing violence and overcoming prejudice.
NPA has continued its clearance efforts, including in Brcko and other
flood-affected communities. For them, removing the last PROM-1
mines still threatening Bosnian civilians is not only a technical challenge
or market opportunity. It requires a fundamentally different approach
from those who had sought to profit from Bosnia's dysfunction. It
requires reform of 'the governance and management structure of mine
action … to provide political leadership, root out corruption [and] seek
new local, national, and international sources of funding'.[39] They still
believe the last of the minefields can and will be cleared.

Chapter 5

DETRITUS
WAR ON TERROR, AFGHANISTAN

It was probably booby-trapped. On 15 April 2002, as a US Army EOD team began dismantling a Taliban cache of rockets captured in Kandahar, it exploded, killing four soldiers and injuring a fifth. This was a turning point in the war. When the US government first intervened in Afghanistan following the 9/11 terrorist attacks, its soldiers initially endured few fatalities from hostile fire. Of the first thirty-four US personnel to be killed in 'Operation Enduring Freedom' (between October 2001 and February 2002), twenty-nine were caused by accidents, crashes or other 'non-hostile' incidents; three resulted from 'friendly fire'. But by March and April 2002, Americans were facing more belligerent opposition, with all but one of the thirteen fatalities killed in hostile engagements. Booby-trapping old munitions soon became a favoured tactic of the Taliban and other militias fighting the United States and its coalition forces in Afghanistan. By the end of 2016, these and other IEDs had killed 1,403 coalition military personnel, almost half of all its fatalities.[1] Civilians have borne the brunt of IEDs, with more than 33,672 killed or injured by them in Afghanistan between 2011 and 2018 alone.[2]

IEDs were easy to make from the military detritus scattered throughout the country after almost four decades of continuous warfare. In March 2017, the Afghan government reported that since 1989, civilian mine action agencies had destroyed more than 18.2 million explosive remnants of war (ERW), including UXO, abandoned shells, mortars and other munitions, plus 1.3 million landmines. The Ministry of Defense had destroyed another 31,634 tonnes of ERW.[3] Afghanistan's ERW were often jumbled alongside everything else discarded on former battlefields. A thriving industry encourages Afghans to take dangerous risks in collecting scrap metal, whether by dismantling shells or braving a landmine and ERW-contaminated junkyard. They are not the only ones drawn to ERW, despite the risks. Visiting Kabul in the autumn of 2006, I was picked up from my hotel by an EOD contractor who offered to give me a tour. As we were driving to the former battlefield he was helping to clear of ERW inside a military area, he pointed out a massive dumping ground. Scrap metal dealers were collecting old military equipment abandoned after the Soviets fled Afghanistan. There were armoured vehicles, pieces of helicopters, ammunition cases, communications gear and even an entire airplane, punctured with bullet holes. I expressed awe at the sheer quantity of materiel and so he pulled over so I could take some 'pickies'. He jumped out of the jeep and escorted me along the dirt path leading into the dump. I was enthralled, taking photographs of the chilling glamour all around me. Then we both stopped dead in our tracks. Right next to the barbed wire fence at the edge of the dump were several clearly visible landmines peeking, exposed by erosion, through the dirt. 'They're PMNs', my guide told me, 'Soviet mines'. I felt the hairs rise on the back of my neck.

*   *   *

During the late 1980s, the US government bought almost every healthy mule in the American South and flew them under cover of darkness to Pakistani Air Force bases. Here they were pressed into service by the US-supported rebels in Afghanistan, transporting supplies and ammunition across the mountains into the fight against the Soviet occupation. But there was a problem. As Larry Crandall, a US aid official described it, 'You bring a mule all the way from Tennessee, you train a guy, you deploy that mule and you've got several thousand dollars of investment there right away. And if the first time it walks across the border into Afghanistan it steps on a landmine and blows its leg off, it's useless, you've got to shoot it.'

American involvement in the Afghan proxy war was much more direct than in Cambodia. Soviet efforts to establish in Afghanistan a secular, totalitarian state provoked a nationalist and religious backlash. Aid from the United States, Pakistan and its allies militarized this fundamentalist rebellion, encouraging its most violent tendencies. The US government supported the *mujahidin* ('holy warriors') – a diverse group of rebels, dominated by Islamists, who were fighting both the Soviet client regime in Kabul and the Soviet troops deployed to protect it. The US agencies used every possible sleight of hand to support the mujahidin in what was, up to that point, 'the biggest paramilitary affair in CIA history'.[4] From 1980 to 1991, the United States pumped $2.75 billion worth of arms and aid into the mujahidin effort, which received broad and bipartisan support at all levels of the US government. The US assistance was matched dollar for dollar by Saudi Arabia and augmented by support from other Western and Islamic countries and China. Much of the covert aid – cash, arms and training – was channelled through the Pakistani Inter-Services Intelligence (ISI) agency, to seven resistance parties based along the border in northern Pakistan. The ISI favoured the Hezb-e-Islami ('Party of Islam'), led by a brutal religious extremist, Gulbuddin Hekmatyar, which received the 'lion's share' of CIA assistance – over $600 million.[5]

While the CIA funnelled arms through the Hindu Kush mountains, the US civilian foreign aid programme (USAID) operated a cross-border 'humanitarian' programme from Pakistan that did little to hide its partisan 'non-lethal' support for the anti-Soviet mujahidin parties.[6] I met Crandall, the former head of the USAID Pakistan–Afghanistan cross-border programme in 2006, at his suburban home in McLean, Virginia. Surrounded by souvenirs from around the globe – rugs, statues of the Buddha, silks and batiks – he narrated how he had integrated his above-ground programme with the CIA's parallel underground operation. USAID funded the construction of roads and bridges, Crandall told me, for both humanitarian and military purposes, facilitating the movement of mujahidin personnel, supplies and arms. When he wrote up reports for Congress to justify appropriations, 'no mention would be made of potential military use. But everybody knew it.' Crandall described the relationship between the CIA, Pakistani ISI and USAID as 'one big happy family'. They built their close cooperation on 'friendship, but also a very clear objective – we wanted to win'. What was in it for Crandall? He had begun his career in USAID's counterinsurgency effort in Vietnam. He took the fall of Saigon personally and wanted to 'bloody the nose' of the Soviets.

A top priority for the US government was to develop 'better routes for infiltration' into Afghanistan.[7] The famous Khyber Pass – traversing the Hindu Kush range between Pakistan and Afghanistan – became choked with caravans carrying arms, food and vital commodities. Without them, rebels operating in-country would have no supplies and no escape. Crandall used the USAID budget to buy pick-up trucks for the mujahidin but 'there were so many places where there were no roads and no opportunity of making any roads'. The CIA had been bringing mules for the mujahidin traffickers from China across the Wakhan Corridor – a thin finger of Afghanistan reaching out into China. However, the Chinese government was charging a premium and Crandall said 'everybody thought their mules were crappy': 'They were scrawny and sickly looking and very unimpressive animals.' With the help of his logistics contractor, he found a Tennessee mule trader who scoured Missouri, Arkansas and his own state, rounding up hundreds of mules to send across the world. Crandall discovered that mules get seasick, so he decided to fly them. This was more complicated than it sounds, as mule urine corrodes the fuselage of an ordinary plane. He needed planes lined with plastic to drain off the urine of the frightened animals. Basically, Crandall needed a flying toilet. At the cost of a quarter of a million dollars a flight, Crandall started shipping 110 mules from the American South about every month. The planes flew into Pakistan at night without lights with the ISI keeping a close eye. Pakistani government officials were so disgusted by the amount of waste the mules excreted during the flight, they insisted the manure be flown to Algeria for cleaning, instead of dumped in Islamabad.[8] By the end of the project, Crandall had distributed 1,850 mules to the mujahidin.[9] To teach the mujahidin how to care for and use the mules, Crandall set up an 'Animal Holding Facility' outside Peshawar, Pakistan, eventually run by a logistics contractor, RONCO Consulting Corporation. Officially, the mules were for transporting humanitarian cargo, 'but no one bothered to tell the mujahidin at the border that they might be violating [US]AID rules by adding a mortar or box of AK ammo to the load'.[10]

There was another problem, however. Drawing on their experience of fighting the German invasion with megalithic minefields during the Second World War, Soviet helicopters littered thousands of small, aerially dispersed mines along the mountain passes. These 'butterflies' were particularly insidious, made of plastic and small enough to fit in a child's hand. They caused horrific wounds. According to Ian Mansfield, the Soviets primarily used anti-personnel mines because they 'knew that the mujahideen generally operated on foot'.[11] The Soviet occupation also used landmines to make life unlivable in mujahidin-held areas, 'to depopulate villages to prevent effective local support'.[12] US officials believed that in addition to the humanitarian costs, these mines were a strategic threat to the US-sponsored mujahidin.[13] Few countries in the world have borne the brunt of landmines more than Afghanistan, where mines exacted a tremendous human toll on the rebels and the refugees coming across the border.[14]

Giving blood one day at the Red Cross hospital in Peshawar, Crandall noticed that it was 'filled with landmine victims'; he felt moved 'to do something about landmines'. Crandall had, of course, other motives too. He was fed up of losing his mules. He wanted to keep supply lines open. And demining civilian areas might have useful propaganda value.

So he searched for ways to demine the trails in and out of Afghanistan.[15] The Pentagon was skittish about getting involved – 'they wanted this to be seen as a hands-off operation'. But in talking with the RONCO veterinarian at the Animal Holding Facility, he learned that the Royal Thai Army had been demining areas along the Cambodian border since 1987. The vet had worked with a US Army programme that had helped Thailand develop a countermine unit, using mine detection dogs.[16] He suggested Crandall get in touch with the Thai government. Using dogs would be more appropriate than bulky military demining machines, he told Crandall, attracting less enemy attention and avoiding the difficulty of transporting them through the mountains. Conveniently, Crandall had friends in the US Embassy in Bangkok, who introduced him to the right people in the Thai military. In 1989, Crandall persuaded the Thai generals to let him pay to fly fourteen trainers and their dogs who had been demining the Thai–Cambodia border, to help the mujahidin against the Soviets. 'Suddenly on the streets of Peshawar there were a dozen Thais running around in civilian clothing looking very uncomfortable,' laughed Crandall. He eventually let the Thai trainers return home and directed RONCO to transform the Animal Holding Facility into one of the first civilian-run demining programmes in the world. For several years, demining dogs in Afghanistan only responded to Thai commands, and their Afghan trainers had to learn Thai phrases to speak to them.

By April 1991, RONCO reported that its teams, working in collaboration with mujahidin, had destroyed 'in excess of 3,000 explosive devices' while clearing '736km of roads and two airstrips'.[17] The mujahidin commander in that area, Haji Zarbad, escorted the team in and out of the country and provided them with food and accommodation; when I visited in Afghanistan in 2006, I found him still working with the mine dog programme. USAID was impressed, calling the project a 'huge success'.[18] This was the first time the United States had contributed to the creation of a civilian landmine clearance programme and it established a pattern. Over the next couple of decades, the United States became the largest government donor to 'humanitarian demining' in the world. But much of its assistance was tied closely to its strategic interests and often implemented by private security contractors. When asked about the seeming contradiction between the US aid programme's humanitarian rhetoric and its close collaboration with mujahidin warlords in Afghanistan, Crandall snapped, 'our attitude was: don't worry about the niceties, just get the goddamn job done. We weren't interested in all the handholding, this was serious business. The main objective was to strengthen the Afghans so they could defeat the Soviets. And the bottom line is very clear – we beat 'em.'

But at what cost? The Soviet withdrawal precipitated a sudden loss of American interest in Afghanistan. Many of the unpleasant people the United States had empowered remained behind, along with readily available weapons. Into the power vacuum rushed a vortex of internecine fighting. Hekmatyar's forces flattened much of Kabul, shelling without regard for civilians.[19] The city was criss-crossed with minefields, laid by feuding militias. The fighting also created 'a growing problem with unexploded ordnance', writes Ian Mansfield, with Kabul 'rapidly becoming a city of rubble, which was also littered with thousands of [ERW]'.[20] However, RONCO pulled out in 1994 and US aid, including for demining, all but dried up. Afghan deminers who worked on US-funded projects told me they felt abandoned, even used, by the Americans. Hekmatyar, once the CIA's favourite commander, has slipped back and forth across the border for years, allying with Al Qaeda and the Taliban – he was designated a terrorist by the US State Department in 2003 – before making a deal with the Afghan government in 2017.[21]

*　*　*

With the proxy wars raging, and encouraged by trends of globalizing communications and privatizing social services, the 1980s invigorated the humanitarian movement. The 'without borderists' used media-savvy, political lobbying and celebrity backing to raise millions of dollars to brief relief to war zones around the world, whether the local authorities approved or not. Afghanistan became a cause célèbre across the Western and Islamic world, drawing a multitude of disaster junkies, martyrdom-seekers and philanthropists. Some of them were compelled by the landmine and ERW problem. Agencies like the ICRC and Handicap International (now Humanity and Inclusion) provided medical care and prosthetics to landmine and ERW victims. NGOs began incorporating mine and ERW awareness education into other community development programmes. Rae McGrath, an aid worker with World Vision International in Afghanistan and former British soldier, organized one of the first NGO demining projects in early 1988, despite accusations of imprudence from other NGOs. This inspired him to found MAG, intending to support UN relief and reconstruction work in conflict zones like Afghanistan.[22]

Colin Mitchell and Guy Willoughby, two former British Army officers who had worked in the Afghan aid effort, were shocked by the humanitarian impact of mines and felt that rather than leaving it to the military, demining ought to be 'an act of charity'. In 1987 they set up the HALO Trust. Following an assessment in June and July 1988, they recruited a Kabuli doctor, Farid Homayoun, and set up an office in Shahr-e-Naw, in the town centre of communist-controlled Kabul. Throughout 1988 and 1989, HALO provided mine awareness briefings to the expatriate community in Kabul and ran maternal and child health clinics in the city. Undeterred by press reports calling them 'bizarre' and 'quixotic',[23] HALO began a nascent demining programme with ex-British Army volunteers, many of whom learned mine-clearing in the Falklands War. Their first projects involved EOD at the German and Japanese embassies and Hoechst Pharmaceutical Co. in 1989. HALO's major breakthrough came when they obtained Soviet minefield records from the Afghan government. While these were later found to be inaccurate, persuading the Kabul government to allow a Western NGO to photograph secret Soviet documents signalled a shift in thinking about the mine problem as a humanitarian rather than military issue. By the end of 1989, the *New York Times* was describing Willoughby and another Englishman, Paul Jefferson, working their way through minefields in Pul-i-Khumri in a pilot project intended 'to test the accuracy of Soviet mine maps and to show the Afghan Army's engineering corps how the job is done'.[24] In the politically charged context following the Soviet withdrawal in early 1989, HALO's programme aroused suspicions. Some agencies cast a disapproving eye on the fact that HALO was the only demining group, and one of very few Western NGOs, that coordinated its efforts with the communist government. 'Our job is to get things going and to save lives, rather than dithering about the politics of giving aid to the regime,' Willoughby retorted. 'There may be 20,000 Communists, but there are over one million displaced people in Kabul alone who need our help.'[25] HALO is now one of the biggest international demining NGOs in the world and, when I visited their Kabul office in 2006, had some 2,000 Afghan employees.

In 1989, the UN launched a massive programme of assistance – Operation Salam – intended to help the Afghan people return home and rebuild their country. The UN initiated a series of ill-planned mine clearance endeavours. They also struggled to find funding for demining from foreign aid donors. As Ian Mansfield, an early UN mine action official recalled, 'The vast majority of countries viewed landmines as a military problem, and not a humanitarian one.'[26] Following a damning evaluation, a former UN manager told me that they decided 'the best way to go about this was to stimulate the development of Afghan demining NGOs'. The UN opted against using the private contractor model because '[they] wanted to create capacity that would be available to Afghanistan after the UN had finished and we didn't want to carve it out for international commercial companies to make a lot of money'. They also wanted to make sure that the programme was 'deliberately not military in character'.[27] The UN would fund, coordinate, train and supervise the programme, through a Pakistan-based Mine Action Center for Afghanistan (UNMACA). Throughout the 1990s, this UN-coordinated, Afghan-run system struggled with lack of funding and navigating the complexities of working in an active conflict zone. However, the lack of interest from other governments, perhaps counter-intuitively, fostered the development of strong and independent Afghan leadership in demining their own country.

After attending the 1995 Phnom Penh ICBL conference, Afghan advocates and mine action professionals returned home and set up the Afghan Campaign to Ban Landmines (ACBL), with UNMACA support.[28] They participated in the successful global civil society campaign for the treaty, but at home faced a hostile political environment. Following the collapse of the Soviet-sponsored government in 1992, the victorious mujahidin factions turned on each other. Their use of landmines was pervasive, cementing Afghanistan's reputation as the most mine-contaminated country on earth. In 1994, the Taliban, an armed movement of fundamentalist students radicalized in the refugee camps in Pakistan, swept up through southern Afghanistan, promising to impose strict interpretations of Islamic law to end the corruption, abuses and in-fighting of the discredited mujahidin. They also reportedly used anti-personnel landmines.[29] By 1997, they had captured Kabul, and instituted a reign of terror, with violent punishments for those listening to music, men who shaved and women who did not wear the *burqa*. They harboured the Al Qaeda international terrorist network, destroyed sublime remnants of Afghanistan's Buddhist past and massacred thousands of the Hazara people, an ethnic group whose Shia faith they saw as heresy.[30] The Taliban seemed like the least receptive audience for the ACBL. What would they care about international law or what NGOs say?

As it happens, more than one might expect. ACBL, in collaboration with campaigners in Pakistan, worked to convince the Taliban – both its leadership and rank-and-file fighters – that landmines were immoral.

They spoke with military commanders and political leaders, publicized the Ottawa Convention in the media, convened a 'Prayer Day for Mine Victims' and hosted events featuring Islamic clerics who called upon religious injunctions to protect civilians. Given that mines could not discriminate between victims, ACBL insisted, they could not comply with Sharia laws of war. They distributed 2,000 copies of a calendar featuring religious verses exhorting charity and the prevention of harm, as well as anti-landmine messages.[31] UNMACA also made contact with the Taliban, urging them not to use landmines and to respect the work of the mine action programme.[32] In October 1998, the Taliban's Supreme Leader Mullah Muhammad Omar issued a unilateral decree, declaring the production, trade, stockpiling and use of landmines as 'un-Islamic and anti-human' and expressing support for the Anti-personnel Landmine Ban Treaty. It made the use of landmines punishable 'in accordance with the Islamic law'.[33] This did not halt the Afghan mine action programme's many challenges. Foreign aid donors were reluctant to fund projects – including mine action – in a country controlled by a regime they did not recognize. The Taliban refused to allow mine action organizations to employ women as mine risk educators and occasionally harassed deminers whose ethnicity was not Pashtun. The mine action programme struggled with a major moral dilemma when the Taliban offered UNMACA an office in Kandahar in a girls' school they had shuttered.[34] And other mujahidin factions continued to lay mines. However, between issuing its declaration and the American intervention in 2001, *Landmine Monitor* found no confirmed Taliban use of anti-personnel landmines.

By the time I visited Kabul in 2006, thousands of Afghans were employed by the UN-coordinated, Afghan-run system of local NGOs that had been steadily clearing up millions of mines and ERW. Mohammed Sediq Rashid (he goes by Sediq), an Afghan senior manager at UNMACA while I was in Kabul, was one such person. Thin and poised, with trim beard and neatly combed hair, he answered my questions thoughtfully, in a measured tone. Sediq had joined the Afghan demining programme from its very beginnings in the late 1980s as a technical surveyor, identifying minefields and battlefields contaminated by ERW and trying to discern their boundaries through careful research of military maps, local conflict dynamics and interviews with local people. This required him to travel through the lines dividing the mujahidin groups, whose uneasy unity fragmented after the fall of the communist government. During the early 1990s, Afghan politics was a complex and violent system of conflict and collusion between the numerous rival militias. 'These parties divided the country, even families, and the members of one party were not able to go to the area of the other,' Sediq told me. To navigate this complexity, UNMACA and the demining NGOs cultivated an identity set apart from the politico-military factions. Flying a 'flag of impartiality and neutrality', Sediq said, 'was the key factor in our success'.

By the time the Taliban took over Afghanistan, the deminers were able to persuade both the Taliban and the armed groups opposing it that demining was a public good that benefited everyone. The Taliban largely left deminers alone, accepting their work as a form of jihad against an un-Islamic, if mechanical, enemy.[35] 'You could travel day and night and nobody was going to stop you,' said Sediq. 'We were crossing the borders between the Taliban and the Northern Alliance' with few incidents. The Taliban even donated land to some of the Afghan demining NGOs. The mine action programme's perceived neutrality was crucial in maintaining its ability to work extensively throughout the country. Expressing a sentiment that most Afghan mine action personnel hold, Dr Farid of HALO Trust said, 'The important thing is to keep neutrality, so you are not seen as pro this or against that group. That's the key thing, having a neutral, impartial humanitarian organization.'[36]

The claim to be neutral invites scepticism. To be alive necessarily means that we take up space, use resources, have thoughts and prioritize some values over others – this inevitably draws us into conflict and cooperation with other people; hence politics. However, as I listened more carefully to Sediq and other Afghan deminers, I realized that when they spoke of neutrality, it was not a passive attempt to 'not get involved'. They had made the active political choice of an alternative, cosmopolitan identity. To be a deminer was to adopt an identity 'under the umbrella of the United Nations', as Sediq put it, that transcended narrow ethnic and political boundaries. For example, the HALO Trust hired employees from a diverse range of Afghanistan's ethnic groups and political backgrounds (including both former communists and former mujahidin), as well as a small group of expatriate advisers that worked under Afghan leadership. This isn't to say that there weren't problems of efficiency and occasional corruption, but nevertheless the underlying ethos was one of service, rather than money-making.

'In the Qur'an there is a phrase that if somebody kills an innocent person, it means he has killed everybody in the whole planet, and if somebody saves a life, it means he has saved all the inhabitants of the world,' Sediq told me. 'People have a very strong belief in that, even removing a stone or a thorn, something from the way of the people, is a very good thing. If you remove a mine from the way of the people, that's a very great thing.' I heard this Qur'anic verse[37] from almost every Afghan demining professional I interviewed. Demining, Sediq explained, 'is conceived of as a *jihad* because we are destroying the enemy of everyone'. Masculinity, piety, service and jihad derived not from wielding weapons to kill, but rather in saving lives, removing weapons from the earth. To be a deminer, for Sediq, was to be a '*real* mujahidin', one who put the humanitarian needs of civilians first. While some of the mujahidin fighting the communist regime 'did a lot of bad things' and 'lost completely their reputation among the local community', Sediq believed demining needed to be 'a community-based programme' that earned 'the respect of the local' people.

The UN and NGO systems were also linked to a global community engaged in mine action practice and advocacy. I had actually first met Sediq in Geneva, at a meeting regarding the landmine ban, which the UN, civil society and the International Red Cross and Red Crescent Movement had persuaded the Afghan government to join on 11 September 2002. Addressing concerns by aid agencies that the landmine ban did not sufficiently address other forms of explosive detritus, the UN convened negotiations in Geneva on a fifth protocol to the CCW to address the serious humanitarian harm caused by ERW. Adopted in 2003, the ERW Protocol established international normative expectations that governments should cooperate to survey, mark, clear, remove and destroy ERW contamination, provide assistance to victims and educate civilians about the risks.

But when I interviewed him in Kabul in late 2006, just as the new ERW Protocol entered into force, Sediq was worried that Afghanistan's cosmopolitan and humane vision of demining and EOD was under threat. Desperate to stem the bloodletting, the United States found itself with too few troops trained in EOD to defuse, clear, secure and destroy the unexploded and abandoned ordnance causing accidents on their new Afghan bases and being used to build IEDs. Instead of turning to the Afghan demining groups, the United States used private security contractors, like my guide to the military dump. 'Kabul is the Klondike of the new century', observed the political scientist Michael Ignatieff, with the 'feverish excitement of a boom town'.[38] EOD and demining contractors were big beneficiaries of the new privatized nation-building.

Meanwhile, according to the UN, the Taliban's compliance with global norms against victim-activated explosive devices eroded once the United States drove them from Kabul. They began using IEDs widely, rigging up abandoned shells and leaving them in the roads travelled by US troops. The states parties to the landmine-ban treaty interpret victim-activated IEDs as functionally equivalent to an anti-personnel landmine and therefore illegal. The Taliban also began targeting deminers working on projects they perceived as benefiting the new Afghan government or foreign troops.[39] Nevertheless, in 2012, the Taliban claimed it only used command-detonated – not victim-detonated – IEDs. While this appears to be factually wrong, it indicates that at least some Taliban fighters may acknowledge the existence of the norm, if only in the breach.[40]

* * *

RONCO returned to the country in January 2002, led by former British soldier and experienced mine action manager Bob Gannon. They conducted 'closely integrated operations' with the US military, clearing ERW and landmines from the bases at Bagram and Kandahar and 'securing stores of ammunition' in an effort to deny weaponry to insurgents and criminals.[41] Gannon told me that they 'went round the country looking for stockpiles and getting commanders to declare stockpiles and then checking them'. He said, 'We had a list from the Ministry of Defense of what was to be kept and the rest was taken away to be destroyed.' By 2006, RONCO reported that their EOD teams had destroyed 'over two million items of explosive ordnance, including in part 22,000 mines, 84,000 rockets, 915,000 projectiles, 100 missiles and ... 30 man-portable air-defense systems posing a significant threat if obtained by terrorists', as well as 'hundreds of tons of small-arms ammunition also found in bunkers or caches'.[42] They also supplied bomb-sniffing dogs to private security companies guarding US government compounds. RONCO was soon joined in Afghanistan by other commercial demining outfits.

While these efforts might have had incidental benefits for Afghan civilians, they were not attuned to the humanitarian dimensions of demining and ERW clearance. Based in exclusive expatriate compounds, many companies had no pretence of impartiality – they were close to the US government and some carried guns openly. The manager of DynCorp's Afghan demining programme, which was providing EOD support to US-funded forced poppy eradication teams and also destroying arms stockpiles,[43] told me, 'All of my people are armed' and 'everyone, including the military retirees go through a weapons training upon arrival'. If the DynCorp mine action staff got into trouble during the ERW clearance work, they could call on an armed DynCorp 'rapid reaction force'.

To understand the rationale for the return of the privatized model of ERW clearance to Afghanistan, I visited the USAID Demining Coordinator, an Army Civil Affairs officer from Missouri I will call The Colonel. His moustachioed face, topped with a greying buzz cut, emerged, with little interruption, from a thick neck. He squinted through the big wire-framed glasses of a desk clerk. In his email, as we set up a time to meet, he told me he was based 'at the CAFE – Compound Across From Embassy' – which turned out to be exactly what its name suggested. The US Embassy in Kabul, one of the biggest in the world, had blocked off an entire street and filled it with concrete blocks, razor wire and menacing armed guards, many working for companies like ArmorGroup that also did ERW and landmine clearance. As US personnel exited their compounds, they tore out of the street in convoys of SUVs and Humvees, bristling with weapons. On one side of the road was the embassy proper, on the other was CAFE – which housed elements of the 'non-essential' US presence, including staff of USAID. As I passed through the preponderance of X-ray machines, pat downs and questioning at the main door, I noticed a sign: 'Personnel transiting from one compound to another <u>must</u> use the tunnel. No exceptions.' US government personnel were not even allowed to cross their own highly secured street – they had to traffic through an underground passageway. US embassy personnel were exposed only to preselected, non-threatening Afghans – those allowed through the gate.

Once inside, The Colonel showed me around. CAFE was a bland non-place – a landscape of containers, air-conditioning, cubicle dividers and framed photos of suburban families. He took me to the school-like cafeteria that served imported food and we sat on opposite sides of a flimsy folding table. A US-dollar-dispensing ATM squatted frumpily in the corner. The Colonel told me that USAID's contributions to landmine clearance efforts were linked to its reconstruction contracts. The engineering firms tasked by USAID to build roads, clinics, schools and other infrastructure needed a way to remove the threat of landmines from their worksites. Initially, The Colonel said, USAID did this by channelling money for demining through UNMACA and the local Afghan demining NGOs. However, by the time I arrived in Kabul, USAID officials had changed their minds. Rather than invest money in building UNMACA's capacity (the approach favoured by most donor countries), USAID instead decided to circumvent it and create a parallel, privatized system, channelled through large-scale reconstruction contracts, mostly for roads. While road building might seem innocuous, it was an important element of the US 'pacification' effort. The US government paid contractors to develop Afghanistan's roads, enabling the rapid movement of troops and binding the hinterlands into global markets.[44] Much of the road building was concentrated in the south and eastern parts of the country, which were most affected by the insurgency. As President Bush declared, 'Where the road ends in Afghanistan the Taliban begins.'[45] From June 2006 onward, The Colonel told me, USAID would give the money for demining to the road-building contractors, which would sub-contract work to demining companies. USAID would encourage the Afghan demining NGOs to spin off commercial outfits to compete in the tendering process. In the words of a US Embassy Kabul cable titled 'Humanitarian Mine Action in Afghanistan – Going Commercial', the 'Commercialization of Afghan Demining NGOs' would supposedly turn 'Landmines to Dollars.'[46]

The impetus for this change in policy, The Colonel explained to me, was that by 'just giving out sacks of money to NGO organizations, through UNMACA…we were creating an even bigger welfare state than exists here now, where it's just "well, you guys, really don't have to do anything, we'll just give you the money"'.

'But the Afghan NGOs are hardly sitting idle,' I interrupted. 'They do demining in return for USAID's money.'

'Yeah, they had to do it,' he acknowledged, 'but all this money, a percentage of it goes to UNMACA for the administration purposes, then they will subcontract down and what we want to build, we want private Afghan businesses to take over and run their own country. We don't want to be here for twenty years doling out money to the NGOs to run Afghanistan.'

But wouldn't the private demining companies also take an administrative cut? No, said The Colonel, saying that the process of competition has 'forced them now to be business entities, which is probably the end state that we want to see anyway'. Competitive tendering, he said, would spur Afghan deminers 'to come up with their own business plan, to look at the whole big picture of, "hey if we're going to get into this whole capitalism thing we need to do it right"'. He continued, 'Here's the money, compete for this, do business for this, work for this, think for it, you know, not just kind of hanging off the government dole out there, you know, waiting for it, but actually put together your own businesses and make something of the country. You know, we could do it like it's been done here for the last thirty years, where everybody makes the same amount of money for doing everything.' He laughed to himself and told me, 'Well, that's called Communism, and we're trying to get away from that.'

The Colonel said the new USAID policy was already successful: 'Several different groups that previously were just standing there waiting for the money to be given to them, are now actively putting together a business plan, and have come to [an engineering firm], for instance, and said, this is what we can do.' The Colonel explained, 'We don't want this to be a non-stop, continuing welfare operation where we just hand out money to do it. Now they're actually competing, they've put together business plans and they're competing successfully. And that's good to see, we're really happy about that. That's what we want to happen.' He finished his homage to free enterprise with a rhetorical flourish: 'We don't want to babysit this country for the next twenty years, we want this country to stand up on its own, with its own business. Well, to do that they have to have private enterprise.' The Colonel was convinced that under the new system, Afghan deminer's 'wages will go up and their standard of living will go up'. But wouldn't their wages go down, because competition reduces prices not increases them? 'Then good,' he responded. In other words, no matter which way the price moved, it would be a win for USAID. If it went up, deminers would be paid more. If it went down, USAID saved money.

Shortly before my interview with The Colonel, I visited a commercial demining project in Afghanistan. I had watched the company's employees openly violating normal safety procedures, including not wearing appropriate protective gear, inadequately spacing personnel to limit casualties and using inappropriate equipment. An EOD technician from a different organization who was with me at the time confirmed that what I was seeing was highly irregular. A UNMACA safety inspector had blown the whistle on them months earlier. But UNMACA struggled to regulate the commercial projects on US military bases. Most of their inspectors were Afghan and had trouble getting permission to visit the bases. Some commercial contractors were also reluctant to have oversight. 'Why the hell do we need to have the UN check our work?' fumed one company's baseball-capped manager. 'We know what we're doing, it's just a waste of my time.' The UN also had little input into which companies were selected by the US military.

I asked Bob Gannon, manager of RONCO's Afghanistan ERW clearance demining programme at the time, what he thought of the criticisms levelled at private clearance operators. He argued that by supporting the US and Afghan governments, the commercial

companies were doing more for Afghanistan's future than the UN and
NGO system: 'If you can get a stable government in a country then it's
going to go a long way towards bringing proper peace. And the way
to get a stable government is to make sure the government's got the
land, the property it needs to put good governance in place.' Since most
of the contractors were involved in clearing military bases for the US,
NATO and Afghan security forces, Gannon felt commercial deminers
were laying the foundation for greater security and thus economic
development. And the scale of Afghanistan's security crisis required a
rapid response, for which he felt the private sector was better suited: a
commercial company gets 'paid to do a job. The quicker you do that
job, the better your profit is, the longer it takes you to do that job, the
more it eats into your profit.' Nevertheless, he admitted that the margins
were slim; he told me, 'If you can make 10 percent you're doing well.
Obviously we'd like to make more.' But if strong ethical standards are
not in place, he warned, 'commercial demining will always go to the
lowest bidder'. This meant he had seen other contractors 'do some stuff
which if they can sleep at night then good luck to them'.

Looking at the data shows that the claim that commercial clearance
was cheaper and faster was not entirely accurate. On the whole, the
commercial companies were more 'cost-efficient' because they were
doing easier tasks than those assigned to the NGOs by UNMACA. 'A
lot of the work the commercials are doing – you know there's nothing
there', a commercial demining manager admitted to me. They also
tended to focus on ERW disposal – a much easier and safer task – than
clearing landmines. 'Of course,' he preferred these tasks because 'they've
got bigger profits'. Even though commercial outfits were generally doing
less dangerous work, on the whole, the quality and safety of their work
was sloppier, and they were having proportionally more demining
accidents.[47] One Afghan demining NGO director remarked to me that
the commercial companies 'are not magicians' and thus it should not
be a surprise that increased speed and thrift might come at the cost of
quality and safety. Scholarly studies of privatization have shown that it
is not uncommon to see a reduction in quality when social services are
contracted out to commercial actors.

*   *   *

When contractors and The Colonel spoke of commercialization as
a panacea, it seemed as if empirical reality was less important than
a commitment to the dream of self-sufficiency, the free market and

private entrepreneurship – an Afghan version of the American Dream. It reminded me of the Bush-era White House official who, in all earnestness, told a journalist that those in 'the reality-based community' – who 'believe that solutions emerge from … judicious study of discernible reality' – would never understand what the Administration was doing. 'That's not the way the world really works anymore,' the official told the aghast journalist. 'We're an empire now, and when we act, we create our own reality. And while you're studying that reality – judiciously, as you will – we'll act again, creating other new realities.'[48]

In Afghanistan, expatriates' misperceptions were supported, incarnated and maintained through Kabul's archipelago of fortresses and a network of restaurants, hotels, 'safe taxis' and even hairdressers that catered to foreigners' tastes, cultures, aspirations and security. In a November 2009 evaluation of the US mine action funding in Afghanistan, the Department of State's Office of Inspector General found that US demining official personnel had 'only infrequently been outside Kabul on mine action visits' and barely spoke to embassies of 'key allies' or even other US government agencies.[49] They, like most expatriates, inhabited enclave worlds, shielded within perimeters of stark concrete walls, rolls of barbed wire and hired guns.

Victorian-era British and Russian imperial agents saw Afghanistan as the field of a 'Great Game', a 'Tournament of Shadows'. In George MacDonald Fraser's satire *Flashman*, the Anglo-Afghan War is the title character's power-trip playground, where a coward could make his name: 'there was power,' writes Flashman in his fictional memoir, 'the power of the white man over the black … and none of the restrictions of home'. Flashman's self-aggrandizement is abetted by the fact that his superior officers 'studied the country only from the cantonment at Kabul' and thus 'knew no more about it than you would learn about a strange house if you stayed in one room of it all the time.'[50]

Filing a story for *Vanity Fair* shortly before I arrived in Kabul, the late Christopher Hitchens wrote, 'Those of us who have tried to cover the new "Great Game" as it has unfolded … have forgathered … in the Flashman Restaurant of the Gandamack Lodge, in Kabul … . These are places where the borders are "porous," as the newspapers like to say, but where the boundary between fact and fiction is the most porous of all.'[51] I, too, stayed at the Gandamack, where one could order a full English breakfast, complete with transgressively real bacon. Sitting on the restaurant veranda, my plate resting on a placemat depicting British pubs, I tucked my silver knife into the Wilkin & Sons Ltd Victoria

Plum Conserve, made in Tiptree, Essex. My room invoice proclaimed
the inn a 'rice-free zone' and the lobby was kitted it out in what one
guest called the 'Colonial Raj' school of interior design. Most Afghans
I would meet, who took my order in expatriate restaurants, washed my
clothes, cleaned my room and cooked my meals were carefully chosen
and trained to maintain the delicate fiction that people who looked like
me were in control of this particular corner of Afghanistan. Similarly,
inside their high concrete walls, the interactions between expatriate
and Afghan staff in many international organizations, including several
demining groups, were carefully stage-managed – the real authority
to make policy remained with the white people. In the imaginations
of the interveners, Afghans implemented and served – or resisted. As
Michael Ignatieff observed, 'Nation-building isn't supposed to be an
exercise in colonialism, but the relationship between the locals and
the internationals is inherently colonial. The locals do the translating,
cleaning and driving while the internationals do the grand imperial
planning.'[52]

Yet there was ambivalence, for expatriates were fascinated by the world
outside the fence. For the thousands of North Americans and Europeans
who piled into Kabul after 9/11, the city represented a place where the
rules of mundane existence back home did not apply, where one could
make a reputation, seek adventure and live in hedonistic abandon. Expats
had the chance to inhabit a world of warlords, bandits and quicksilver
contractors. As he tried on his newly purchased local garb, an aid worker
friend gleefully told me, 'I look like a mujahid.' He explained that he loved
his Afghan clothes because he 'never got to play dress up as a kid'. As an
American aid worker mused to me, 'Kabul is a strange, strange place.'
The roads were jammed with cars cutting in front of each other, zippy
motorcycles weaving in and out of traffic and people wandering around
in the middle of the road. Street vendors hawked their merchandise of
pungent foods and prepaid cellphone cards. Beggars stretched out hands,
car stereos blasted Persian and Hindi pop music. There was energy and
vitality, the hum of business being done, set against the harsh beauty of
the mountains. Everywhere there was dust – dust on the furniture, dust
in the folds of clothing, dust between the pages of books, dust in the air
refracting sunsets into brilliant red, orange and golden rays, lighting up
the mine-infested hill beyond the guesthouse's garden. And there was
danger, exquisitely unrequited.

The most striking decorational feature throughout the Gandamack
Lodge was the volume of weaponry hanging from window wells and
walls – swords, Lee Enfield rifles, machine guns, that elephant gun in

the bar. There was even a cannon sitting in the garden, dating back to the British colonial Afghan campaigns. Returning to the Lodge one evening, I walked into the entrance hallway to a find a British cameraman and his fixer playing with the Lee-Enfields, posing and snapping pictures of one another. The camera flashed like a strobe light, while the cameraman raised a gun in the air and brandished a wad of $100 bills. He pulled the rifle's trigger to hear it click impotently and exclaimed, 'This would be so illegal in Britain!' It reminded me of the documentary footage I once saw of Charlie Wilson, the playboy Texan congressman primarily responsible for appropriating funding for the CIA effort to arm and train the Afghan mujahidin in the 1980s.[53] Wilson, himself a fan of *Flashman*, was dressed in Afghan clothing, riding on a white horse, with a bandolier across his chest. The film cuts to him firing a celebratory barrage from an anti-aircraft gun, a big grin on his face while his body vibrates violently from the recoil.

I met one manager of a demining outfit who figured out how to take advantage of expatriate titillation by explosive ordnance by leading 'Pointy Tours' (as in 'don't touch that, it's pointy') of the immense arms dumps his company was charged with securing. The Pointy Tours became rather popular and made him a minor celebrity in the expat scene. Separately, one afternoon, I joined an excited group of expatriates on a tour of one of the Afghan demining sector's biggest attractions – the OMAR Mine Museum. The headquarters compound of the Afghan demining NGO OMAR (Organization for Mine Clearance and Afghan Rehabilitation) in Kabul has the surreal and fantastical quality of a James Bond film set. It sits next door to the infamous Ghazi Stadium, where the Taliban conducted their grisly spectacle of public executions and corporal punishment. As we entered through OMAR's front gate, on our right, placed on a concrete pedestal, was a medium-sized passenger plane, brightly painted with a mural declaring 'Destruction of One Landmine Is To Shut A Door Of Poverty, Disability and Begging'. Inside, the plane had been converted into a classroom for mine action training, with a blackboard at the front of the cabin and the standard rows of cramped economy class seats for the participants. To the right of the airplane classroom, as if providing it with protective firepower, were three rusting fighter jets. A pet monkey sat brooding on one of them looking like a pilot considering his next mission, a chain tied to his neck. Someone quipped that one day he would cast off his bonds and escape in one of the MIGs. The paths through the surrounding garden were lined with anti-aircraft guns and defunct Soviet ballistics. Along one compound wall, sat a row of decrepit MI-24 Hind helicopter gunships, once a deadly scourge to the anti-Soviet mujahidin, now looking like decaying old men at a military retirement home. We took turns having our photos taken next to rusting missiles; I snapped one of some joker hugging a Scud.

Feeling like one lives in a 'place in-between' (to steal a phrase from Rory Stewart's Afghan memoir[54]) means the standard restrictions, the ethical guideposts melt away into the mists of moral twilight that exist at the edge of two cultures, neither in nor out. This suspension of rules is actually formalized for many expatriates who enjoy diplomatic immunity or Status of Forces agreements that allow them to remain above and beyond the reach of Afghan rule of law. But this lack of accountability had political and social consequences. Three years after I left Kabul, photos of employees of a demining and security firm whose barracks I had visited were splashed across the front pages of the major world newspapers:

> The images ... show naked men, employees of the security firm, whose genitals are only barely covered with a kind of black beer mat. The men are drinking, dancing naked around a fire, licking each others' nipples and grabbing each others' testicles. They perform sex acts, pour vodka down each others' naked backs and drink it from the buttocks.
>
> It now appears that some of the men in the photographs were forced by their supervisors to take part in the demeaning sex games. They found it amusing to watch them be subjected to the 'hazing', the ritualistic humiliation used to initiate someone into a group. ... 'They were living out some sort of delusion,' [said] one of the whistleblower guards.[55]

A year later, in a report that read like a noir action thriller, the US Senate Committee on Armed Services Inquiry into the Role and Oversight of Private Security Contractors in Afghanistan 'uncovered evidence of private security contractors funneling U.S. taxpayers dollars to Afghan warlords and strongmen linked to murder, kidnapping, bribery as well as Taliban and other anti-Coalition activities. It revealed squandered resources and dangerous failures in contractor performance.'[56] The report described how a major private security company's demining subsidiary, funded by the UN and US Air Force, became entrenched in the political economy of the conflict. Instead of hiring security guards themselves, the company paid a 'warlord' they called 'Mr White II' (codenamed after the gangster in Quentin Tarentino's *Reservoir Dogs*) 'thousands of dollars a month to provide security guards and vehicles'. The company admitted that they had 'no idea' how Mr White II used the money and how much he paid the sub-contracted guards. In August 2008, Mr White II, who was the nephew of a major Taliban commander and rumoured to be involved in the drug trade, was killed by a US Army raid of 'a Taliban meeting' at his house. Seven other employees were killed in the raid, which also uncovered a significant cache of 'weapons, explosives, [and] intelligence materials'. This included 'anti-tank landmines, landmine fuses…AK-47s, machine guns, 4,000 rounds of machine gun ammunition, body armor and other military equipment'. The Inquiry suspected that money from these demining contracts had been funding Taliban operations. Over internal objections, the demining company then hired Mr White II's brother – Mr White III – even when he was suspected of involvement in the placing of IEDs targeted at US troops.[57] When asked for comment by the BBC, the firm stated that their 'personnel remained in close contact with US special forces personnel to ensure that the company was constantly acting in harmony with, and in support of, US military interests and desires'.[58] But the report concluded, 'The proliferation of private security personnel in Afghanistan is inconsistent with the counterinsurgency strategy' and that the 'Afghan warlords and strongmen operating as force providers to private security contractors' – including those doing commercial demining – 'have acted against U.S. and Afghan government interests'. This posed 'grave risks to U.S. and coalition troops as well as to Afghan civilians'.[59]

In September 2016, Robert Gillam and Simon Davies of Mondial Defence Systems, based in Dorset, England, were jailed for paying two bribes (of £72,000 and $75,000) in 2009 to the off-shore Singapore account of Bob Gannon, RONCO's then Afghanistan manager. In return they won a contract worth more $5 million to supply EOD equipment in Afghanistan and Iraq. Gannon thanked Gillam in an email on Christmas Eve 2009, 'Bob Great news—this seems to have done the trick—santa left his parcel. Much appreciated.' The bribes were discovered in a joint investigation between London police, the FBI and the US government's Special Inspector General for Afghanistan Reconstruction (SIGAR). Gannon himself had spent a year in jail and was sentenced to an additional two years of supervised release, expulsion from the US and fines of almost $194,000, plus the sale of his house. He is barred from ever working on US military contracts again.[60]

*   *   *

In the expat's micro-colonies I frequented during the winter of 2006, the ERW lurking just beyond the barbed wire fence – evidence of a historical legacy that predates the US occupation – might as well not have existed, unless as a prop in social media photographs. The heartbreak of the local demining NGOs – as well as their dedication and successes – could be easily ignored. The commercial companies primarily demined the 'insides' of these enclaves – military bases, airports and other secured compounds accessible only to the military, political and economic elite. As the US government focused on 'self-referential' demining of its compounds and the roads that connected them, it refused to sign the landmine and cluster munition bans, reserving the right to use explosive force on those who lived outside the perimeter fence. There were rumours that one company had cleared a potentially contaminated part of a military base simply by scraping off the top soil, chucking it into a truck and unloading it at an illicit dump. Even if this wasn't true, it seemed like a compelling metaphor – expelling insecurity from the green zones and imposing the detritus on the unlucky bastards stuck outside the compound walls.

While expatriates at the Gandamack played with conspicuously displayed yet harmless weapons, outside, Afghan deminers faced hidden but deadly ERW. Alone in a 1 metre wide 'lane' – at least 25 metres from their nearest colleague, they faced the mind-numbing task of scraping away sun-baked mud for 6 to 8 hours a day. Weighed down with Kevlar, a heavy helmet and an inconvenient facemask, they sweated in their multiple layers of protective equipment. Unless they were in an unusually hazardous area, they could go hours, days, even weeks before ever coming across an explosive device. But the moment they allowed their attention to wander could be their last. Most ERW are straightforward to deal with if you know what you are doing, but every now and then, something goes wrong. There is a booby trap, the fuse is corroded, a landmine is upside down. A mishap in the minefield can be devastating. In 2005, the year before my visit, nine deminers were killed and twenty-one injured in demining accidents.[61]

When I interviewed him now more than a decade ago, Sediq had prescient fears that the growing involvement of these foreign private security firms in demining would erode Afghans' trust in demining and ERW clearance as a charitable public service and 'damage its impartiality'. Local NGOs, less protected and more exposed than their commercial and international counterparts, were the soft underbelly of the demining system and were suffering the brunt of the increasing politicization. In the two years before I arrived in Kabul, NGOs were five times more likely to face a criminal or terrorist attack (it was difficult to tell the difference) than commercial demining groups. According to Sediq, 'Deminers are heroes who risk their lives each day to save innocent lives and free Afghanistan of landmines and unexploded ordnance to return the cleared land back to their countrymen. They should be praised for their hard work and not attacked.' For Sediq, it seemed, Afghan deminers were among the last of the noble. In light of the tragedies visited upon them in recent years, he wanted to extend his 'heartfelt thanks to the deminers for their unwavering courage, sacrifice and commitment to their country'.[62]

Hiding in their fortresses, those who benefited most from the war in Afghanistan could avoid seeing the explosive detritus that was killing people outside the compound wall. But for Afghan deminers, weapons were not a thrilling game. Beyond the fence, there were people – landmine survivors, deminers, aid workers and activists – who braved the dangers of explosive detritus and blowback, remaining committed to a humane, non-violent and cosmopolitan Afghanistan. In saving even a few lives, they sought to save the world.

Chapter 6

RED ROADS
EVERYWHERE WAR, SUDAN AND SOUTH SUDAN

UN peacekeepers began deploying throughout South Sudan after the 2005 Comprehensive Peace Agreement (CPA), which laid the foundations for its later independence from Sudan in 2011. As they moved, peacekeeping troops worried about the rumours of pervasive landmine contamination. To offer guidance in avoiding mines, especially on the roads they began to patrol, the peacekeepers established a Mine Action Office (UNMAO). Before this, mine action donors had largely ignored Sudan. But from 2003 to 2010, annual international contributions for mine action in Sudan (including both north and south) expanded from about $10 million to almost $83 million, making it the second largest programme in the world, after Afghanistan.[1]

Surrounded by computer equipment and cables in his office in Khartoum, Sudan's capital, UNMAO's director Jim Pansegrouw told me that the focus on roads 'worked out very, very well', because the 'major routes that humanitarians want open are the major routes that the [peacekeeping] mission wants open as well'. UNMAO developed a Road Threat Map, colour-coding highways based on an assessment of landmine risk. Where there were reports of mine contamination, roads were rendered red, cleared roads were green and roads that, following survey, appeared mine-free were coded yellow. 'I always err to the conservative side,' said Pansegrouw, explaining why so many roads were initially deemed 'red'. Officially, UN regulations proscribed travel on red roads.[2] While sensible, many of 'the uninitiated', as a UNMAO official described them, misunderstood this system. To a layperson, the Road Threat Map – especially in its early editions – suggested that significant lengths of South Sudan's roads could kill you.

But a 'red road' was not necessarily mined; it just had not been confirmed as mine-free. Suspicion of landmine contamination in a very small section could lead to hundreds of kilometres of a road being labelled red. These routes were not necessarily the ones most likely to be mined. Rather, many were located in marginal and 'inaccessible' locations that were difficult to verify. They were the 'unknown' and 'unsurveyed' places beyond the expanding reach of the peacekeepers, beyond the boundaries of the international community's authority. 'There are vast areas in Sudan which we don't know anything about', Pansegrouw told a press conference in late 2005. 'We have not visited [or] made an assessment of the whole of Sudan.'[3] Though they were irritated if I suggested it, mine action agencies also benefited from depicting an extensive mine threat – it helped their fundraising.

While designating wide swaths of territory as red was inaccurate, it served as a powerful symbol of the feeling of insecurity that pervaded post-CPA South Sudan. Trust was low and the exact boundaries of risk were unclear. The Sudan People's Liberation Army (SPLA) – South Sudanese rebels fighting for autonomy from the oppressive northern regime – committed 'widespread and persistent' human rights violations, including 'summary executions, arbitrary arrests, and the theft of food', use of landmines and 'diverting relief' provided by humanitarian agencies.[4] Some 20,000 child soldiers served in the SPLA's ranks.[5] After the CPA, what was now called the Sudan People's Liberation Movement (SPLM) essentially became the government of South Sudan. Aid donors told me they were working with the SPLM to build their capacity in governance and influence them in a democratic direction. However, advocacy groups continued to express concerns about the SPLM's disregard for human rights, 'impunity' and corruption: 'soldiers and other security forces commit serious crimes, often opportunistically, against civilians.' According to Human Rights Watch, 'The crimes include beatings, robbery, intimidation, land-grabbing, and sexual violence.'[6] Following South Sudan's independence, civil war broke out in December 2013 between feuding factions of the SPLM. More than 50,000 have been killed, 2 million displaced.[7]

Speaking publicly about landmines and releasing maps of contamination in this context was 'very sensitive in the beginning', said Pansegrouw. While the CPA had drawn a line between a warring past and a peaceful future, no one really knew where the boundaries of safe/unsafe, trustworthy/untrustworthy, stable/unstable existed. Even if these boundaries were invisible, they remained terrifying and devastatingly real. Confidence in the peace process remained wary. The landmine threat may sometimes be a projection of our fears, but this is no less frightening. This environment made Juba, South Sudan's capital, an unsettling place to live and work when my spouse Emily and I visited in 2007. We lived next door to a high-ranking SPLA officer who hosted loud drunken parties. Walking in the streets around our compound, Emily had to dodge leering alcoholic soldiers. We felt always on edge.

Uncertainty – and the anxiety it produces – has been a feature of mines and booby traps since their earliest uses. The landmine's clandestine nature is as crucial to its function as the victim-activated trigger and resulting explosion. This subterfuge, seen as unchivalrous, spurred the early moral outrage against them. In 1862, *Harper's Weekly* called landmines 'infernal machines', because they did not allow their victims 'a chance of escape'.[8] An American officer in the Second World War said that it was the minefields he 'hated most' about the war: 'It's an eerie feeling because it is something unseen. It's there and it's not there, you know?'[9] But the minefield has a mirror twin – the object or area masquerading as dangerous that is actually safe. A Union officer in the US Civil War observed that landmines did not actually have to be present to degrade morale. The suspicion that mines 'were scattered in every direction would necessarily produce its effect on the troops who never knew when to expect an explosion or where to go to avoid one'.[10] Another account described Confederate soldiers realizing that it was enough to suggest the existence of mines, by establishing 'dummy minefields', to change the route of a Union assault.[11]

The first US Army Field Manual on *Land Mines and Booby Traps*, published in 1943, shows that the US military internalized this lesson. The guide recommended interspersing dummy minefields with real ones 'to confuse and delay the enemy'. Laying real and fake minefields 'greatly increases the effectiveness of both since the enemy cannot easily tell them apart and is forced to consider clearing the entire area'. Soldiers in the know should nevertheless still pretend that the dummy minefield is real, never passing through them, in case one's opponents are watching. The manual suggested scattering the dummy minefield with 'old pieces of metal and empty ration cans' to increase false alarm signals on deminer's metal detector. It should come as no surprise that the chapter closes with a suggestion that the dummy minefields 'contain a few scattered antipersonnel and antitank mines'. Like a mobius strip, the dummy dummy minefield turns in on itself in a perverse double-bluff. The enemy soldier who initially believed the minefield was real is led to believe it is fake, only to discover that it is real in a final explosive climax. But the manual retains vestiges – even in such sordid fakery as a dummy minefield – of fair play. For while framed as making dummy minefields 'look as real as possible', the manual advises the engineer to include 'the erection of standard marking fences'. This is part of the trick, but it simultaneously offers a bounded uncertainty. Second World

War-style minefields – even when they weren't real – were supposed to be separated from civilian space, at least according to the stated policy, placed between your side, the enemy and non-combatants. [12]

In the years since the publication of the 1943 manual, there has been a kind of synthesis of the booby trap and the dummy minefield. Contemporary war – and peace – is characterized by the indistinctness and indefinite nature of its time and space. In places like South Sudan, one never really knows whether one is in the minefield. Scholars of emerging patterns of warfare have challenged us to rethink our implicit assumptions, in which we see battlefields – or minefields – as 'containers' – clearly defined areas of violence that are, by their nature, separate from civilian areas. In anti-colonial struggles, proxy wars, post-communist collapse, terrorist attacks, drones strikes and the 'New Wars', violence is shape-shifting and there are rarely clear divisions between 'safe territory' and the 'war zone'. US secretary of defense Donald Rumsfeld mused in his famous 2002 'unknown unknowns' speech that 'the absence of evidence is not evidence of absence. … Simply because you do not have evidence that something exists does not mean that you have evidence that it doesn't exist.'[13] Far from the pseudo-poetry of the Pentagon, the experience of 'low-intensity' conflict is nevertheless one of unrelenting unease. Even if South Sudan's minefields are less dense than in Afghanistan, for the peacekeepers deployed in 2005, all moments, all roads, seemed like potential explosive traps, haunted by the possibility of killing. Unlike dummy minefields laid deliberately by specific soldiers, this pervasive instability meant that rumours of minefields may have a thousand sources, as civilians, militia, aid workers, reporters and peacekeepers try to place mental boundaries around which areas are more precarious than others.

The geographer Derek Gregory calls this 'Everywhere War', the weaponization of 'radical uncertainty'. Violent surprise punctuates through the pervasive ambiguity in moments of dislocating trauma – the terrorist attack or missile fired from above the clouds. Even when a 'frontline' or border exists, they are 'trickster figure[s]', ever mobile.[14] One day a route is passable, the next it is a trap whose 'contours ensnare both those involved in war and those who witness it'.[15] Like popular notions of Schrodinger's Cat, all space is unsettled – both military and civilian at the same time – until it collapses into the observable moment of a landmine erupting from a road.[16] Sudanese security institutions have benefited from maintaining this state of unease in the areas seen as most threatening to their rule. Unsurprisingly then, Pansegrouw told me there was 'some unhappiness' in certain quarters when UNMAO began publishing the Threat Map and deminers began surveying and clearing roads. Reducing uncertainty could undermine the control of those who benefit from disorder.

Humanitarian landmine clearance is, in part, about the management of surprise. One cannot assume that an entire country is mined. Faced with deep unknowingness, deminers must establish the limits of safe territory. Demining agencies engage in a process of 'survey' and 'land release' to determine what land should be subject to full clearance (with deminers metal detecting and/or prodding through the entire area) and what can be considered outside the minefield. There are two basic kinds of minefield survey: non-technical and technical. In non-technical survey, a demining team's 'community liaisons' or 'surveyors' will research the terrain and history of the conflict. They gather any existing minefield maps (rare in Sudan and South Sudan). They observe what land is under regular cultivation and what is left abandoned. They collect information about where landmine and ERW accidents have occurred. And they speak to former fighters (ideally those who laid mines) and the local population. This helps them determine the rough edges of the minefield, designating what is called a 'Suspected Hazardous Area' (SHA). Ideally, this is followed by technical survey, in which trained deminers will try to reduce the boundaries of the minefield using sampling methods. The team may also run explosive-sniffing dogs or a machine with a flail across areas where there seems to be a low risk of mines. The machines do not clear at a sufficiently high-level of confidence that one can say the area is guaranteed cleared, but it provides additional confidence that it is unlikely to be mined. If the machine runs into a mine, the surveyors will adjust the boundaries of the minefield and do new sampling to see if there is further contamination. The remaining land, which must be fully demined, is called a 'Confirmed Hazardous Area' (CHA).

The process of survey is inevitably influenced by assumptions, prejudices, treasured beliefs and who in the community is listened to and who is ignored. However, this deeply human and iterative series of informed judgement calls is consolidated into 'information management systems'. In the digitized maps of Sudan and South Sudan's mine action agencies, the messy social complexity of minefields was abstracted into 'polygons' outlined in bright red lines, exact boundaries designated by GPS coordinates. This gave their work the appearance of precision, concealing uncertainty and enabling international officials to project technocratic competence even as South Sudan mine action spent more per mine cleared in 2005 than almost anywhere in the world.[17]

But the very exactitude of their databases actually revealed how much was unknown. Out in the communities I visited around Juba, there were no neat polygons defining the boundaries of safe space, only a hazy moving cloud of uncertainty, which some people, though not everyone, felt might be lifting. And the survey process was not always as straightforward as the standard operating procedures might suggest, as political and military factions try to influence the process. Early in the Nuba Mountains mine action programme, for example, the Sudanese government prevented NGO minefield surveyors from using GPS. In recent years, it has become clear that the level of mine contamination in South Sudan was much lower than was initially thought and funding has reduced to levels more consistent with the other mine-affected countries.[18] In 2015, the UN Mine Action Service estimated that South Sudan had 98 square kilometres of Suspected Hazardous Areas and recorded seventy-five casualties (seven killed; thirty-one injured) of landmines and ERW.[19] This is clearly a serious humanitarian threat, and there are worries that renewed fighting is increasing ERW and possibly landmine contamination. However, it is still a smaller problem than in Afghanistan, for example, with 594 square kilometres of SHA and 1,296 casualties in 2015.[20] 'There are no big minefields, no massive contamination' in Sudan and South Sudan, Pansegrouw told me, 'perception is the biggest blockage.'

In *Peaceland*, her study of peacekeeping and other international interventions in conflict zones, Severine Autesserre noted that expatriate's security procedures, separation from the surrounding population and lack of detailed local knowledge often lead them to overestimate risks.[21] Overestimation had its consequences, as 'remote' communities whose roads were difficult to verify as safe were further marginalized by risk-averse humanitarian agencies. A persistent feature in Sudanese politics, both during and after colonial control, is the systematic privileging of cities, particularly along the Nile, over the 'peripheral' areas of South Sudan, Nuba Mountains, Darfur and Blue Nile State. Marginalized regions were subjected to violence and abandonment, grievances that fuelled insurgencies. Much of the protracted conflict in Sudan (and now South Sudan) has roots in these stark economic inequities.[22] Disregarded zones are the most likely to need humanitarian assistance, but they were also often most likely to be rendered 'inaccessible' by the 'red road' designation on the Road Threat Map. Some aid agencies subverted this system by travelling on well-used red roads or sub-contracting transport to local companies willing to travel down them. But, as one independent evaluation of Sudanese mine action observed in 2007:

> Perceptions of risk ... sometimes inflated by the mine action community in order to attract donor attention ... create special problems for development in mine-affected areas. ... Many such [humanitarian] agencies simply adopt a policy of avoiding communities in which there are suspicions of contamination, with the result that these communities are 'doubly damned' (i.e. not only do they suffer from contamination but they are also denied development assistance).[23]

Another evaluation worried that while inflation of the mine problem benefited the government and mine action agencies 'by luring the sympathy and financial assistance of donors', it made dealing with the very real threat of the mines that did exist 'more difficult to plan', as it was unclear where to dedicate resources.[24] One international NGO worker told me that 'people so grossly overestimate the impact of landmines in Sudan' and South Sudan because there was an incentive to 'over-assess the problem'. This created the erroneous impression that the region was 'completely flooded with landmines, landmines all over the place', when 'it's very low actually'.

This pattern is not unique to South Sudan. In the early 1990s, the UN made estimates of the global scale of landmine contamination that were entirely based on conjecture. They believed that Afghanistan had around 10 million mines, and this was used as a benchmark. Countries were ranked according to how demining professionals believed they compared to the level of contamination in Afghanistan and given estimates of their own (e.g. Angola, 15 million; Cambodia, 7 million; Mozambique, 2 million). This was totalled to around 100 million mines in the ground – some versions of the statistic went as high as 120 million. These figures were used extensively by the ICBL in their campaign. Their statistical charisma has proved irresistible to journalists. I still get news media inquiries asking me about 'the 100 million mines around the world', more than two decades later. These figures are completely – wildly – incorrect. In 2008, mine action expert Mike Croll attempted a revised global estimate using a more systematic method and came up with the figure of 5 million deployed landmines worldwide. Even this is only a guess, because we will only know how many landmines there were once they have all been destroyed.[25]

Over-representing the scale of landmine contamination can generate fatalism about our ability to deal with it. Slow progress means South Sudan is also likely to miss its deadline for mine clearance in 2021. In 1993, the UN estimated it would take 1,100 years to clear up the global mine problem.[26] However, more recent evaluations suggest that the world's minefields could be cleared up quickly and efficiently if there is focused political and economic attention.[27] For example, once considered among the world's most mine-affected countries, Mozambique declared itself mine-free in 2015. Similarly, Croatia, which struggled to make much headway on its mine problem in the 1990s and early 2000s, is now back on track. The total area Croatia cleared (41 square kilometres) or released through new, more rigorous, surveys (27 square kilometres) in 2015 alone – 68 square kilometres – is equivalent to 70 per cent of South Sudan's total SHA.[28]

*   *   *

While understandably focusing on numbers and GPS points, missing from many mine action surveys is a thorough analysis of the social, cultural, political and economic dimensions of the minefields. In her scholarly analysis of international aid agencies addressing conflict, Autesserre found that 'quantitative measurements became so dominant' in evaluating progress, that many miss important information on 'local histories, politics, and customs'.[29] Most senior mine action advisers have a military background, rather than in development, anthropology or political science. Pansegrouw, for example, served as a countermine specialist in the South African defence forces, including during the apartheid regime's counterinsurgency in Namibia. He later worked for a South African landmine company that rebranded as a demining firm after the political transition.

The kind of abstraction that turns a field of killing machines into a 'polygon' also influenced how demining agencies interacted with the conflict surrounding them. Determining that the CPA had ended the war between Sudan and South Sudan, humanitarian agencies unwittingly engaged local structures they thought were peaceful, but were actually entwined in violence. To avoid being accused of intelligence gathering and to persuade militaries to facilitate the work of minefield surveyors, demining operators often end up with close relationships with security forces. A fixation on landmines themselves can draw one into conversations with those who like to plant them, rather than the people who are most affected by them.

In South Sudan, demining agencies struggled with pervasive government graft, as well as arbitrary and extrajudicial violence.[30] The Mine Awareness Trust, an NGO that tried to start a programme in late 2002, pulled out of South Sudan, citing 'frustrations caused by NGO registration and corruption'. Following a review of their programmes in 2006, Landmine Action determined that the productivity levels and the fraught organizational politics were too much for them to handle as a small mine action organization. They withdrew and handed over some of their South Sudan projects to HALO Trust. However, despite being one of the world's largest demining organizations, with experience in some of the most complex political situations in the world, HALO was not able to report any concrete successes from the programme in the year they were operational. Following bitter disputes with local authorities, HALO was expelled from the country.[31]

When I visited in 2007, one of the few international demining NGOs that had avoided challenges from local political authorities was Norwegian People's Aid (NPA). They were given more room to operate because of NPA's prolonged and close relationship with the SPLA since 1986. NPA has long espoused that it is impossible for a humanitarian agency to remain neutral in a conflict zone. NPA's top managers believed it would be dishonest, if not a mark of moral cowardice, to say that one is neutral in the face of violence: 'Not taking stand against oppression is also to take sides.'[32] In keeping with its leftist roots, NPA never pretended to be neutral in the conflict between the north and south and, during the 1990s, operated outside the officially sanctioned Operation Lifeline Sudan aid programme, delivering humanitarian assistance in direct cooperation with the SPLA. NPA's first country director in the 1980s, Egil Hagen, a former Norwegian ski commando and counterespionage agent, was nicknamed the 'Rambo of Relief' for his militant 'one hundred percent' support for the SPLA: 'Relief in war situations *is* politics,' he said.[33] In remarks prepared for the 2005 funeral of SPLA founder Dr John Garang, former NPA secretary general Halle Jørn Hanssen wrote that he had become 'personal friends' with Garang. Hanssen said that NPA 'were resolute solidarity partners' in the SPLA's 'struggle for liberation' because 'the struggle was just' and the basic 'values and ideals are ours as well'.[34]

This unbending loyalty helped NPA in the post-CPA era. NPA's demining programme was able to draw on experienced and dedicated local staff from other long-standing NPA programmes in South Sudan. NPA was well respected by the South Sudanese population and SPLM administration. Several high-ranking South Sudanese government administrators, including in the Demining Commission, were former NPA employees. This meant that of all the interviews I did with international demining NGOs working in South Sudan, NPA had the friendliest relationship with the SPLM administration, voicing few major points of contention. This saved them considerable time, money and energy. NPA deminers were also able to take advantage of NPA's well-established logistical system in the South, with an archipelago of offices and bases to house and support them. In comparison with the more ad hoc *bricolage* of other demining agency compounds, when Emily and I visited NPA's demining team in Yei, near the Ugandan border, they had a fully kitted-out mechanics workshop, library, bar and a pleasant series of cabins in which they hosted us for the night.

However, the SPLA's actual behaviour has not always matched NPA's romanticism, which has led some to question whether their solidarity crossed the boundary into complicity. In the 1990s, while NPA was campaigning for a ban on landmines, the SPLA was busy using them. An independent evaluation of NPA found that their explicitly political stance: 'always risks to legitimise [*sic*] violence and political forces which are not necessarily representative and can divert humanitarian logistics to military ends'.[35]

Mine action programmes in the north faced different but similarly complex political challenges. Ahmed Haroun, the northern government's humanitarian affairs minister and secretary general of its National Mine Action Committee, was indicted in 2007 by the International Criminal Court (ICC) in The Hague for his role in 'crimes against humanity' in Darfur. Before becoming the top Sudanese official responsible for demining and other humanitarian activities, Haroun had been minister of state for the interior and managed the 'Darfur security desk' from 2003 to 2004, coordinating the various forces, both regular and irregular, involved in the government's 'counterinsurgency' effort. In this role, according to his ICC indictment, Haroun managed the 'recruiting, arming and funding' of proxy militias, called *janjawid*, and incited them to rape, kill and displace civilians.[36] Haroun had been identified by HRW as early as December 2005 as one of the 'important figures in the coordination and planning'[37] of what the US State Department has called a 'genocide'.[38] Moreover, Haroun's implication in militia violence was not new. He had played a key role in coordinating Khartoum's campaign in the Nuba Mountains in the 1990s.[39]

Haroun's indictment caused dilemmas for UNMAO, which was responsible for coordinating the international response to Sudan and South Sudan's landmine and UXO problems. Haroun had represented

Sudan at annual review conferences of the landmine ban treaty[40] and was UNMAO's primary counterpart in the Sudanese government. The UN had even paid for Haroun to go on a 'capacity building' trip to Jordan.[41] When I interviewed Pansegrouw not long after Haroun's indictment, he told me that he had previously had 'very regular meetings' with Haroun, since 'mine action reports to him directly'. Haroun's ICC warrant had made 'it a bit awkward' and their meetings were 'less regular now'. But UNMAO officials still coordinated with him. 'Yes, we do talk,' Pansegrouw admitted, but only 'in certain circumstances', saying he had to 'notify' and 'ask permission' from the Deputy Special Representative of the secretary general in Sudan each time in advance. Nevertheless, the indictment hadn't had 'a big impact, yet' on the mine action sector.

In December 2007, the ICC tried to trap Haroun as he planned a pilgrimage to Mecca. Several countries had coordinated to divert his plane and arrest him, but he received a tip and disembarked before taking off.[42] Haroun has remained defiant, claiming that his indictment is a neo-colonial plot and that he draws inspiration from Saddam Hussein's 'strong confident steps towards the gallows'.[43] 'My conscience is clear. I have no regrets,' he told the *Guardian* newspaper. 'It reminds us of the 19th century, when the white people were dominating here in Africa.'[44] In May 2011, Haroun was declared the Governor of South Kordofan in an election the SPLA denounced as rigged, raising concerns that he could reignite the conflict in the Nuba Mountains.[45] By June, reports of 'aerial bombardment' and 'ethnic cleansing' were filtering out of South Kordofan.[46] While not independently confirmed, there were reports of fresh mine-laying in the town of Kadugli.[47] In April 2012, shortly after reports alleged Sudan was using cluster munitions in South Kordofan,[48] Haroun was caught on tape telling troops to 'take no prisoners' in their fight against rebels. 'You must hand over the place clean,' he continued, 'Swept, rubbed, crushed. Don't bring them back alive. We have no space for them.'[49] According to HRW, there appeared to be 'a deliberate strategy of the Sudan government to treat all populations in rebel held areas as enemies and legitimate targets, without distinguishing between civilian and combatant'.[50]

Nevertheless, the UN maintained its surreptitious links to Haroun, even flying him to a 'peace meeting' in the conflict-stricken Abyei state, arguing that his participation 'was critical to … stop further clashes and killings'. A spokesman of the ICC was unimpressed: 'I have real concerns. Ahmed Haroun is a charged war criminal linked to the worst abuses in Darfur. … I think the U.N.'s posture should be of keeping a distance from him.'[51] International mine action officials pointed out to me that there have been few reports of the Sudanese government using landmines in the Darfur conflict. They believe that, even if only in a small way, through links to people like Haroun, international organizations and local civil society have been able to persuade the Sudanese government to commit to the global norms on landmines.

Nevertheless, just because they mostly stopped using landmines does not mean the Sudanese government has become more careful in avoiding civilian casualties. In fact, targeting civilians seems to have been an integral part of the government's strategy. As it had in the South, the Khartoum government responded to armed rebellion in Darfur with a combination of aerial bombardment coordinated with janjawid raids against civilians accused of supporting the rebellion. Some 2.7 million people were displaced from their homes and 300,000 people killed in the Darfur conflict.[52] Critics of the landmine ban have argued that it, and other similar instruments of international humanitarian law, may have the perverse impact of legitimizing military action. By suggesting that war can be waged 'humanely' or according to 'civilized standards', state signatories to the landmine and cluster munitions bans may be able to distract attention from the fact that war is always inhumane, always uncivil.[53] By allowing the Sudanese government to seem like it is adopting the moral high ground of conduct in war, one could argue that the landmine ban provides a fig leaf for Khartoum's unwillingness to protect civilians. 'What're a few thousand mines, when you have 100 million dollars' worth of fighter jets, bombers, helicopter gunships and nearly that sum invested in assault rifles, mortars and machine guns?' asked actress and human rights campaigner Mia Farrow when Haroun attended a ceremony announcing Sudan's destruction of its stockpile of anti-personnel landmines.[54] Moreover, while the landmine problem has been relatively small in Darfur, 'the use of heavy weaponry by armed government-supported militias' has caused a 'significant' problem of unexploded ordnance that 'poses a constant threat to civilians and the delivery of humanitarian aid'. And given that 'security conditions in Darfur are so severe', in 2011 UNMAO decided 'that it would be unsafe for international NGOs' to do the clearance operations necessary to deal with the UXO problem. Instead, the UN contracted a company, Exploration Logistics, to do 'battle area clearance', but it was 'dependent on the availability of force protection, permission from the Government of Sudan, and accessibility to contaminated regions'.[55] Access was thus controlled by Khartoum, the very structures responsible for the problem.

*   *   *

The complexity of Sudan and South Sudan's conflicts meant that some expatriate mine action workers – often only in the country for a short time – grew quickly exasperated. One demining executive vented to me that parts of South Sudan's mine action programme were infected with 'CLING' – 'Corruption, Laziness, Ineptitude, Nepotism & Greed'. Many international staff gave up on trying to understand what was happening. Rather than carefully discerning each new judgement call, they dismissed the entire country as a dangerous and unknowable place: an unending political red road. One international company even tried to hire staff entirely from outside the country. A mine action researcher told me that he felt international NGOs in South Sudan had a tendency 'to only understand partnership [with local NGOs] in a white man's burden sense'.[56] Autesserre has observed a widespread tendency in international organizations operating in conflict, to act as if 'foreigners know and decide, while local colleagues obey and execute'.[57] One national demining manager said he found this attitude 'quite insulting because the South Sudanese who lived here throughout the over two decade long war ... have a very clear knowledge of the landmine problem'.[58] Several local people told me they found the racism of certain expatriate workers infuriating. 'Some of the people [NGOs sent] were probably not culturally sensitive enough,' admitted Pansegrouw.

There is a long history of powerful foreigners imposing pre-existing categories and modes of thinking on Africa and of dismissing it as incomprehensible when the external frameworks fail. But, to paraphrase David Keen, a graduate school mentor of mine, if Sudan seems chaotic to you, you must ask whether the problem is the chaos in your own thinking. Focusing only on 'technical survey' prevented many expatriate humanitarian deminers from understanding that minefields were embedded in a complex of political violence so powerful that it could even sustain the perception of minefields where they did not exist. Pansegrouw believed that 'mine action programs that fail here never fail technically or logistically'. They failed, he said, because they were managed poorly. Sudanese and South Sudanese officials pointed out to me that since few expatriates spoke local languages, it was no surprise they had little clue of what was happening. Autesserre has found that 'lack of linguistic competency is one of the most significant hindrances' to international peacebuilding programmes in 'conflict zones all over the world'.[59]

Lack of interest in bridging the cultural gaps between themselves and local workers prevented expats from seeing that landmines – whether genuine or not – were manifestations of much more deeply buried problems. These included the legacy of colonial divide-and-rule, post-independence exploitation, arms proliferation, exclusionary patronage networks and the privatization of violence. Understanding these issues takes time. But time, for many expatriate aid workers (whether in mine action or other sectors), was in short supply. The humanitarian profession is transient, as media and donor attention jolts from one place to another. Few but the truly committed dedicate more than three years to one place.[60] 'Given that they are recruited on the basis of their technical expertise', such as demining, 'rather than their country knowledge, interveners know little about their area of deployment when they arrive in the field,' writes Autesserre.[61] Without a sustained commitment to a community, it is difficult to bridge the boundaries that separate the expatriate from the local or even understand where those boundaries lie.

Margaret Mathiang, then Deputy Chairperson of the South Sudan Demining Commission (SSDC) (now called the South Sudan Mine Action Authority (SSMAA)), told me that many expatriates communicated a lack of interest in South Sudanese people. They seemed unwilling to learn about the intricacies of the country or even have 'interaction with their own [South Sudanese] deminers'. As we spoke in her office in Juba, she explained that she and her South Sudanese colleagues felt proud to be 'liberators' of their people. She perceived potential for 'a period of peace and we want to enjoy the fruits of our struggle of two decades of war and suffering'. When international staff spoke disparagingly of South Sudan, or even comported themselves in an undignified way, it cheapened the South Sudanese people's achievement. Mathiang said some of her colleagues were 'disgusted' by the vulgarity of some of the expatriates, saying that South Sudanese people have fought for 'two decades for our rights, we don't want someone coming from far away to use the "F" language'. Mathiang indicated that crudeness displayed a lack of appreciation for the dignity of South Sudan and its people. Demining professionals in Khartoum told me similar stories, saying that they disapproved of expatriates' drinking habits, which they saw as disrespectful of their religion.

Mathiang acknowledged that some of these challenges were about 'cultural differences', but also suggested that more fundamentally, there was an issue of power and justice. Mathiang did her master's thesis on the effective reintegration and participation of people with disabilities in development of post-war South Sudan. After leaving the SSDC, she was appointed Undersecretary of the National Ministry of Gender, Child and Social Welfare. In the course of our conversation, she often reflected on patterns of marginalization in the demining sector. She felt insulted by 'colonial language' that suggested expatriates 'think they are superior and better'. Management of mine action, she said, 'should not only be in the hands of the international organizations, the bidding done in New York with no involvement of us'. Relating the difficulties of mediating a demining group's workplace dispute between international and local staff, she told me that whatever the particularities of who had said what to whom, inequality was a core problem. Local deminers were paid 'very little money, less than $200 ... , [for] a very dangerous job'. It's 'exploitation', she told me. By contrast, expatriate technical advisers could earn up to six figures, tax-free if employed by the UN. These salaries, as well as a desire to stay in 'suitable hotels', said Mathiang, contributed to the high cost of demining in South Sudan. Distance from the people they serve meant that managers of demining agencies also 'don't inform the authorities or the communities of what they are doing' effectively. Poor communication meant that local people may not understand which areas have been demined, leaving them fallow and unused.

When I raised these concerns to expatriate demining managers, many dismissed them as populist political rhetoric – anti-colonial posturing. But in my conversation with her, Mathiang offered examples of demining agencies that were 'closer to the people' and augmented minefield survey with careful attention to social and cultural nuances. She said that South Sudanese mine action benefited when it drew on the knowledge of technical experts from around the world. She appreciated the NGOs and UN agencies that dedicated time and resources to training local staff. She told me that she had started asking all international demining agencies, 'What have you done in capacity building?' She believed SSDC's advocacy was working, saying, 'Most organizations are now cooperating and are trying their best to employ South Sudanese in key positions, like team leaders or assistant team leader, so they can learn from those people.' She also argued that international demining agencies should leave their equipment behind when they pulled out of the country, to contribute to local institutions. But for Mathiang, capacity building could not only be one way: 'also they need to learn from us, we need to share experiences.' South Sudanese 'people are not wild people', she told me, saying that organizations which 'treat them well' have fewer difficulties than agencies with a hierarchical management style. She told me that an important indicator of an agency's commitment to inclusion was how much they were 'engendering the process of mine action'. She said she was 'impressed' by a one particular NGO, in which women 'were leading the demining process'.

The participation of a wider range of people shifted how demining agencies thought about their priorities. Mathiang said that while surveying and clearing roads remained crucial, listening to local communities along the routes changed how this work was framed and thought about. Instead of being primarily about the security of UN peacekeepers, road clearance, according to Mathiang, should 'facilitate the return of the internally displaced and the refugees from neighboring countries' and help the World Food Program's 'activities for the hungry and the needy'. The work of demining also needed to reach beyond the verges of roads and into 'communities are still living with mines, still living with the threat of unexploded ordnance'. But to succeed, 'it has to be directed right', with the input and participation of those most affected by the dangers.

Recognizing this need, several organizations began calling on demining operations to institutionalize greater qualitative analysis of their surroundings. Many international demining NGOs like MAG and NPA have incorporated 'community liaison' teams into their operations to ensure that they are working closely with and learning from the people they intend to serve. The Assistance to Mine-Affected Communities project at the Peace Research Institute, Oslo (PRIO) conducted in-depth social science field research on mine action and worked with operators to help them better understand 'social structures and dynamics within which mine action agencies operate'.[62] This was vital, they said, to 'maximize the positive impacts of mine action on peacebuilding'.[63] In Sudan and South Sudan, they published reports and offered advice on how mine action interacted with conflict dynamics in the Nuba Mountains,[64] potential for mainstreaming gender considerations across mine action programmes and the importance of building national capacity.[65] For example, a PRIO report by Rebecca Roberts and Mads Frilander raised the following concerns:

> The lack of previous long-term close-contact engagements in Sudan means that external actors do not have a good working knowledge of how to operate effectively in the country. Most external organizations, including those involved in mine action, are having to learn how to work in a new cultural, political and legal environment that has been shaped by a complicated protracted conflict. Often, even basic information related to normal daily activities is lacking.[66]

However, the report also found that when humanitarian mine action agencies paid close and careful attention to their surroundings, they were able to have a modest but nonetheless positive impact. The 1980s and 1990s conflict between the Sudanese government and the SPLA had been particularly bloody in the Nuba Mountains. This diverse borderland in South Kordofan state is technically in 'the North' but, due to its political and economic marginalization, has proved a fertile recruiting ground for the SPLA. South Kordofan is often called one of Sudan's 'transitional zones' – frontline areas that do not fit neatly into the division of the country into a north and a south. But at stake are the 115,000 barrels of crude oil produced daily in South Kordofan.[67] During the 1990s, widespread support for the rebels in the Nuba Mountains drew the ire of the Sudanese government, which took advantage of the region's isolation from the international media to unleash a horrific campaign of collective punishment, including 'aerial bombardment, isolation, shortages, land expropriation ... forced population movements'[68] and the 'systematic elimination of educated Nuba and village leaders'.[69] According to the International Crisis Group, the area remains 'deeply scarred', 'fragmented' and 'polarized' by the conflict.[70] The Nuba Mountains region also suffered some of the worst landmine contamination in all of North and South Sudan. The 2009 South Kordofan Landmine Impact Survey found that almost 300,000 people were living in mine-affected communities, many of whom were unable to access 'rainfed agricultural land, roads and housing' because of the explosive hazard.[71] Recently, the political tensions resulting from the disentanglement of North and South Sudan have threatened further violence. Many people in the Nuba Mountains feel used and abandoned by their former patrons in both the North and South and worry that tensions between the two governments could spill over again into their communities.[72]

But it would be inaccurate to dismiss the Nuba Mountains as a hopeless backwater, destined for war. Local support for ending the conflict made the Nuba Mountains a driver of the peace process as a whole in the early 2000s. Listening to their missionaries in East Africa, the evangelical Christian coalition that had helped elect George W. Bush pressured the US government to broker peace between the Sudanese government and the SPLA. This resulted in an unexpected ceasefire in the Nuba Mountains in 2002 that 'dramatically' improved the 'security situation'.[73] In the hopeful days after the ceasefire, many international actors saw the Nuba Mountains as a way to demonstrate 'peace dividends' of freedom of movement, economic development and social linkages. The ceasefire set up a Joint Military Commission (JMC), made up of both local and international troops, to oversee the truce. The JMC saw demining of roads as crucial both to its own mission and to opening the Nuba Mountains to the potential for peaceful exchange. The US government quickly gave a contract to RONCO which supported the JMC ceasefire monitoring teams, by 'opening up roads ... so they could reach the isolated villages'.[74]

International demining NGOs also wanted to capitalize on the opportunity for peace. Rae McGrath, founder of MAG, had been trying to establish a locally staffed mine action programme in Sudan since 2001, to demonstrate that donors could engage in mine action while conflict was still ongoing. He felt demining should begin while it was needed most, rather than waiting for peace, by dismantling explosive boundaries. Through the British NGOs Oxfam and Landmine Action, and with funding from the European Commission, McGrath arranged a series of 'crosslines' meetings between local mine action actors and set up the Sudan Landmine Information and Response Initiative (SLIRI), a joint information gathering project with northern and southern mine action groups. Following the ceasefire, this project shifted the emphasis of its 'crosslines' work to the Nuba Mountains, training joint teams of surveyors and deminers from both sides of the conflict.

Similarly, DanChurchAid (DCA) set up a programme working with JASMAR, a local mine action NGO with close ties to the Sudanese government, and OSIL, an NGO established by the SPLA. 'Every aspect of the programme' was designed to 'contribute to the peace and confidence-building effort' by developing 'increased trust and reliance' between the employees of the two NGOs.[75] A DCA expatriate manager told me that the programme benefited from DCA not being '100% a demining organization'. Extensive experience in humanitarian relief, health, food security and human rights, 'gives the organization the capacity to think 360 degrees, to see all the problems related to the population', rather than fixating on landmines. They also had strong commitments to treat local staff well. While 'in the everyday operation it's very secular', the manager told me, 'an organization that is called Danish *Church* Aid' has to make 'ethical choices'. These included a pay scale that did not discriminate between expatriates and national staff and generous health benefits.

While their programmes faced significant difficulties – spending time negotiating disputes between local deminers – both Landmine Action and DCA had some important successes. As a result of their work, 'professional working relationships have been developed at the national, intermediate and local levels, and in some cases personal friendships have followed.'[76] In reflection, said Pansegrouw, 'I think the relationship that was built across the lines ... and the fact that these guys were talking to each other showed that it can be done ... that two opposing groups can work together, they can talk some of their problems out.' Despite still being at war, the crosslines contacts in Nuba Mountains demining meant that in 2004 the Sudanese government, SPLA and United Nations Mine Action Service (UNMAS) signed a memorandum of understanding establishing the framework of a mine action programme for Sudan. This was one of the first major agreements signed between the warring parties and meant that negotiations on the mine action sections of the CPA were completed a year earlier than the rest of the peace agreement. Sudanese mine action professionals told me that if they had not been involved in the SLIRI crosslines programme in the Nuba Mountains, they would have found it harder to trust their counterparts when negotiating the CPA. As a result, researchers at PRIO concluded that mine action in the Nuba Mountains was 'symbolically important' and 'laid foundations for further peacebuilding'.[77]

Involvement in crosslines mine action also had an impact on military behaviour in Sudan and South Sudan. In 2001, as Landmine Action was opening its SLIRI project, the SPLA signed the Geneva Call Deed of Commitment (an equivalent of the landmine ban treaty for non-state actors like guerilla groups).[78] Garang said the decision was motivated by concerns 'about the plight of the civil population and the unsettling realisation that we might end up with mined land rather than the homeland we are fighting for'.[79] A year into the Nuba Mountains demining programme, the Sudanese government ratified the landmine ban treaty. Lobbying by the Sudanese Campaign to Ban Landmines 'managed to transform the image' of landmines within Sudan from 'a military and security issue' to a 'humanitarian' concern.[80] This was a significant civil society victory – the government has long been suspicious of NGOs, in fact, any group seeking to limit the power of the military. There have been no independently confirmed uses of landmines by the Sudanese military since 2004 (though there were several unconfirmed reports between 2011 and 2013).[81] 'We demonstrated that it is possible to talk and work together on a very contentious subject,' Pansegrouw said, even though both sides saw landmines as 'military secrets'. While the political situation in the Nuba Mountains has recently deteriorated, the crosslines mine action programme and the Nuba Mountains ceasefire are indicators that this is not inevitable. In September 2017, South Sudan acceded to the Convention on Cluster Munitions.

In reflecting on the value of mine action in Sudan and South Sudan, Pansegrouw acknowledged that neither programme had performed well if assessed on the number of landmines cleared – a common metric of demining progress. But, 'I do think it's worth it,' he said, if you could measure mine action 'in terms of perceived danger that has been reduced'. Mathiang had similar reflections. Without getting 'rid of all the obstacles' posed by 'the existence of landmine and explosive remnants of war', she said, South Sudanese people would not be able to enjoy the 'fruits of our liberation ... and rebuild'. Mathiang longed for South Sudan 'to be like any other country which is developed'. Abolishing the persistent fear of mines, she told me, is 'like a foundation for making all this true'. In other words, the contribution of mine action was not simply about digging old weapons out of the earth. It also proved capable of alleviating the profound anxieties of 'Everywhere War', placing clandestine knowledge on public maps, bringing people who are enemies into humane conversation and diminishing the uncertainty about where is and is not safe.

Chapter 7

KILLER ROBOTS
DIGITAL WAR, THE UNITED STATES

Pursuing a sniper, Dallas police surrounded the suspect, a veteran of the US campaign in Afghanistan, who was shooting at officers escorting a July 2016 Black Lives Matter protest. When negotiations with him broke down, he again opened fire, killing twelve police and two members of the public. Improvising a tactic first used in the Iraq War, police officers attached plastic explosives to a Remotec Andros MarkV-A1 bomb disposal robot and navigated it, via remote control, close to the sniper. Detonating the charge, they killed him.[1] While it was the first such robotic police killing in America, similar technologies are being deployed to deadly effect by US military and intelligence agencies in Central Asia, the Middle East and Horn of Africa. 'We use the predator drone to target people overseas, and now we see the police force using a [robot] to target someone in a US city,' Peter Asaro told the *Christian Science Monitor*. 'We don't want to see this as a model,' he said. A professor at New York's New School specializing in the ethics of robotics and vice-chair of the International Committee for Robot Arms Control (ICRAC), Peter is increasingly unnerved by the 'weaponization of robotic platforms, as these technologies become more sophisticated and more autonomous'.[2] But the Dallas Chief of Police, David Brown, was unrepentant: 'I would use any tool necessary to save our officers' lives. ... And I'm not ashamed to say it.'[3]

I met Peter four years earlier, while researching the Pentagon's quiet efforts to develop new robotic landmines, called the Spider (XM-7) and the Scorpion Intelligent Munitions System. I read an intriguing article by Peter, which argued that 'humans have the right not to be killed by a machine' and that the existing laws of war inadequately protect us from the humanitarian consequences of increasingly autonomous weapons systems.[4] He worked only a couple miles uptown from my Pace University office, at the New School for Public Engagement, and also lived in Brooklyn. I invited him out for coffee in Park Slope. Peter, a savvy user of the web and social media, told me that he was not anti-technology. Rather he wanted a relationship between humans and machines that values human life. As he puts it, 'It's OK for a plane to fly itself. It's not OK for a plane to decide who to shoot at.'[5] It was disturbing enough for the police in Dallas to use a remotely operated improvised bomb, but what if a future emerged in which the robot sought out suspects to kill on its own, without direct human control?

If put into production, the Spider and Scorpion systems (developed by the same arms contractors that made the bombies now littering Laos) would form so-called 'smart minefields', which could be turned on and off by a soldier operating a laptop, broadcast their location over a coded signal, detect the presence of vehicles and self-destruct after a specified period of time. Though a 'man-in-the-loop' adaptation of the Spider (called the Matrix) saw a limited deployment in Iraq, advocacy from the US Campaign to Ban Landmines and Patrick Leahy, a senator from Vermont, managed to cut funding for both the Spider and Scorpion.[6] 'The United States shouldn't be making and using weapons that can't discriminate between a soldier and a civilian,' said Steve Goose of Human Rights Watch.[7] In 2009 budget documents, it appeared the US government had quietly dropped plans to allow these systems to operate without a 'man-in-the-loop'. Nonetheless, in May 2012, the US Army put in a $58.2 million order to Alliant Techsystems for the Spider.[8] As this book went to press, the Trump White House lifted Obama-era restrictions on US use of these and other landmines.[9]

The Spider and Scorpion 'smart' landmine systems represent only a small corner of the rapidly developing field of military robotics. Sometimes these innovations are used to create remote-controlled robots that can aide in EOD. When the New York Police Department (NYPD) used an ANDROS series robot, fitted with a surveillance camera, mechanical arm and caterpillar tracks, to defuse a car bomb in Times Square in 2010, local media depicted it as a 'high-tech hero'.[10] The image of a friendly electronic public servant is encouraged by the manufacturer, Northrop Grumman, which touts the ANDROS as the inspiration for the cute automaton protagonist in Disney's movie *Wall-E*.[11] However, the very 'robo-partner' used by the NYPD to save people's lives can also be used to kill. Dig around the manufacturer's website and you will soon find that the ANDROS can be fitted with a grenade launcher.[12]

For years, the Pentagon has listed its funding of research on explosive detecting robots as part of the US government's contribution to 'humanitarian demining'. But the sensitive equipment of robotic demining machines often breaks down, requires expensive parts and is often unnecessary in post-conflict countries where there is no shortage of unemployed people who can be trained to be deminers. 'It is perhaps no coincidence that some of the most popular areas of research in relation to landmine detection, such as thermal imagery, have considerable and, it could be argued, far greater, military potential,' suggests mine action expert Rae McGrath.[13] Communications scholar Ian Roderick argues that 'the veneration of the EOD robot' is a form of 'fetishism', which enables the Pentagon to wage war while simultaneously claiming to 'save lives'.[14] At best, EOD robots simply extend the reach of a deminer or bomb disposal officer – they are essentially a robotic arm, not a magical demining machine.

After 9/11, faced with the threat of IEDs, landmines and unexploded cluster munitions in Afghanistan and Iraq, EOD robots went to war. And many of them did not remain innocuously 'humanitarian'. In Iraq, US soldiers strapped Claymore mines to EOD robots and drove them around, looking for insurgents. It was only a matter of time before defence contractors were mass producing military robots armed with machine guns. By 2009, Brookings Institution researcher P.W. Singer reported that the United States had deployed over 12,000 ground robots in Iraq, which were engaged in 'street patrols, reconnaissance, sniping, checkpoint security, as well as guarding observation posts'.[15] 'These are big, big, meta-changes that are happening in war that we've got to wrap our heads around,' says Singer, who authored a seminal book on military robotics, *Wired for War*.[16]

* * *

The European empires tested new repressive ideologies, techniques and technologies on their colonial subjects – far from the scrutiny of domestic opposition. However, the effects of these political and military methods, once perfected, had a tendency to 'boomerang' back into Europe, initially used on marginizalized people: the poor, women, Jews, Roma, the mentally ill and criminals. Concentration camps, identity cards, racist pseudoscience and machine guns, first innovated as means for controlling/slaughtering 'far away' people soon wrought devastation 'at home'.[17]

The modernization of political repression has seen a shift from rule by maiming to more subtle systems that surveil and control our movement. The rise of industrial modern society in Europe was accompanied by a move away from public torture and execution to controlling people's movement through space and time in prisons, mental institutions, schools and hospitals. This encouraged people to govern their own behaviour through habit and self-regulation.[18]

Similarly, a handful of contrarian landmine experts argue that major military powers are giving up their mine stockpiles not because of the ban treaty, but because they now have access to more sophisticated methods of automated and remote-control violence.[19] Unlike the all-or-nothing explosiveness of the landmine, unable to distinguish between a car and tank, security services are now developing complex systems of networked digital surveillance to watch and channel our movements.

For example, the Lower Manhattan Security Initiative (LMSI), a $150 million joint effort by the NYPD and several of the dominant corporations in New York's Financial District. LMSI surveils the section of the island stretching from City Hall to Battery Park, including Wall Street, the former World Trade Center site and access to the Brooklyn Bridge. At the LMSI Coordination Center, a 10-minute walk down Broadway from Pace, a mix of police and private security personnel watch over the input from over 3,000 closed circuit television cameras, most privately owned, as well as radiation detectors and car licence plate readers. This avalanche of data is processed by 'advanced video analytic software' that 'can alert police in real-time' to a variety of 'suspicious' objects or activities, including unattended parcels, movement in restricted areas and unusual loitering. LMSI has now been expanded up to Midtown, to include Times Square, Penn Station and Grand Central.[20] The initiative is also building a 'ring of steel' around Lower Manhattan – mobile road barricades as well as flood barriers in the train tunnels to New Jersey, that can seal off the Financial District at a moment's notice.[21] Commenting on the initiative, then mayor Michael Bloomberg proclaimed, 'We will take whatever steps necessary, regardless of cost in Federal or City funds, to protect New York from terrorists.'[22] However, it was also used to surveil the lawful demonstrations of Occupy Wall Street in 2011.[23]

This massive security complex is not just fixed in place. NYPD helicopters, loitering over the city, are fitted with a high-powered digital 'eye in the sky' that can zoom in to follow a car or person on the move. New York's *Gay City News* found that the NYPD explored using aerial surveillance drones able to record video through apartment windows, raising privacy concerns within the gay, lesbian, transgender and queer community.[24] 'With the wars [in Afghanistan and Iraq] winding down,' wrote Nick Paumgarten of *The New Yorker*, 'the drones, field-tested at taxpayer expense, are coming home and looking for jobs.'[25] Bard College's Center for the Study of the Drone has found that 201 law enforcement agencies in the United States now use the kind of EOD robots used in the Dallas killing.[26] The NYPD also has six 'underwater drones' – VideoRay Remotely Operated Underwater Vehicles (ROVs) – which engage in marine surveillance, aiming to detect narcotics, IEDs and radioactive material through searching 'suspicious boats under bridges' and 'unidentified floating package[s]'.[27]

LMSI shares with minefields an attempt to limit the movement of unwelcome intruders and punish those who dare to cross the boundaries. The violence remains largely implicit, veiled. But should you forget that you are in regulated space in Lower Manhattan, there are prominently placed cameras, signs warning you that you are being watched, in addition to police and private security guards. The incessant reminders to remain vigilant put you on alert, not only to the behaviours of others, but also to your own – you know not to leave your bags unattended in City Hall Park, you know not to act erratically around Ground Zero, you stiffen your spine as you walk by the phalanx of police officers watching as you exit the subway station. By diffusing dominance through a complex of human, institutional and technological networks operating in and through the spaces of Lower Manhattan, LMSI does not need to resort to more violent methods of social control. A minefield represents a failure of dominance, the failure to persuade and condition people to govern their own behaviour. One does not need landmines if one has more subtle forms of control.

Nevertheless, the digitization of security has a sharp end. As the American public's tolerance for long-term military deployment has eroded, the Bush, Obama and Trump Administrations outsourced counterterrorism operations to covert networks of drones and their operators. Predator and Reaper drones allow soldiers or contractors in a shipping container 'office' in upstate New York to fire on people half a world away. From 2002 to the time of writing, the CIA and US military had conducted at least 6,786 drone strikes in Afghanistan, Pakistan, Somalia and Yemen, killing between 8,459 and 12,105 people, of whom between 769 and 1,725 were civilians and between 253 and 397 children.[28] Drones allow soldiers to project violence far beyond what their bodies can do alone. In addition to the physical distance between a pilot in the desert of Nevada and the casualty in Yemen, 'killing by remote control', as anti-drone activist Medea Benjamin calls it, may increase the psychological distance between the killer and killed.[29] Computing, surveillance and navigation technology are so cheap now that almost anyone can afford their own robots, their own drones. Singer believes we are on the cusp of a widespread proliferation of military robotics that will transform the way war is fought, not just by industrialized superpowers but by militias and terrorist networks too.[30]

Landmines were invented in so-called 'developed countries', but as they became cheap commodities, they proliferated into areas considered the world's peripheries. There is no reason to believe that this will not happen with military robots, putting powerful weapons in the hands of people with a kaleidoscope of agendas. Hezbollah has used drones to both surveil and attack Israel.[31] Insurgents in Iraq developed systems to remotely detonate IEDs with a mobile phone. 'Robotic technology removes the person from the emotional equation of war,' writes Notre Dame scholar David Cortright, who worries that robotic weapons stretch 'the disconnection between war and society', which 'reduces the political inhibitions against the use of deadly violence'.[32]

An example of this depersonalization of killing is the US practice of so-called 'signature strikes', in which people are targeted by drones for fitting a demographic 'profile', rather than being a known fighter. Human rights experts worry that we are a short step from encoding such behaviours into a computer program that selects targets automatically. While weaponized EOD robots and the military's Predator drones require operators 'in-the loop', at the cutting edge of military robotics there is an emerging class of robots that act autonomously, identifying 'enemy targets' through surveillance systems and delivering a violent response without human approval. The South Korean arms company DoDaam Systems has developed a networked machine gun turret – the Super aEgis II – 'that can detect and lock onto human targets from kilometers away, day or night and in any weather conditions, and deliver some heavy firepower'.[33] It can operate with a person 'in-the-loop'. But the Super aEgis II can also operate automatically, in what the manufacturer has called 'Slave Mode Operation'. DoDaam also offers a machine-gun-armed mobile robot that can patrol an area autonomously using GPS and automatically attack a person it encounters.[34] The Chinese Navy is developing a mobile robotic sea mine that can navigate to 'programmed destinations', detect the location of passing ships and fire a torpedo in response. They are researching ways to make such robotic mines able to detect and fire missiles at passing helicopters.[35] US defence researchers are seeking ever-increasing autonomy for lethal drones.[36]

Autonomous weapons systems would multiply in their digital complexity the lethal binary logic of the landmine: IF the victim trips the trigger, THEN explode. Killer robots are to the landmine as the mechanical light switch is to the microchip; both are capable of processing binary code but on totally different orders of magnitude. Landmines and autonomous armed robots derive from the same desire to control space, to project violence beyond the capacity of a human body and to deliver a hostile automated response. Both transform the Other into a stimulus, an incoming piece of data, rather than a human being with a family, a history, a culture, hopes and dreams. But autonomous armed robots are the landmines of the digital, globalized, mobile future. While the future of killer robots roaming the earth sounds like science fiction, Singer warns, 'Do not believe that isn't coming.'[37]

Drawing together the trends in technology that either already exist or are in development, it is not difficult to imagine a future for expeditionary mines that go looking for targets. Mines that navigate using GPS. Mines that can organize themselves into flying swarms, able to communicate with each other. Insect-sized mines crawling around the world, adapting to their surroundings, detecting 'unusual' human movements and triggering a deadly response from a drone hovering nearby. 'Nanobot' mines that sneak through the open windows of a Brooklyn brownstone. Mines that are produced on demand by pre-positioned 3D printers. Mines that patrol underwater, sink ships and perform marine landings on distant shores. Mines that can record and broadcast video of what they are doing for distribution to news channels. Mines capable of charging their batteries by resting on powerlines, or in the case of one system currently in its experimental stages, able to feed off the flesh of dead soldiers on the battlefield – using the breakdown of organic material to generate electricity.

In the Information Age, there is also no reason for mines to remain constrained to the physical world. Already, malware programs such as viruses, worms and trojans lie in wait in uncharted territories of the internet. One could imagine more sophisticated versions that would turn another military's equipment against its owners. According to the *New York Times*, in early 2008, President Obama 'secretly ordered increasingly sophisticated attacks on the computer systems that run Iran's main nuclear enrichment facilities, significantly expanding America's first sustained use of cyberweapons'.[38] The US- and Israeli-designed Stuxnet worm took over 1,000 Iranian uranium enrichment centrifuges, damaging them by making them spin out of control. The programme became public when Stuxnet escaped the networks it was targeted against and started replicating itself, infecting 45,000 computers around the world.[39]

The notion of a 'minefield' is rooted in an outdated concept of war constrained to two-dimensions – a 'battlefield'. Today, the pointy heads in the Pentagon talk about multidimensional 'battlespace', incorporating land, sea, air, outer space and cyberspace.[40] We may not be far from a future of metastasized mines, where the concept of the mine as a deadly trap meets the instant mobility and replicability of the computer virus, turning our surrounding everyday environment, machines and networks into deadly hazards. The mine would become decentred, with no one thing that can be removed and defused. The minefield would be replaced by minespace – triggered by 'suspicious signature patterns' identified by algorithms data-mining the deluge of data from email, surveillance cameras, mobile phones and credit card records. It would identify and track target persons by taking over the GPS in their phone. It might kill them with a high-powered laser, a drone-fired missile, an underwater-launched torpedo or poison administered by a robotic insect. All this would occur without a 'human-in-the-loop'. But just as likely as the totalitarian dystopia of this meta-minefield is a fragmented future, where those with sufficient capital can seal off privatized enclaves of privilege – spaces where only people with certain biometric specifications are allowed and 'Others' are literally not allowed to enter alive. Or a future where the violent technology becomes so cheap that anyone can jerry-rig an explosive Roomba and there is an armed drone above every home.

Artificial intelligence pioneer, Professor Stuart Russell at University of California, Berkeley, is particularly eloquent about the dystopian possibilities of proliferation:

> A very, very small quadcopter, one inch in diameter can carry a one- or two-gram shaped charge. You can order them from a drone manufacturer in China. You can program the code to say: 'Here are thousands of photographs of the kinds of things I want to target.' A one-gram shaped charge can punch a hole in nine millimeters of steel, so presumably you can also punch a hole in someone's head. You can fit about three million of those in a semi-tractor-trailer. You can drive up I-95 with three trucks and have 10 million weapons attacking New York City. They don't have to be very effective, only 5 or 10% of them have to find the target. There will be manufacturers producing millions of these weapons that people will be able to buy just like you can buy guns now, except millions of guns don't matter unless you have a million soldiers. You need only three guys to write the program and launch them. ... They could be here in two to three years. ... There are really no technological breakthroughs that are required. ... Every one of the component technology is available in some form commercially.[41]

Ronald Arkin, a computer scientist at Georgia Institute of Technology, argues that killer robots could be programmed to be more ethical and discriminating than human soldiers. He says robots won't react out of fear or prejudice and might process more information quickly than people. He claims it may be possible to encode international humanitarian law into an autonomous military robot's instructions. However, he admits that he assumes his robot soldier would operate in a 'traditional war where civilians have evacuated the war zone and anyone pointing a weapon at U.S. troops can be considered a target'. This seems like wishful thinking; as robotic ethics professor Colin Allen retorted, 'I challenge you to find a war with no civilians'.[42] Arkin's notion of a digital 'ethical governor' constraining robotic weapons relies on an impoverished view of human society. Just as 'autonomy' would entrust the intimately human matter of death to a machine, people like Arkin suggest that the subtle nuances of norms, wisdom and judgement could be transformed from symbols and language into binary code, with clear divisions between 'good guys' and 'bad guys'. But everything we know from studying warfare shows that it is infinitely more complex. In the course of several months, a single person can shift from one side of a conflict to another and in or out of uniform. This is why war is such a confusing human experience. It is not just a series of ones and zeros. Just watching any Hollywood spy film will tell you that a person, as a double agent, can be both a one and a zero at the same time.

Just as Arkin underestimates human complexity, he overestimates the capability of robots. Information technology rarely matches science-fiction fantasies; printers jam, laptops melt down. 'Computer-related technology ... is especially susceptible to malfunctions and "bugs" given their complexity,' wrote the authors of a 2008 report on autonomous military robotics for the US Navy.[43] Though it is reassuring that robots have not yet achieved total perfection, this also raises further concerns. In October 2007, a South African robotic anti-aircraft cannon on a training exercise went haywire, firing hundreds of shells, killing nine soldiers, wounding fourteen.[44] Sometimes aerial robots just drop out of the sky. In June 2012, a massive US Navy Global Hawk, a quasi-autonomous unmanned spy plane, crashed near Salisbury, Maryland.[45] A British advocacy group has recorded almost 250 crashed drones between 2007 and the first part of 2016. This count did not include 'crashes by mini-UAV's like Raven and Scan Eagle as they crash so often it would swamp the database'.[46]

In suggesting that a robot can be just, Arkin disembodies justice, turning it into a technical exercise, rather than a deeply human process. We make moral judgements in conversation between human beings (both past and present). Ultimately our conception of justice lies in the ability to find, discipline and punish a person. When a wrong is committed, we arrest or imprison a human body, make them do community service or pay compensation. Habeas corpus requires a corpus. The laws of war rely on the ability of a judge to pinpoint responsibility for war crimes on specific people. You can't court martial R2D2.[47]

Some have suggested that while we cannot hold a robot responsible for misconduct, we might be able to sue the manufacturer or perhaps the commander of the overall operation. However, military robots are embedded in vast, globalized networks. The military operation might be ultimately responsible to a government employee, but an armed robot could be operated and maintained by private contractors of various nationalities, stationed on bases in numerous countries. As with any high-tech product, its design and manufacture may have been outsourced to people and other robots spanning the globe. 'Unmanned systems don't just affect the *how* of warfighting, they affect the *who* of fighting at its most fundamental level,' says Singer. 'What does it mean to go to war increasingly with soldiers whose hardware is made in China and software is written in India?'[48]

How possible is it to remain humane in warfare, when the human encounter of killing is mediated through a diffuse and shape-shifting global crowd of people and technologies? How do you 'demine' the computer virus, the mobile mine, the mine that endlessly reproduces itself? Proliferated, distributed, diffuse, intelligent and networked mines will require 'deminers' capable of hunting for a moving target, hacking into cyberspace, chasing an ever-changing network of software and hardware. Deminers themselves may need to be augmented, supplemented by demining apps, deminer bots. Deminers are already experimenting with drones and satellites to survey minefields. To struggle against the techno-dystopia in which humanity is coded, dominated and killed by emotionless digital processes – blurs the edges between the deminer and the activist, it requires a multifaceted effort to reorganize political and economic systems in a human-centred way. Mine action will need to become the action of a social movement.

* * *

In June 1995, Mary Wareham, a recent political science graduate from New Zealand, landed in Cambodia for the ICBL Phnom Penh conference. She had just finished a master's thesis on the nascent campaign against landmines, pursued against the advice of her faculty advisers, who thought she was studying something too obscure.

Faxing all the NGOs listed on the attendance list of the London ICBL meeting, she set up appointments with campaigners and travelled on a round-the-world ticket to Europe and North America to learn from them. Returning home, she talked with New Zealand soldiers who had been deployed with UN demining programmes in Afghanistan and Mozambique. She also observed meetings of the New Zealand campaign and began to help out. She even joined the official New Zealand delegation to a CCW meeting in Geneva. But Cambodia was the first landmine-affected country Mary had visited. She arrived in the midst of 'a seminal moment for the campaign', telling me that she felt 'incredibly lucky to have the opportunity to work and hang out with the campaign icons', including Jody Williams, Bobby Mueller of VVAF, Rae McGrath of MAG and Steve Goose of HRW. 'I was only 25 at the time when I started with ICBL, it was quite amazing,' said Mary. 'I got to watch and learn from the best.'

In Cambodia, she visited mine action projects and watched MAG's training academy graduate its first women deminers. 'It was really exhilarating' after having studied the issue from afar to meet Reth and Sister Denise, listen to the wisdom of Maha Ghosananda and find out that people most affected by minefields were the real 'powerhouse of the campaign'; 'landmines were not theoretical for them, they were a real problem'. Mary has been a disarmament activist almost her whole life. She remembers watching ships protest against Pacific nuclear testing from her primary school window in New Zealand and going to the art room to make posters before joining demonstrations. But it was her key insight in Cambodia – that disarmament is more about the impact on people than the weapons themselves – that has driven her campaign work ever since. She has become a pivotal figure in the struggle against automated violence, pressing for bans on landmines, cluster munitions and, now, killer robots. While methods of repression can boomerang from the world's peripheries into the core, Mary's career has been a vector transmitting humane advocacy from places such as Phnom Penh to the centres of global power.

In 2012, I attended a summit Mary convened in New York City to commemorate the twentieth anniversary of the ICBL's launch, bringing together campaigners, activists and academics working on a range of disarmament, security and arms control issues. As we sat facing her in the metal folding chairs of the Church Center, looking out at the UN Secretariat building, Mary was constantly in motion, urging us to think about what we had learned over the last two decades. Over the course of the conference, the NGOs in attendance adopted a

'Communique' outlining a vision for 'humanitarian disarmament', a global effort 'protecting civilians from the harmful effects of armed violence' and 'ensur[ing] the rights of victims'. The manifesto argued that 'the strongest and most significant disarmament achievements' have involved 'genuine cooperation and substantive partnerships between governments, international organizations, and civil society'. Even though it is the states that make treaties such as the landmine and cluster munitions bans, non-governmental actors must recognize their 'critical role', providing 'monitoring and research', 'advocacy' and 'operations in affected countries'.[49] At one of the summit's evening meals, the eminent international human rights lawyer Philip Alston, author of a groundbreaking 2010 UN report on armed drones,[50] challenged the conference attendees to apply their experience banning landmines and cluster munitions to do something about robotic weapons. Behind the scenes, Mary and her HRW colleagues met with other NGOs to consider how the humanitarian disarmament vision could respond to the emerging challenges of high-tech killing. Mary said the aim was to create 'a global coordinated campaign like the ICBL and CMC to go out and get a ban' on killer robots.

Over the past few years, human rights groups had been contacted by computer scientists, artificial intelligence experts and tech ethicists distressed at the growing autonomy of weapons systems. They were disturbed by the tech industry's complicity with arms developers and many of them turned down military funding for their work.[51] Joining forces with lawyers, social scientists and activists, including Peter Asaro, a number of these 'robotic refuseniks' launched the International Committee for Robot Arms Control in 2009. With the slightly odd acronym ICRAC, they called on 'the international community to urgently commence a discussion about an arms control regime to reduce the threat posed by' military robotics. They wanted governments to consider the 'prohibition of the development, deployment and use of armed autonomous unmanned systems'.[52]

Shortly after we first met, Peter introduced me to ICRAC co-founder and chair Noel Sharkey, godfather of the robotic refuseniks. A professor of artificial intelligence and robotics at the University of Sheffield, he grew up in Northern Ireland, gaining a sober appreciation for the tragedy of war. His thorough technical understanding of robotics – Noel has two doctoral degrees among the daunting string of letters after his name – has led him to conclude two things: one, that a future of autonomous weapons systems is closer that we might think, and two, that 'the idea of a robot making decisions about human termination is terrifying'. 'Policymakers seem to have an understanding of AI [Artificial Intelligence] that lies in the realms of science fiction and myth,' he says. Counter to Ron Arkin's idea of a robot capable of making ethical judgements, Noel is convinced that 'machines could not discriminate reliably between buses carrying enemy soldiers or schoolchildren, let alone be ethical'. Noel believes it is 'imperative that we create international legislation and a code of ethics for autonomous robots at war before it is too late'.[53]

When I first met him at an event in Washington DC, Noel, sporting a silvery pointed beard and white pony tail, was dressed in all black, with a matching black trench coat. A BuzzFeed journalist later described him as playing 'the part of the campaign's brilliant, absent-minded professor'.[54] His Twitter profile – @StoptheRobotWar – displayed a photo of his face superimposed onto that of the Terminator. Naturally, when Peter introduced me to him, I was a little intimidated. But as we shared drinks in a nearby pub, I found Noel to be a kindly and encouraging scholar – humane, in fact. He showed interest in my research, the progress of my career and empathized with the challenges of being a junior academic.

When Mary convened the backroom conversations at the Summit in October 2012, she invited ICRAC to offer their expertise to the gathering of representatives from NGOs with extensive experience of humanitarian disarmament, including Article 36, Mines Action Canada, Nobel Women's Initiative, PAX, Pugwash and HRW. HRW was selected to lead an international coalition seeking a pre-emptive ban on autonomous weapons systems. Mary was appointed coordinator. She quipped, 'Who could say no to running something called the Campaign to Stop Killer Robots?' She told me that after spending her life 'banning things already in use', she wanted to work on something 'preventative', pre-empting future harm. A month later, on 19 November, HRW released a landmark publication modelled on their early reports on landmines, entitled *Losing Humanity: The Case against Killer Robots*. On the same day, Mary moved back from New Zealand to work in the offices of HRW's Arms Division in the Dupont Circle neighbourhood of Washington DC.

The *Losing Humanity* report generated considerable media coverage, some of which had little to do with its primary purpose. The cover of the publication was illustrated with a cartoon of a robot taking charge of a command centre, with images of drones and devastation on the screens arrayed before it. A wide-eyed general looks alarmed, as he exits the room. In her campaign work, Mary has specialized in savvy cultivation of the news media. As we talk, I notice that on the wall of Mary's office and propped up on her desk are striking pictures of mine and ERW survivors. She is herself an impressive photographer. But, she told me, the challenge in building public opprobrium against autonomous armed robots is that, unlike landmines and cluster munitions, they have not been widely deployed. It is difficult to illustrate, in advance, the harm they might cause. How could the Campaign 'shift the conversation so it's not just about the technicalities of international law?' One cannot point to casualty statistics, ask a survivor to address sceptics with their life story or illustrate the dangers with photographs of the humanitarian costs. They also didn't want the report to imply that existing systems were the problem and so they couldn't put a photograph of a weapon on the cover. So, HRW decided to use a cartoon.

Unfortunately, many people don't accept the premise that killer robots could be a real problem – to many, autonomous military robots sound too much like *Doctor Who* to take seriously. The cartoon on the front of the HRW report may have contributed to the impression that killer robots were a fantasy. Much of press coverage of the report was initially vapid, relying on tropes from *Terminator* or *I, Robot*. This gave the DC defence intellectuals a strawman to tut-tut at. ICRAC were depicted as 'a fringe group of nutty professors'. One journalist who later wrote excellent coverage admitted that 'plenty of people, including myself, laughed' at the HRW's decision to warn the world about killer robots; 'they seemed insane'.[55]

However, this all distracted from the substance of the *Losing Humanity* report, which was meticulously researched by HRW and the Harvard Law School's International Human Rights Clinic, led by Bonnie Docherty, a lawyer who has contributed much to the intellectual foundations of humanitarian disarmament. The report reviewed examples of the 'precursor' weapons, illustrating a trend towards the increasing delegation of military functions to robots and computer programs. The authors of the report marshalled an impressive array of both technical evidence and legal arguments to refute claims that autonomous armed robots could act 'ethically'. Reviewing the rules governing armed conflict, HRW argued that weapons that make autonomous decisions over the use of lethal force 'would not be consistent with international humanitarian law and would increase the risk of death or injury to civilians during armed conflict'. As a result, the report called for the negotiation of an international, legally binding 'pre-emptive prohibition' on the 'development, production and use' of fully autonomous weapons systems.[56]

HRW also recommended that individual governments adopt relevant 'national laws and policies'.[57] In this, by virtue of good timing, they had a quick win. Three days after the launch of the *Losing Humanity* report, the US Defense Department issued Directive 3000.09 on 'Autonomy in Weapon Systems'. The policy, which is not law and can be changed by future administrations, requires that 'autonomous and semi-autonomous weapon systems shall be designed to allow commanders and operators to exercise appropriate levels of human judgment over the use of force'.[58] The Pentagon's 'appropriate levels of human judgement' represents a different standard than HRW's position that to be lawful, all weapons must exhibit 'meaningful human control' over 'individual attacks'.[59] Directive 3000.09 also has some unnerving loopholes. The activist Mark Gubrud has argued that the policy 'basically green-lights the development and use of both lethal and nonlethal SAWS [semi-autonomous weapons systems] for all targets'.[60] Nevertheless, Mary told me that the US policy raised the profile of the issue and made it easier for HRW to convince the public that killer robots were worthy of serious attention. 'We think this is a problem,' she said she would tell sceptical journalists, 'and so does the Pentagon.'

Five months later, HRW, ICRAC and numerous other NGOs officially launched the Campaign to Stop Killer Robots in London on 22 and 23 April 2013, with a conference and events at the Frontline Club and Parliament. Still struggling with how to represent the campaign visually, they selected an abstract logo of red cross-hairs inside a black cog. It communicated a sense of machinic danger without a cartoon's potential for misunderstanding. In their public events, rather than represent a robotic threat, the campaigners opted to have Jody Williams and Noel Sharkey pose for photos outside parliament with a friendly looking 'robotic campaigner' – an image that has persisted in news stories even today. At the parliamentary event, Admiral Lord West, former First Sea Lord and chief of the naval staff of the UK, declared, 'I find the idea of artificial intelligence doing targeting and weapon delivery quite abhorrent and I believe we need to do something to make that illegal globally and I think it is extremely dangerous.'[61]

Again, the nascent Campaign benefited from serendipitous timing. The UN's Special Rapporteur on Extrajudicial, Summary or Arbitrary Executions, Christof Heyns, had been conducting a series of consultations on killer robots. As a legal scholar, Heyns enjoys engaging with the academic community and invited me to participate in a small seminar of professors researching the development of killer robots. The experts represented a range of different opinions, strongly held and persistently expressed. Heyns sat at the front of the room, lobbing questions and taking notes on the resulting heated arguments. On 30

May 2013, Heyns presented the results of his research, the first ever UN report to consider what he called 'lethal autonomous robotics', to a meeting of the UN's Human Rights Council in Geneva. The report stated that the possibility of weapons that could 'select and engage targets without further human intervention' raises 'far-reaching concerns about the protection of life during war and peace'. While phrased carefully in diplomatic language, Heyns made clear his conclusion that 'robots should not have the power of life and death over human beings'.[62] 'Machines lack morality and mortality,' he wrote, which is 'among the reasons landmines were banned'. A decision to use violence, he asserted, must be taken by 'a human being ... as part of a deliberative process of human interaction', taking legal and ethical responsibility for 'each life lost'.[63] In the ensuing debate, the first ever official, public deliberations on killer robots, diplomats from twenty countries, as well as the UN Office for Disarmament Affairs, EU and Organization of the Islamic Conference expressed their views.[64]

During the exchange, France, which had assumed the presidency of the CCW, suggested that the issue be discussed at the upcoming November 2013 CCW conference in Geneva. ICRAC urged governments 'to be guided by principles of humanity' and maintain 'meaningful human deliberation and control over the use of violence ... [as] the cornerstone of any eventual global policymaking on robotic weapons'.[65] By the end of the conference, the CCW's members agreed, by consensus, to return to Geneva in May 2014 for an 'informal meeting of experts' on 'lethal autonomous weapons systems' (with the misleading acronym 'LAWS'). The once marginal group of 'robotic refuseniks' had arrived; they were seated at the diplomatic table. 'It was pretty impressive,' Mary reflected. 'We jumped forward a few years.' She said that the informal reaction of diplomats when they saw who was part of the campaign was to groan that 'here they come again, banning another weapon'. But she believes this reputation made states realize that they needed to pay attention if they wanted to maintain control of the process.

While the Campaign had successfully framed initial public discussion of autonomous weapons systems, the policy wonks began to mobilize. Kenneth Anderson and Matthew Waxman, two legal scholars, wrote a widely circulated report saying that 'lethal autonomous machines will inevitably enter the future battlefield'.[66] Noel Sharkey has responded to such deterministic narratives by saying 'autonomous robot warfare' is 'evitable' – we have some control over our technological future.[67] Human history is not the predetermined narrative arc of a video game. Just because a technology exists does not mean it will 'inevitably' be used. Human societies have chosen not to use certain armaments, including landmines, cluster munitions and chemical, biological and nuclear weapons. Nevertheless, Anderson and Waxman argued that technological progress could increase 'precision', providing 'humanitarian advantages' that make 'some proposed responses – such as prohibitory treaties – unworkable as well as ethically questionable'. While they recommended that the US government 'develop internal norms, principles, and practices' for the 'design and implementation' of autonomous weapons systems, they describe as 'extreme' those 'critics of autonomous lethal systems … demanding some grand international treaty or multilateral regime to regulate or even prohibit them'.[68] Similarly, an article posted by the Heritage Foundation, a conservative think-tank, asserted that 'there is no need to panic', describing the Campaign's 'agitation' as 'premature', potentially 'stifling legitimate research and development' to expand America's high-tech arsenal.[69]

As the naysayers became louder, the Campaign realized, as it prepared for the first expert meeting in May 2014, that diplomatic progress on killer robots depended on who governments chose to advise them. When the French government, as CCW president, released the list of seventeen experts whose testimony would be featured at the May 2014 meeting, all of them were men. When the Campaign inquired, they were told that there were no suitable women. This was preposterous. Mary was the coordinator of the international coalition that had mobilized global public concern. Jody Williams – a Nobel Laureate – was a prominent supporter. There were numerous other women academics, lawyers and scientists working on this issue.[70]

During the expert meeting, a group of women from the Campaign met at a Geneva restaurant to strategize. 'We had to make it clear to states that they couldn't put as at the back of the room to listen to male "experts" telling us killer robots are great because they don't rape,' said Mary. She was tired of the condescension from powerful men who had dubbed the women in the ICBL and Cluster Munition Coalition 'ban bunnies'. While fighting for the ban, the Campaign also needed to resist the systematic exclusion of women in discussions of both weapons and robotics. As a result, the Campaign decided to develop two lists. The first featured the many highly qualified women working at the nexus of technology, security and global policy.[71] Mary has continued to maintain this list, with the tongue-in-cheek title 'Binder of Women', featuring experts from all over the world.[72] The second list was a pledge to be signed by men, committing themselves not to speak on all-male panels regarding global peace and security policy.[73] On a personal note,

I have found that this promise has made me more aware of both my complicity in gender discrimination and need to challenge it.

The experience of discrimination spurred the Campaign to examine its own inclusiveness. Mary said it was crucial to build 'a broad case for a ban backed by a diverse crowd', including advocates from the Global South, people from the private sector, faith leaders and youth, not just Western experts. She told me that 'we know from previous campaigns that they need to be representative of all corners of the world. We need to be welcoming of men and women, gay and straight.' For Mary, the struggle against discrimination could not be separated from pursuing disarmament. 'Diversity is a winning strategy because it makes people realize that they only represent a corner of the world.' It shows up the provincialism and narrow-mindedness of traditional 'male power politics'.

The 2014 CCW expert meeting did have the positive outcome of putting numerous countries on record with statements about killer robots. Mary thanked the delegates for their engagement in the conference, saying that 'this week's deliberations showed us that there is great concern' with killer robots.[74] Since then, the CCW has held additional expert meetings in Geneva in April 2015 and April 2016. Governments have also expressed concerns about killer robots in the UN General Assembly's committee on Disarmament and International Security. At the time of writing, twenty-nine countries had backed the call to ban autonomous weapons systems.[75] The Campaign was thus able to get killer robots on the multilateral agenda with surprising speed.

However, within a couple years, diplomatic momentum began to flag. 'We've hit a rough patch,' Mary admitted to me. In 2015, the UN rolled out new programme management software, called Umoja, which enabled more accurate tracking of its income and expenditure. This was a welcome development for many, especially in UN country offices; the UN has often been accused of a lack of transparency. However, Umoja's protocols prevent the UN from moving forward on multilateral meetings if budgeted funds are not available, creating widespread disarray.[76] The new accounts showed that the CCW was $336,322 in the red, with several countries in arrears, most notably Brazil, which owed 70 per cent of the missing funds.[77] As a result, even though the CCW's five-year Review Conference in December 2016 approved upgrading discussion of 'LAWS' to a more formal process, meetings planned for April were postponed to August 2017 and then cancelled, ostensibly due to lack of sufficient funds.[78] There is perhaps irony that the effort to deal with the increasing outsourcing of human deliberation to digital processes was held up by the UN's accounting software. In an email leaked to *Foreign Policy*, a high-level UN official complained about 'enforced servitude to Umoja', which has 'damaged both morale and staff productivity'.[79] The Campaign found itself in the position of lobbying Brazil to pay its dues and pushing other governments to find a way forward. 'We used to switch off when the CCW talked about finance,' Mary confessed. But now they don't have that luxury.

In September 2017, the UN announced that Brazil had paid up its arrears, as had Russia, which meant that the CCW process could continue.[80] Mary worries, however, that such a backlog could happen again and that the distraction of bureaucratic details allows governments to stall on progress towards a ban. She believes that if the political will really existed, governments would find their way around accounting glitches: 'we're not the ones who should resolve this.' Instead, the Campaign must focus on building political mobilization. 'We are sincere in our desire for it to succeed in the CCW,' Mary told me, but 'now it's time for us to step up our impatience.' Even if countries fail 'to find a solution to their financial woes', this shouldn't mean they 'stop addressing concerns' with killer robots.[81] Indeed, Stuart Russell warned, 'We need to be quite concerned about the developments on the ground just outpacing what is happening at the CCW ... because it will become very hard to unwind once countries start committing large parts of their defense posture to autonomous weapons.'[82] Mary has put delegates on notice: 'If the CCW is unable to act,' she warned, the world would have to 'find other ways to maintain the momentum toward a ban.'[83]

Drawing on the ICBL's strategy, Mary and the Campaign are taking their case directly to the global public. Their education of journalists has paid off, with stories becoming more sophisticated, rather than alarmist, ironic or gee-whiz. Mary was particularly pleased with an 8,000 word 'deep dive' piece by *BuzzFeed*, following the 2016 expert meeting.[84] 'While diplomacy is faltering,' she said, 'there is more national campaigning and private sector interest.' Technologists and scientists have also become more outspoken, with more than 3,000 of them – including Stephen Hawking, Elon Musk and Steve Wozniak – signing an open letter calling for 'a ban on offensive autonomous weapons beyond meaningful human control'.[85] Most news stories focused on the high-profile men who signed the letter, but Mary points out that numerous prominent women scientists were also signatories, including Professor Barbara Grosz of Harvard University, Kathryn McElroy of IBM Watson and Professor Martha E. Pollack of the University of Michigan. Several companies are reviewing their investment, research, development and production policies regarding killer robots. In April 2014, ClearPath Robotics, a Canadian technology firm, was the first to commit to 'value ethics over potential future revenue' by refusing to manufacture 'weaponized robots that remove humans from the loop'.[86] Two years later, the ethics committee of the Norwegian sovereign wealth fund – the world's largest – announced that it would scrutinize investments in any company developing killer robots.[87] By August 2017, 126 founders and directors of technology companies in twenty-eight countries had signed a letter 'raising … alarm' at the trend towards lethal autonomous weapons systems:

> Once developed, they will permit armed conflict to be fought at a scale greater than ever, and at timescales faster than humans can comprehend. These can be weapons of terror, weapons that despots and terrorists use against innocent populations, and weapons hacked to behave in undesirable ways. We do not have long to act. Once this Pandora's box is opened, it will be hard to close.[88]

According to an Ipsos opinion poll conducted in twenty-six countries, 61 per cent of the global public is now in favour of banning killer robots.[89] UN secretary general António Guterres has specifically called on states 'to ban these weapons, which are politically unacceptable and morally repugnant'.[90] This public pressure has not yet resulted in action in the CCW. In a 2019 meeting, while the majority of countries were in favour of moving forward with negotiating a prohibition, the United States and Russia abused the consensus rules to block further progress.[91] However, there was discontent in the diplomatic community, as pro-ban governments began to brainstorm new ways forward.

* * *

At meetings with the broader 'humanitarian disarmament' community, I have occasionally heard grumblings that focusing political attention on high-tech weapons – a sexy topic for journalists and policymakers – has distracted from lower-tech methods of slaughter. In Syria, the Assad government has used mines and cluster munitions and deployed other inhumane weapons against civilians. By laying siege to rebel-held cities such as Aleppo, the Syrian military has, as Secretary General António Guterres put it in May 2017, turned urban infrastructure into 'death traps' for civilians.[92] By closing borders, walling off entry points and condemning people to purgatorial refugee camps, Western countries have colluded in trapping Syrians fleeing the violence. In response, many of the same groups that campaigned for the landmine, cluster munition, killer robots and nuclear weapons bans have been collaborating in an effort to prevent the use of any explosive weapons – whether low- or high-tech – in populated areas. They have persuaded many countries, NGOs and UN agencies to call for such a commitment.[93] But the success of disarmament campaigners in banning one category of inhumane weapons after another faces new political challenges as they continue to ban ever more complex manifestations of violence. A small but influential group of these campaigners have begun discussing about reviving a much older legal obligation on government to pursue 'General and Complete Disarmament'. For now, they are often dismissed – unfairly, perhaps – as an unrealistic fringe.[94]

Mary, whose other responsibilities at HRW includes research and advocacy on landmines, cluster munitions and incendiary weapons – not just killer robots – argues that pitting these campaigns against each other is counterproductive. It doesn't have to be 'an either/or thing' she says. In her own work, when she starts to feel burned out by one issue – 'documenting the use of the most heinous weapons can be distressing work' – she can turn to another. 'It's possible to become jaded. It becomes dangerous', and so self-care is crucial. 'You have to celebrate the small successes.' In the concept of humanitarian disarmament, she sees a way to push for humane limits on violence across the board. Indeed, progress in defining legal limits on one type of killing can, if advocacy is coordinated well, build norms and political will to address other kinds of weapons. This also builds a broader community of support, enabling her to 'work with like-minded people who are dedicated and committed'. She sees the bans on landmines and cluster munitions not as piecemeal efforts that fail to address larger problems, but rather as 'standard bearers for efforts to prevent and reduce harm from indiscriminate weapons'.[95] She hopes that sometime soon, a ban on killer robots will join this developing tradition, constraining new forms of remote and automated violence: 'We have to be the voice of reason, but not compromise.'

SURVIVORHOOD
AN EPILOGUE, UNITED NATIONS

Emily and I had just spent the last three weeks at UN headquarters in New York, as diplomats finalized negotiations of a legally binding international treaty banning nuclear weapons. Those of us working with the International Campaign to Abolish Nuclear Weapons (ICAN), who had pushed so hard for this agreement, felt giddy. As 122 governments voted to adopt the treaty, defying the boycott of the nuclear-armed and allied countries, we thundered our applause. The last couple years, 2016 and 2017, had been difficult for disarmament campaigners. A newly installed Trump traded erratic nuclear threats with the North Koreans, ramped up arms sales and dropped the largest ever conventional bomb on Afghanistan. Russia's statements on nuclear weapons at the UN had grown alarmingly cavalier. Myanmar laid new mines as part of its ethnic cleansing campaign against the Rohingya minority. The British and US government continued to sell arms to Saudi Arabia, despite its bombing of civilians in Yemen with cluster munitions.

But the nuclear weapons ban conference felt like a *kairos* moment, when the world quickens and serendipity has a chance. As the negotiation drew to a close on 7 July 2017, Ambassador Elayne Whyte Gomez, a Costa Rican diplomat and chair of the conference, thanked 'all of the victims who have shared their personal stories with us … and have been an ongoing inspiration for our work'. She turned to recognize Setsuko Thurlow, an eighty-five-year-old *hibabusha* (atomic bomb survivor). The light on the microphone before Setsuko turned red. Wearing reading glasses and dressed elegantly in a purple jacket, UN pass clipped to its lapel, she began to address us, 'Delegates, NGO colleagues, dear friends, I never thought I would see this moment.' The flashes of press photographers illuminated her face.[1]

On the morning of 6 August 1945, Setsuko Nakamura was thirteen years old and was at the army headquarters in Hiroshima, where, like many high school students, she had been assigned to help the military staff. 'At 8:15 a.m., I saw a bluish-white flash like a magnesium flare outside the window,' she told a meeting of Physicians for Global Survival in 2003. 'I remember the sensation of floating in the air. As I regained consciousness in the total silence and darkness, I realized I was pinned in the ruins of the collapsed building. I could not move. I knew I was faced with death.' A man urged her to stay conscious and directed her to crawl through openings in the rubble. 'By the time I got out, the ruins were on fire. This meant that most of my classmates who were with me in the same room were burned alive.'[2] As she saw the 'outside world', she found it transformed in unrecognizable horror:

> Streams of stunned people were slowly shuffling from the city centre toward nearby hills. They were naked or tattered, burned, blackened and swollen. Eyes were swollen shut and some had eyeballs hanging out of their sockets. They were bleeding, ghostly figures like a slow-motion image from an old silent movie. Many held their hands above the level of their hearts to lessen the throbbing pain of their burns. Strips of skin and flesh hung like ribbons from their bones.[3]

As she delivered her statement to the UN, her choked voice found a steady rhythm, a timbre of inner resolve. It drew tears to my eyes; it still does as I now transcribe the footage. 'As we gather in our celebration of this extraordinary achievement, let us pause for a moment, to feel the witness of those who perished in Hiroshima and Nagasaki, both at that time in 1945 and over these 72 years. Hundreds of thousands of people.' She swallowed and for a second her face looked drawn, affected. Her eyebrows rise, forehead wrinkles, 'Each person who died had a name. Each person was loved by someone.'[4]

After the war, Setsuko attended the church of Reverend Kiyoshi Tanimoto, a major character in John Hersey's devastating 1946 book *Hiroshima*, which opened Americans' eyes to the humanitarian consequences of the atomic bombings.[5] Many American students are still assigned the book in high school. Reverend Tanimoto convinced Setsuko's parents to let her marry a Canadian man, James McKitrick Thurlow, who was teaching English in a Christian school. She later emigrated to Canada, becoming a social worker and advocate for the rights of Japanese immigrants. Among the few survivors who broke the stigma against speaking openly about being a *hibakusha*, she became a compelling campaigner for nuclear disarmament.[6] 'I feel it's really important to tell my story,' she once told a journalist. 'I made a vow to my loved ones, my schoolmates, to family and friends, that their deaths would have significance. It would not be in vain. I would not forget this. I would do my best till my last breath.'[7]

Despite – or because of – the catastrophic impact of the Hiroshima and Nagasaki bombings, those calling for the abolition of nuclear weapons at the end of the Second World War were ignored. The Bomb proliferated, first to the USSR, then to the UK, France, China, India, Pakistan, Israel, South Africa and North Korea. The Cold War trapped the United States and Soviet Union in a game of nuclear chicken, placing ever more warheads – aimed at each other's cities – on high-trigger alert. In the event of nuclear war, New York City would have been eviscerated. Cinephiles may be familiar with the 'Doomsday Device' in Stanley Kubrick's *Dr. Strangelove*, which automated a catastrophic retaliation if the Soviet Union came under attack. Few realize that the Soviets actually built a system called Perimeter or Dead Hand, described by one of its developers as 'very, very nice' because it 'remove[d] unique responsibility from high politicians and the military', automating the decision to launch a nuclear counter-attack.[8] Electronic sensors would supposedly detect an incoming missile and a computer would initiate a response. As the United States developed actual atomic landmines, mutually assured destruction turned the entire world (and parts of outer space) into a nuclear minefield. One false move and the atomic trap might wipe out humanity.

There were an astounding number of close calls and near misses.[9] That these accidents did not lead to conflagration is near miraculous, given the tight integration of automated response systems. On several occasions, it was the intervention of people – relying on common sense and justified fear of the consequences – that prevented automated systems from plunging us into nuclear war. The spread of nuclear weapons was slowed by the 1968 Nuclear Non-Proliferation Treaty (NPT), which committed the nuclear-armed states to disarmament and everyone else to a renunciation of the Bomb. It was grassroots and diplomatic pressure from non-nuclear-armed countries that pushed the superpowers to the negotiating table to make these agreements. Indeed, civil society had raised concerns since the beginnings of the Manhattan Project. The anti-nuclear movement culminated in a million-strong anti-nuclear demonstration in New York City in 1982. However, arms control measures such as the NPT never succeeded in fulfilling the superpowers' promises of a nuclear-free world. Such treaties enabled them to pose as responsible reducers of nuclear risk without having to give up their arsenals. There are still almost 15,000 nuclear weapons in the world, the vast majority – 13,800 – wielded by the United States and Russia.[10]

Nevertheless, Setsuko's defiance pointed to a way out of nuclear sclerosis. 'I've been waiting for this day for seven decades,' she told the nuclear ban negotiators, increasingly strident. 'And I am overjoyed that it has finally arrived. This is the beginning of the end of nuclear weapons!' The nuclear ban conference had been boycotted by the United States, Russia and other governments that continue to claim that nuclear deterrence provides them with security. However, drawing on the model of the landmine and cluster munitions treaties, the rest of the world's countries decided to move forward without the major military powers. Documenting the catastrophic humanitarian and environmental consequences, they have declared nuclear weapons inhumane. ICAN campaigners wanted to force those who wield the Bomb to answer questions about ethics, public health and ecology, not just the size and quantity of their missiles. Establishing a powerful stigma through the ban reframes the nuclear-armed states as pariahs, out of step with the world's values. 'Nuclear weapons have always been immoral, now they are also illegal,' declared Setsuko in her speech. The new treaty enables governments to criminalize any efforts by their citizens to assist with or finance nuclear weapons programmes.

Taking a humanitarian approach to nuclear weapons required governments to pay attention to the plight of survivors. During the negotiations, I worked with ICAN's 'positive obligations team', persuading delegates not only to prohibit nuclear weapons but also to address the harms already caused. Millions of people have been exposed to nuclear violence, both in Japan and in more than 2,000 nuclear tests, whose total explosive force of 29,000 Hiroshima bombs devastated swaths of Algeria, Australia, China, Kazakhstan, Kiribati, Marshall Islands, French Polynesia and the United States.[11] In many parts of the American West, people living downwind of nuclear test sites or in the watershed of uranium mines and processing sites suffer the quiet radioactive violence of the nuclear arms race. From 1945 to 1992, the government detonated 1,040 nuclear devices within or above the continental United States, mostly at the Nevada Test Site.[12] Between 1992 and March 2016, the US Department of Justice approved 3,963 Radioactive Exposure Compensation claims for 'onsite participants' in nuclear tests and 19,555 claims from 'Downwinders' (those exposed to fall out from the Nevada Test Site) who had 'contracted certain cancers and other serious diseases as a result of their exposure'.[13]

The preamble of the nuclear ban treaty acknowledges the 'unacceptable suffering of and harm caused to the victims of the use of nuclear weapons (hibakusha), as well as of those affected by the testing of nuclear weapons'. It also honours their 'role of public conscience in the furthering of the principles of humanity as evidenced by the call for the total elimination of nuclear weapons'. Given that nuclear tests were often conducted in areas considered peripheral by the world's powerful leaders, the preamble recognizes 'the disproportionate impact of nuclear-weapon activities on indigenous peoples'. As they drafted the treaty, we successfully cajoled delegates into including increasingly strong language, drawn from the landmine and cluster munition bans, obligating assistance to victims and remediation of contaminated environments. 'We will not return to funding nuclear violence instead of human needs,' declared Setsuko. 'We will not return to irreversibly contaminating our environment. We will not continue to risk the lives of future generations.'

Setsuko ended her speech with a challenge: 'To the leaders of the countries across the world, I beseech you: If you love this planet, you will sign this treaty!' She concluded by urging us: 'Together let us go forth and change the world!' Campaigners jumped to their feet, clapping, crying, as Setsuko removed her reading glasses, nodded and turned to face each corner of the room, mouthing 'thank you'. She stood, and joined the applause, in gratitude for the work of the activists and diplomats who had made this historic moment possible. Thanking her for her 'extraordinary words', Ambassador Whyte said she wanted to address her final reflection to the 'person we have just heard, who was a source of inspiration for this process ... representing so many victims'. Ambassador Whyte quoted Setsuko's words from an earlier address to the conference in March:[14] '"Those who survived became convinced that no human being should ever have to experience the inhumanity and unspeakable suffering of nuclear weapons." Ms Thurlow, today, finally, we can tell the world that we have a treaty that prohibits nuclear weapons. Thank you very much for not letting us rest.'[15]

Four months later, ICAN campaigners in the Geneva office received a phone call from Oslo, congratulating them on being awarded the 2017 Nobel Peace Prize for their 'work to draw attention to the catastrophic humanitarian consequences of any use of nuclear weapons' and for their 'ground-breaking efforts to achieve a treaty-based prohibition of such weapons'.[16] ICAN later announced that Setsuko would jointly accept the prize, along with the campaign's executive director Beatrice Fihn. 'I am so deeply humbled,' said Setsuko. 'It has been such a privilege to work with so many passionate and inspirational ICAN campaigners around the world over the past decade. The Nobel Peace Prize is a powerful tool that we can now use to advance our cause.'[17]

* * *

At the end of the flag-lined avenue exiting the UN building in Geneva is a four-story sculpture of a wooden chair, one of its four legs shattered. *The Broken Chair* by Daniel Berset was installed in 1997 at the spot where, during the ill-fated CCW landmine negotiations, activists had built a mountain of shoes representing those who lost limbs to a mine and where Reth confronted entering delegates. It serves as a visual testimony to the suffering of landmine survivors. When I look up at the sculpture in the dimming sunlight after a long day of mealy-mouthed meetings on killer robots, its oblique symbolism has a bracing clarity. I feel ashamed of the ultimate inadequacy of each campaign against inhumane violence. Even with the many impressive achievements of disarmament movements, it seems difficult to celebrate when there is an endless litany of sorrow: school shootings, terrorist attacks, the ongoing slaughter in Syria, nuclear sabre-rattling. Even our successes are sometimes ambiguous. No arms control agreement, treaty or programme will ever be perfect. Even the best laws need reinterpreting, updating and amending as the world remakes itself anew. Sometimes, when I look at *The Broken Chair*, the optimism of Setsuko's speech seems absurd. The chair's leg remains broken, just as new bodies are shredded each day by our explosive belligerence. As I have travelled from one minefield to the next, I am always disappointed by how violence is always more complex than I expected.

In struggling against modern industrial slaughter, we must first reject the temptation to believe in cheap solutions that promise to make everything better.[18] In Sophocles play, Oedipus believed that his gumption, acumen and charisma would overcome political obstacles and bring peace to Thebes. In today's international arena, our delusions include 'smart landmines', 'surgical strikes', 'ethical robotic weapons', 'nuclear deterrence', as well as the panaceas of privatization, globalization and civil society. But in our despair, we must come up with a better choice than that of Jocasta, who takes her own life upon learning that her lover Oedipus was her own son. I am not drawn to suicide, but there is a spiritual suicide in despondent apathy. I am tempted sometimes to resign myself to fatalism. Why bother fighting against landmines when there is always someone willing to manufacture new ones? What is the point of a disarmament treaty when someone will figure out the loopholes or invent some new way to maim people? Why celebrate policy successes when someone like Trump can overturn them in spite?

But this is not the choice Oedipus makes. Instead, recognizing his own complicity in the Theban tragedy, he blinds himself and goes into exile. In this grim piece of performance art, Oedipus humbles himself, ritually marking onto his body the violence of fate's minefield. He makes himself in the image of the blind prophet Tiresias, a liminal, damaged person. But he still chooses life over death. He chooses survivorhood, the life of the marginal refugee, instead of that of a king. Similarly, despite its completion at the landmine campaign's apogee, *The Broken Chair* represents restrained sorrow, not triumphalism. Its very vulnerability calls on the policymakers entering and exiting the UN to choose a more humane future.

On the day the Antipersonnel Landmine Ban Treaty opened for signature, just shy of twenty years before Setsuko's speech, Reth, seated in his Mekong wheelchair, offered reflections on the success of the campaign to an interfaith celebration in Ottawa. 'Some people call me a "landmine victim." So I am,' he acknowledged; but, he said, 'So are you in a different way.' He recognized that he carried physical marks of the blast on his body, but asserted that 'we are all landmine victims' when we allow the '"mental landmines" of ... producers and exporters and fearful governments' to persist, when we 'refuse to ban, to de-mine, to assist communities and people suffering'. Therefore, while his 'handicaps are quire visible to you', they can 'remind us of the invisible handicaps we all have [,] ... landmines inside [that] can lead us to war, to jealousy, to cruel power over others'. In resisting these the 'landmines of the heart', the cowardice embodied in automated killing, 'we all become landmine survivors'.

The world is ensnared by proliferating vectors of remote and automated violence. But the wisdom of Reth and Setsuko, the image of *The Broken Chair* and Oedipus's humbling all point to a way out of the trap. Exiting the political minefield requires us to listen to those most affected by it, see them as people, not targets. We must seek exile from our hubris, searching for meaning in our very brokenness, and use our vulnerability to humanize the suffering of the survivors in our midst. In doing so, we can dismantle all that traps ourselves and others in webs of violence. We built the Bomb. We can defuse it. We laid the minefield. We can demine it and transform political minefields too.

ACKNOWLEDGEMENTS

Given that a major premise of this narrative is that both the deminer and the writer are embedded in a network of social relations, I must acknowledge the contributions of the community of people who made this book possible. Of course, responsibility for any errors, inaccurate representations or misremembered details remains with me alone. I want to thank Joanna Godfrey, Olivia Dellow, Tomasz Hoskins, Maria Marsh and Abigail Fielding-Smith, editors at I.B. Tauris, for their patience in shepherding this book into production. Alex Jeffrey, Hugh Griffiths, Zlatan Music and Catherine Zimmer must be singled out for their particular contributions to my thinking. I am deeply grateful to Mary Kaldor, Vesna Bojicic-Dzelilovic, David Keen, Kristian Berg Harpviken, Dennis and Lorna Labayen, Bob Mesle, Bill Russell and Bill Juhnke, my intellectual mentors. Thanks to John Kavanaugh for listening. Much love to David, Laura, Jewell and Andrew Bolton.

I have appreciated the opportunity to explore my ideas in public. Occasionally, the text of this book draws on news media, policy reports and academic articles I have published elsewhere, including in *The Examiner* (Independence, MO), *Political Geography* and the *Marine Technology Society Journal*, as well as blog posts for *MAG America*, *IB Tauris*, *Sustainable Good*, *Political Minefields*, and *Global Policy* and reports for UNICEF and Counterpart International. An early draft of the book received helpful feedback from the members of the Brooklyn Writer's Guild.

Simon Conway, Bob Eaton, Tim Lardner, Richard Moyes, Ted Paterson, Nathalie Prevost and David Rowe all played a crucial role in helping me navigate the world of mine action, along with Damir Atikovic, Liza de Benedetti, Mike Boddington, Per Breivik, Tun Channareth, Denise Coghlan, John Flanagan, Zoran Grujic, Shohab Hakimi, Matthew Hovell, Darvin Lisica, Fred Maio, Rueben McCarthy, Rae McGrath, Per Nergaard, Dijana Pejic, Mark Russell, Mohammed Sediq, Aksel Steen-Nilsen, Tatiana Stephens, John Stevens, Colin Wanley, Mary Wareham, Evy Van Weezendonk and Guy Willoughby. I needed a similar set of guides to the broader world of humanitarian disarmament and have been lucky to work with and/or learn from Peter Asaro, Ray Acheson, Beatrice Fihn, Charli Carpenter, Zoya Craig, Bonnie Docherty, Beatrice Fihn, Steve Goose, Dimity Hawkins, Daniel Hogsta, Erin Hunt,

Channapha Khamvongsa, Anna Macdonald, Elizabeth Minor, Richard Moyes, Raluca Muresan, Allison Pytlak, Noel Sharkey, Seth Shelden, Susi Snyder, Portia Stratton, Kathleen Sullivan, Mary Wareham, Helena Whall, Jody Williams, Tim Wright and Wim Zwjinenburg.

Thanks, too, to Sahar al-Nouri, Martin Bell, David Brock, Thoric Cederstrom, Girish Daswani, Arvinn Eikeland Gadgil, Erica Field Jones, David and Shauna Holmes, Ian Johnson, Sam Jones, Jennie Lewis, Gene Ritter, Sarah Knuckey, Ajla Silajdzic and Nathan Stock. My research was generously supported with funding from the UK Economic and Social Research Council; Pace University's Dyson College of Arts and Sciences, Scholarly Research Committee and Wilson Center for Social Entrepreneurship; Pro Victimis Foundation; Landmine Monitor; Verizon Foundation and Friedrich-Ebert-Stiftung. I received in kind or institutional support from Outreach International, London School of Economics and Political Science, Counterpart International, Control Arms, Article 36, HALO Trust, Norwegian People's Aid, Mines Advisory Group, International Campaign to Abolish Nuclear Weapons, International Committee for Robot Arms Control and Landmine Action. This project at Pace University has been supported by a community of scholars and staff on the New York City campus, particularly my colleagues Abbey Berg, Sarah Blackwood, Peter Dachille, Sally Dickerson, Katherine Disher, Amy Freedman, Sharon Graham, Nira Herrmann, Jessica Lavariega Monforti, Joe Ryan, Kevin Shaefer, Al Ward and Adelia Williams. I am very grateful to my student research assistants: Caitlin Boley, Gabrielle Chalk, Chanda Daniels, Katelyn James, Cayman Mitchell, Cassandra Stimpson and Sydney Tisch.

Ultimately, however, I dedicate this book to Emily Welty – lover, best friend, colleague, soulmate, fellow advocate and sojourner – I give thanks daily for the grace of you.

ACRONYMS

ACBL	Afghan Campaign to Ban Landmines
ADSID	Air-Delivered Seismic Intrusion Detector
AFSC	American Friends Service Committee
ALS	Amyotrophic lateral sclerosis
AQAG	A Quaker Action Group
ARC	American Refugee Committee
BHMAC	Bosnia and Herzegovina Mine Action Center
BLU	Bomb, Live, Unit
CAFE	Compound Across From Embassy (US Embassy Kabul, Afghanistan)
CBU	Cluster Bomb Unit
CCBL	Cambodia Campaign to Ban Landmines
CCW	Convention on Certain Conventional Weapons
CHA	Confirmed Hazardous Area
CIA	United States Central Intelligence Agency
CLO	Community Liaison Officer
CMAC	Cambodia Mine Action Center
CMC	Cluster Munition Coalition
COPE	Cooperative Orthotic and Prosthetic Enterprise
CPA	Comprehensive Peace Agreement (Sudan/South Sudan)
DCA	DanChurchAid
DMZ	Demilitarized zone
EOD	Explosive Ordnance Disposal
ERW	Explosive remnants of war
EU	European Union
GPS	Global positioning system
HALO	Hazardous Area Life-support Organization
HI	formerly Handicap International, now Humanity and Inclusion
HRW	Human Rights Watch
ICAN	International Campaign to Abolish Nuclear Weapons
ICBL	International Campaign to Ban Landmines
ICC	International Criminal Court
ICRAC	International Committee for Robot Arms Control
ICRC	International Committee of the Red Cross
IED	Improvised explosive device
ISI	Pakistan Inter-Services Intelligence
ISIS	Islamic State of Iraq and the Levant
IVS	International Voluntary Services

JRS	Jesuit Refugee ServiceKR: Khmer Rouge
LAWS	Lethal autonomous weapons systems
MAG	Mines Advisory Group
MCC	Mennonite Central Committee
NATO	North Atlantic Treaty Organization
NGO	Non-governmental organization
NPA	Norwegian People's Aid
NPT	Treaty on the Non-Proliferation of Nuclear Weapons
OHR	Office of the High Representative for Bosnia and Herzegovina
OMAR	Organization for Mine Clearance and Afghan Rehabilitation
PHR	Physicians for Human Rights
PLO	Palestine Liberation Organization
PMN	Antipersonnel pressure mine (Soviet Union)
PoW	Prisoner of war
PRIO	Peace Research Institute, Oslo
PROM-1	Bounding fragmentation mine (Yugoslavia)
SAS	Special Air Service
SHA	Suspected Hazardous Area
SIGAR	United States Special Inspector General for Afghanistan Reconstruction
SLIRI	Sudan Landmine Information and Response Initiative
SPLA	Sudan People's Liberation Army
SPLM	Sudan People's Liberation Movement
SSDC	South Sudan Demining Commission
SSMAA	South Sudan Mine Action Authority
TAEC	Traditional Arts and Ethnology Centre
TNT	Trinitrotoluene (explosive)
UN	United Nations
UNHCR	United Nations High Commissioner for Refugees
UNICEF	United Nations Children's Fund
UNMACA	United Nations Mine Action Center for Afghanistan
UNMAO	United Nations Mine Action Office in Sudan
UNMAS	United Nations Mine Action Service
UNTAC	United Nations Transitional Authority in Cambodia
USAID	United States Agency for International Development
USCBL	United States Campaign to Ban Landmines
UXO	Unexploded ordnance
VVAF	Vietnam Veterans of America Foundation

NOTES

Chapter 1

1   Bosnia and Herzegovina Mine Action Centre. (2002) 'Demining Strategy for Bosnia and Herzegovina: By the Year of 2010'. Draft. Sarajevo, BHMAC. Annex 2.

2   US Embassy Sarajevo. (17 November 2006) 'Demining: Allegations of Fraud and Malfeasance in USG Supported Programs'. Ref. 06SARAJEVO2907.

3   Ashley Rowland. (12 June 2014) 'There Was an Eerie Silence'. *Stars and Stripes*. <https://www.stripes.com/news/special-reports/heroes/heroes-2014/there-was-an-eerie-silence-1.288019>.

4   Unless otherwise cited, details in this paragraph are from: Raad al-Hamdani. (2004) 'Interview'. *Frontline*. <http://www.pbs.org/wgbh/pages/frontline/shows/invasion/interviews/raad.html>; Michael R. Gordan and Bernard E. Trainor. (2007) *Cobra II: The Inside Story of the Invasion and Occupation of Iraq*. New York, Vintage. pp. 322–40, 394–407; John B. Dwyer. (3 April 2005) 'The Battle of Charlie 6'. *The Washington Times*. <http://www.washingtontimes.com/news/2005/apr/3/2005040 3-093740-9355r/>; Rowland, 'There Was an Eerie Silence'; Daniel Hibner. (2008) 'Apache Six, This Is Dog Six'. In *Heroes among Us: Firsthand Accounts of Combat from America's Most Decorated Warriors in Iraq and Afghanistan*. Chuck Larson (Ed.). New York, Penguin. pp. 107–22.

5   Michael Ondaatje. (1992) *The English Patient*. New York, Vintage Books. pp. 192–3.

6   Sandow Birk. (2007) *The Depravities of War*. Maui, Hui Press; Sandow Birk. (2007) 'The Depravities of War'. <http://www.sandowbirk.com/paintings/the-depravities-of-war/>. Accessed 22 August 2017.

7   Details on minefields in Second World War North Africa are from: Mike Croll. (2008) *Landmines in War and Peace*. Barnsley, Pen & Sword. pp. 65–84; John Strawson. (1969) *The Battle for North Africa*. New York, Charles Scribner; Lydia Monin and Andrew Gallimore. (2002) *The Devil's Gardens: A History of Landmines*. London, Pimlico. pp. 59–63.

8   Croll, *Landmines in War and Peace*, p. 78.

9   Rae McGrath. (2000) *Landmines and Unexploded Ordnance: A Resource Book*. London, Pluto Press. p. 12.

10 Strawson, *The Battle for North Africa*, p. 157.

11 In: Croll, *Landmines in War and Peace*, p. 70.

12 Croll, *Landmines in War and Peace*, p. 76.

13 Monin and Gallimore, *The Devil's Gardens: A History of Landmines*, pp. 59–63.

14 A.B. Hartley. (1958) *Unexploded Bomb: A History of Bomb Disposal.* New York, W.W. Norton. p. 25.

15 Hartley, *Unexploded Bomb: A History of Bomb Disposal*, p. 25.

16 Hartley, *Unexploded Bomb: A History of Bomb Disposal*, p. 35.

17 Hartley, *Unexploded Bomb: A History of Bomb Disposal*, pp. 50–1.

18 Hartley, *Unexploded Bomb: A History of Bomb Disposal*, p. 86.

19 Hartley, *Unexploded Bomb: A History of Bomb Disposal*, p. 23.

20 Hartley, *Unexploded Bomb: A History of Bomb Disposal*, pp. 133, 161.

21 Hartley, *Unexploded Bomb: A History of Bomb Disposal*, pp. 160–1.

22 Hartley, *Unexploded Bomb: A History of Bomb Disposal*, p. 196.

23 Hartley, *Unexploded Bomb: A History of Bomb Disposal*, p. 197.

24 Hartley, *Unexploded Bomb: A History of Bomb Disposal*, p. 196.

25 Hartley, *Unexploded Bomb: A History of Bomb Disposal*, p. 196.

26 Hartley, *Unexploded Bomb: A History of Bomb Disposal*, p. 198.

27 Hartley, *Unexploded Bomb: A History of Bomb Disposal*, p. 198.

28 Hartley, *Unexploded Bomb: A History of Bomb Disposal*, p. 200.

29 Hartley, *Unexploded Bomb: A History of Bomb Disposal*, p. 200.

30 Hartley, *Unexploded Bomb: A History of Bomb Disposal*, p. 200.

31 Hartley, *Unexploded Bomb: A History of Bomb Disposal*, p. 202.

32 Hartley, *Unexploded Bomb: A History of Bomb Disposal*, p. 203.

33 Hartley, *Unexploded Bomb: A History of Bomb Disposal*, p. 207.

34 Ondaatje, *The English Patient.* pp. 101, 193.

35 US Army. (1943). *Land Mines and Booby Traps.* FM5-31. Washington DC: War Department. Chapter 5, Section V.

36 In: Croll, *Landmines in War and Peace*, p. 75.

37 Tim Lardner. (2005) *History, Summary and Conclusions of a Study of Manual Mine Clearance.* Geneva, GICHD. pp. 17–21.

38 Croll, *Landmines in War and Peace*, pp. 85–102.

39 Croll, *Landmines in War and Peace*, p. 99.

40 In: Croll, *Landmines in War and Peace*, p. 87.

41 Graham Allison. (2017) *Destined for War: Can America and China Escape Thucydides's Trap?* New York, Houghton Mifflin Harcourt. For a refutation of this point of view, see: Arthur Waldron. (2017) 'There Is No Thucydides Trap'. *supchina.* <http://supchina.com/2017/06/12/no-thucydides-trap/>. Accessed 21 August 2017.

42 Margaret Buse. (June 2000) 'WWII Ordnance Still Haunts Europe and the Asia Pacific Rim'. *Journal of Mine Action.* 4(2). <http://maic.jmu.edu/jour nal/4.2/features/ww2/ww2.htm>. Accessed 7 August 2012.

43 Campaign to Stop Killer Robots. (18 December 2015) '2015: Year in Review'. <https://www.stopkillerrobots.org/2015/12/reviewing2015/>. Accessed 19 August 2017.

44 Marcel Junod. (1982) *Warrior without Weapons.* Edward Fitzgerald (Trans.). Geneva, ICRC. pp. 16–17, 309–10.

45 Third Geneva Convention Relative to the Treatment of Prisoners of War of 12 August 1949. Article 52.

46 ICRC. (1956) *Draft Rules for the Limitation of Dangers Incurred by the Civilian Population in Times of War*. Geneva, ICRC. Articles 14 & 15.

47 UNOG. (n.d.) 'The Convention on Certain Conventional Weapons'. <http s://www.un.org/disarmament/geneva/ccw/>. Accessed 18 August 2017.

48 ICRC. (1996) *Anti-personnel Landmines: Friend or Foe? A Study of the Military Use and Effectiveness of Anti-Personnel Mines*. Geneva, ICRC.

49 ICBL-CMC. (2018) 'Casualties'. *Landmine and Cluster Munition Monitor*. <http://www.the-monitor.org/en-gb/reports/2018/landmine-monitor-2 018/casualties.aspx>. Accessed 7 October 2019.

50 Mike Croll. (1998) *The History of Landmines*. Barnsley, Leo Cooper. pp. 1–24.

51 Statistics gathered from multiple editions of the International Campaign to Ban Landmines' *Landmine and Cluster Munition Monitor Report*, available from: <http://www.the-monitor.org>.

52 1997 Convention on the Prohibition of the Use, Stockpiling, Production and Transfer of Anti-Personnel Mines and on their Destruction. Article 2(1).

53 1997 Convention on the Prohibition of the Use, Stockpiling, Production and Transfer of Anti-Personnel Mines and on their Destruction. Article 6(1).

54 Naeem Inayatullah (Ed.). (2011) *I, IR: Autobiographical International Relations*. New York, Routledge.

55 Setsuko Thurlow. (8 July 2017) 'Hiroshima Victim Setsuko Thurlow's Closing Statement at the #NuclearBan Conference'. <http://www.dianuke. org/watch-hiroshima-victim-setsuko-thurlows-closing-statement-nuc learban-conference/>. Accessed 22 August 2017.

56 Setsuko Thurlow. (27 March 2017) 'ICAN Statements to the Negotiating Conference: Opening Statement'. <http://www.icanw.org/campaign-news/ ican-statements-to-the-negotiating-conference/>. Accessed 24 September 2017.

Chapter 2

1 GAO. (1972) Review of the BLU-63/B Bomblet Program. Washington DC, Comptroller General of the United States. p. 1. <http://www.gao.gov/ assets/210/204551.pdf>. Accessed 12 January 2017.

2 GAO, Review of the BLU-63/B Bomblet Program; Global Security. (2017) 'CBU-58'. <http://www.globalsecurity.org/military/systems/munitions/cb u-58.htm>.

3 Eric Prokosch. (1995) *The Technology of Killing: A Military and Political History of Antipersonnel Weapons*. London, Zed Books. pp. 85, 97.

4 William Shawcross. (1979) *Sideshow: Kissinger, Nixon and the Destruction of Cambodia*. New York, Simon and Schuster. pp. 209–19, 280–99.

5 Raphael Littauer and Norman Uphoff (Eds). (1972) *The Air War in Indochina*. Rvsd Ed. Boston, Beacon Press.

6 Rae McGrath. (2000) *Cluster Bombs: The Military Effectiveness and Impact on Civilians of Cluster Munitions*. London, Landmine Action. <http://www.landmineaction.org/resources/Cluster_Bombs.pdf>. Accessed 7 August 2012. p. 30.

7 Holly High, James R. Curran and Gareth Robinson. (2014) 'Electronic Records of the Air War Over Southeast Asia: A Database Analysis'. *Journal of Vietnamese Studies*. 8(4). pp. 86–124.

8 International Campaign to Ban Landmines. (13 October 2010) 'Lao PDR: Mine Action'. *Landmine and Cluster Munition Monitor*. <http://www.the-monitor.org/index.php/cp/display/region_profiles/theme/619>. Accessed 11 November 2011.

9 Roger Warner. (1996) *Shooting at the Moon: The Story of America's Clandestine War in Laos*. Vermont, Steerforth Press.

10 Fred Branfman (Ed.). (1972) *Voices from the Plain of Jars: Life under an Air War*. New York, Harper Colophon. pp. 2, 5.

11 Bruce Shoemaker. (March 1994) 'Legacy of the Secret War'. *Mennonite Central Committee*. <http://clusterbombs.mcc.org/system/files/Legacy%20of%20the%20Secret%20War.pdf>. Accessed 7 August 2012; Anthea Lawson. (2006) 'Cluster Munitions in Lao PDR'. In *Cluster Munitions in Albania and Lao PDR: The Humanitarian and Socio-Economic Impact*. Rosy Cave, Anthea Lawson and Andrew Sherriff (Eds). Geneva, UNIDIR.

12 Neil Sheehan. (1972) 'Preface'. In *The Air War in Indochina*. Raphael Littauer and Norman Uphoff (Eds). Rvsd Ed. Boston, Beacon Press. pp. vii–viii.

13 Quoted in Prokosch, *The Technology of Killing: A Military and Political History of Antipersonnel Weapons*, p. 53.

14 Roger Warner. (1996) *Shooting at the Moon: The Story of America's Clandestine War in Laos*. South Royalton, Steerforth Press. p. 43.

15 In: Louis Menand. (26 February 2018) 'Made in Vietnam: Edward Lansdale and the War over the War'. *The New Yorker*. p. 67.

16 Karen J. Coates. (July/August 2005) 'Plain of Jars'. *Archaeology*. 58(4). <http://www.archaeology.org/0507/abstracts/laos.html>. Accessed 7 August 2012.

17 Georges Chapelier and Josyane Va Maldergham. (1971) 'Plain of Jars, Social Changes under Five Years of Pathet Lao Administration'. *Asia Quarterly*. 1. p. 75.

18 In: Walt Haney. (1972) 'The Pentagon Papers and the United States Involvement in Laos'. *The Pentagon Papers: Critical Essays*. Vol. V. Senator Gravel Edition. Boston, Beacon Press. p. 276.

19 Haney, 'The Pentagon Papers and the United States Involvement in Laos', p. 277.

20 Channapha Khamvongsa and Elaine Russell. (2009) 'Legacies of War', *Critical Asian Studies*. 41(2). p. 293.

21 ICBL-CMC. (2018) 'Lao PDR: Casualties and Victim Assistance'.
    Landmine and Cluster Munition Monitor. <http://www.the-monitor.org/
    en-gb/reports/2019/lao-pdr/casualties.aspx>. Accessed 7 October 2019.
22 National Regulatory Agency for UXO/Mine Action Center in Lao PDR.
    (n.d.). 'UXO Problem'. <http://www.nra.gov.la/uxoproblem.html>.
    Accessed 4 March 2017; National Regulatory Agency for UXO/Mine
    Action Center in Lao PDR. (n.d.). 'UXO Impact'. <http://www.nra.gov.
    la/uxoimpact.html>. Accessed 4 March 2017. See also: Karen J. Coates.
    (2013) *Eternal Harvest: The Legacy of American Bombs in Laos.* San
    Francisco, CA, Things Asian Press.
23 For further analysis of the experience of survivors in Laos, see: Leah Zani.
    (29 June 2015) 'Bomb Ecologies? Inhabiting Disability in Postconflict
    Laos'. *Somatosphere.* <http://somatosphere.net/2015/06/bomb-ecologi
    es-inhabiting-disability-in-postconflict-laos.html>. Accessed 22 March
    2017.
24 John F. Kennedy. (23 March 1961) 'News Conference 8, March 23, 1961'.
    <https://www.jfklibrary.org/Research/Research-Aids/Ready-Referenc
    e/Press-Conferences/News-Conference-8.aspx>. Accessed 26 February
    2017.
25 William M. Leary. (1999) 'CIA Air Operations in Laos, 1955-1974'.
    Studies in Intelligence. Winter 1999/2000. pp. 51–67. Available from:
    <https://www.cia.gov/library/center-for-the-study-of-intelligence/csi-
    publications/books-and-monographs/Anthology-CIA-and-the-Wars-in-S
    outheast-Asia/pdfs/leary-cia-air-ops-in-laos.pdf>. Accessed 17 March
    2017.
26 Haney, 'The Pentagon Papers and the United States Involvement in Laos',
    p. 281. Emphasis in original.
27 Croll, *Landmines in War and Peace*, p. 126.
28 US Army. (1967) *Viet Cong Boobytraps, Mines and Mine Warfare
    Techniques.* Washington DC, Department of the Army. p. 54.
29 Herman Rapaport. (1984) 'Vietnam: The Thousand Plateaus'. *Social Text.*
    9/10. p. 138.
30 Herman Rapaport, 'Vietnam: The Thousand Plateaus', pp. 143–4.
31 In: AFSC. (1972) 'Automated Air War'. <https://www.afsc.org/video/au
    tomated-air-war>. Accessed 12 January 2017.
32 Michael Herr. (1978) *Dispatches.* New York, Alfred A. Knopf. pp. 14, 66.
33 In: McGrath, *Landmines and Unexploded Ordnance: A Resource Book.*
34 Croll, *Landmines in War and Peace*, p. 125.
35 In: Croll, *Landmines in War and Peace*, p. 125.
36 In: AFSC, 'Automated Air War'.
37 For further details on US involvement in the Lao civil war, see: Haney,
    'The Pentagon Papers and the United States Involvement in Laos', pp.
    248–93; Warner, *Shooting at the Moon: The Story of America's Clandestine
    War in Laos*; Leary, 'CIA Air Operations in Laos, 1955-1974', pp.

51–67; Christopher Robbins. (2012) *The Ravens: The True Story of a Secret War*. Malmesbury, Apostrophe Books; Alfred W. McCoy. (2013) 'Reflections on History's Largest Air War'. *Critical Asian Studies*. 45(3). pp. 481–9; Elaine Russell. (2013) 'Laos – Living with Unexploded Ordnance: Past Memories and Present Realities'. In *Interactions with a Violent Past: Reading Post-Conflict Landscapes in Cambodia, Laos and Vietnam*. Vatthana Pholsena and Oliver Tappe (Eds). Singapore, National University of Singapore Press. pp. 96–134; Joshua Kurlantzick. (2017) *A Great Place to Have a War: America in Laos and the Birth of a Military CIA*. New York, Simon & Schuster.

38 Warner, *Shooting at the Moon: The Story of America's Clandestine War in Laos*, p. 178; Robbins, *The Ravens: The True Story of a Secret War*, p. 78.

39 Haney, 'The Pentagon Papers and the United States Involvement in Laos', p. 275.

40 Warner, *Shooting at the Moon: The Story of America's Clandestine War in Laos*, p. 246.

41 Haney, 'The Pentagon Papers and the United States Involvement in Laos', p. 275.

42 Robbins, *The Ravens: The True Story of a Secret War*.

43 Andrew Cockburn. (2015) *Kill Chain: The Rise of the High-Tech Assassins*. New York, Henry Holt and Company. p. 21. See also: Haney, 'The Pentagon Papers and the United States Involvement in Laos', pp. 273–4; Prokosch, *The Technology of Killing: A Military and Political History of Antipersonnel Weapons*, pp. 109–11.

44 AFSC, 'Automated Air War'. Further details: John H. E. Fried. (1972) 'The Electronic Battlefield and the Dictates of the Public Conscience: The Ramifications of the U.S. "Vietnamization" Policy'. *Revue Belge de Droit International*. 2(2). pp. 431–54; Paul N. Edwards. (1996) *The Closed World: Computers and the Politics of Discourse in Cold War America*. Cambridge, MIT Press. pp. 3–8, 134–45.

45 W. C. Westmoreland. (n.d.) 'Gen. Westmoreland on the Army of the Future'. *NACLA*. <https://nacla.org/article/gen-westmoreland-army-future>. Accessed 30 October 2017.

46 Edwards, *The Closed World: Computers and the Politics of Discourse in Cold War America*, p. 3.

47 Details on the McNamara Line from: Electronic Battlefield Subcommittee. (1970) *Hearings before the Electronic Battlefield Subcommittee of the Preparedness Investigating Committee of the Committee on Armed Services, Ninety-First Congress*. Second Session. Washington, US Government Printing Office; AFSC, 'Automated Air War'.; Edwards, *The Closed World: Computers and the Politics of Discourse in Cold War America*, pp. 3–8, 134–45; Warner, *Shooting at the Moon: The Story of America's Clandestine War in Laos*, p. 202; Anthony J. Tambini. (2007) *Wiring Vietnam: The Electronic Wall*. Lanham, Scarecrow Press; Cockburn, *Kill Chain: The Rise of the High-Tech Assassins*, pp. 17–31.

48 Cockburn, *Kill Chain: The Rise of the High-Tech Assassins*, pp. 22–4.
49 Quoted in: AFSC, 'Automated Air War'.
50 Cockburn, *Kill Chain: The Rise of the High-Tech Assassins*, p. 25.
51 Haney, 'The Pentagon Papers and the United States Involvement in Laos', p. 279.
52 Cockburn, *Kill Chain: The Rise of the High-Tech Assassins*, p. 25.
53 Herr, *Dispatches*, p. 13.
54 Cockburn, *Kill Chain: The Rise of the High-Tech Assassins*, p. 26.
55 Edwards, *The Closed World: Computers and the Politics of Discourse in Cold War America*, p. 4; Prokosch, *The Technology of Killing: A Military and Political History of Antipersonnel Weapons,* p. 110.
56 Holly High. (2008) 'Violent Landscape: Global Explosions and Lao Life-Worlds'. *Global Environment.* 1. pp. 56–79.
57 Edwards, *The Closed World: Computers and the Politics of Discourse in Cold War America*, p. 4.
58 Cockburn, *Kill Chain: The Rise of the High-Tech Assassins*, p. 28.
59 E.g. Shawcross, *Sideshow: Kissinger, Nixon and the Destruction of Cambodia.*
60 George Orwell. (1981) 'Shooting an Elephant'. *A Collection of Essays*. New York, First Harvest. p. 152.
61 Robert E. Low. (1985) 'Explosive Remnants of War: Detection Through the Use of Dogs'. In *Explosive Remnants of War: Mitigating the Environmental Effects*. Arthur H. Westing (Ed.). London, Taylor & Francis. pp. 73–4.
62 This is mentioned in general terms in several US State Department diplomatic cables, e.g.: US Embassy Vientiane. (1974) 'First Call on Foreign Minister'. Declassified Secret Cable to SECSTATE WASHDC. 1974VIENT02960. Section 2, p. 1. Available from: <http://aad.archives.gov/aad/>. Accessed 1 November 2008.
63 Branfman, *Voices from the Plain of Jars: Life under an Air War*, p. 5.
64 Philip Long. (September/October 2005) 'Ordnance Dangers'. *Archeology.* 58 (5). p. 9.
65 Patrick J. Sloyan. (2011) 'Compelling Military Service'. Crimes of War. <http://www.crimesofwar.org/a-z-guide/compelling-military-service/>. Accessed 4 March 2017.
66 Gloria Emerson. (10 January 1971) 'Villagers Say Saigon Perils Their Lives'. *The New York Times.* <http://www.nytimes.com/1971/01/10/archives/villagers-say-saigon-perils-their-lives-villagers-charge-saigon.html?_r=0>. Accessed 4 March 2017; Ronald Moreau. (28 September 2004) 'A Letter from Ronald Moreau in Islamabad (Newsweek Magazine) Tuesday, September 28, 2004'. Gloria Emerson. <http://gloriaemerson.com/memories_gloria.html>. Accessed 4 March 2017.
67 W. D. Nelson. (9 March 1982) 'Reports Deal Possible on MIA Accounting'. Associated Press. Retrieved from LexisNexis <https://

advance-lexis-com.rlib.pace.edu/api/document?collection=news&id=ur
n:contentItem:3SJ4-J6P0-0011-503K-00000-00&context=1516831>.

68 Various declassified US Department of State cables, e.g.: US Embassy,
    Vientiane. (April 1974) 'Explosive Ordnance Disposal (EOD) Teams
    in Laos'. Declassified Cable. VIENTI 03338 260803Z; US Embassy,
    Vientiane. (April 1974) 'Explosive Ordnance Disposal (EOD) Teams
    in Laos'. Declassified Cable. VIENTI 02960 120540Z. Also: Alounkeo
    Kittikhoun. (9 December 1996) Statement of the Lao PDR to the United
    Nations in the Briefing on Unexploded Ordnance in Laos. Document in
    possession of author.

69 Shoemaker, 'Legacy of the Secret War'.

70 Nguyen Công Luan. (2012) *Nationalist in the Viet Nam Wars: Memoirs of
    a Victim Turned Soldier*. Bloomington, Indiana University Press. p. 507.

71 Biographical information about Branfman in the following sections, if
    not otherwise cited, comes from: Warner, *Shooting at the Moon: The Story
    of America's Clandestine War in Laos*, pp. 214–21, 279–84, 307–8, 314–18,
    387–9; Fred Branfman. (2005) 'My Experiences with Laos and Indochina'.
    Truly Alive. <http://www.trulyalive.org/images/pdf/laos/awli1.pdf>.
    Accessed 22 March 2017; Fred Branfman. (1997) 'Journey for Truth:
    From the Cave of Politics to the Sunlight of Spirit: The Story of a Spiritual
    Journey'. *Truly Alive*. <http://www.trulyalive.org/images/pdf/spiritual/aw
    s1.pdf>; Fred Branfman. (1994) 'Something Missing: A Visit to the Plain
    of Jars'. *Truly Alive*. <http://www.trulyalive.org/images/pdf/laos/awli2.p
    df>. Accessed 22 March 2017.

72 Warner, *Shooting at the Moon: The Story of America's Clandestine War in
    Laos*, p. 220.

73 Fred Branfman. (2005) 'My Experiences with Laos and Indochina'. *Truly
    Alive*. <http://www.trulyalive.org/images/pdf/laos/awli1.pdf>. Accessed
    18 March 2017.

74 Branfman, 'Journey for Truth: From the Cave of Politics to the Sunlight
    of Spirit: The Story of a Spiritual Journey', p. 39.

75 'Fred Branfman – Obituary'. *The Telegraph* (14 October 2014). <http://ww
    w.telegraph.co.uk/news/obituaries/11162288/Fred-Branfman-obituary
    .html>. Accessed 22 March 2017.

76 Fred Branfman, 'My Experiences with Laos and Indochina', p. 1.

77 'An Inconvenient Truth: Obituary: Fred Branfman'. *The Economist* (17
    October 2014). <http://www.economist.com/news/obituary/21625649-f
    red-branfman-exposer-americas-secret-war-laos-died-september-24th
    -aged-72>. Accessed 22 March 2017.

78 'Fred Branfman – Obituary'. *The Telegraph*.

79 T. D. Allman. (17 October 1969) 'Ruined Town a Vignette of War in Laos'.
    The New York Times; T. D. Allman. (8 January 1972) 'The War in Laos:
    Plain Facts'. *Far Eastern Economic Review*. p. 16; Fred Branfman. (7 April
    1971) 'A Lake of Blood'. *The New York Times*; Fred Branfman. (16 July
    1971) 'Laos: One Day the Airplanes Came'. *The New York Times*.

80 In: Warner, *Shooting at the Moon: The Story of America's Clandestine War in Laos*, pp. 316–17.

81 Warner, *Shooting at the Moon: The Story of America's Clandestine War in Laos*, p. 318.

82 Branfman, *Voices from the Plain of Jars: Life under an Air War*, pp. 3, 20.

83 Branfman, *Voices from the Plain of Jars: Life under an Air War*, p. 4.

84 In: Branfman, *Voices from the Plain of Jars: Life under an Air War*, pp. 38–9.

85 McCoy, 'Reflections on History's Largest Air War', pp. 481–9.

86 Branfman, 'My Experiences with Laos and Indochina', pp. 24–5.

87 Seymour M. Hersh. (1972) 'An American Who Once Picked the Targets Tells How We Ran the Secret Air War in Laos'. *The New York Times Magazine*. pp. 18–19.

88 James W. Douglass. (1983) *Lightning East to West: Jesus, Gandhi and the Nuclear Age*. New York, Crossroad. pp. 9–12, 24–9, 44–6.

89 Fred Branfman. (1998) 'The Media, The War and 3.4 Million Ghosts: Reflections on the U.S. Press Corps in Indochina'. *Truly Alive*. <http://www.trulyalive.org/images/pdf/laos/awLI7.pdf>. Accessed 22 March 2017.

90 In: Warner, *Shooting at the Moon: The Story of America's Clandestine War in Laos*, pp. 388–9.

91 Swarthmore College Peace Collection. (n.d.) 'A Quaker Action Group'. <http://www.swarthmore.edu/library/peace/manuscriptcollections/Peace%20in%20Friends/Peace_Testimony_Archives.html#A>. Accessed 13 November 2011.

92 Nicole Pasulka. (11 October 2016) 'An American Boat Sailed to Vietnam During the War. Then It Disappeared'. *Atlas Obscura*. <https://www.atlasobscura.com/articles/the-american-boat-that-sailed-to-vietnam-during-the-warthen-disappeared>. Accessed 28 October 2017.

93 Mark E. Dixon. (n.d.) 'Giving Good Meeting'. *Main Line Today*. <http://www.mainlinetoday.com/core/pagetools.php?pageid=6673&url=%2FMain-Line-Today%2FAugust-2008%2FGiving-Good-Meeting%2F&mode=print>. Accessed 7 August 2012; Ewen MacAskill, Edward Snowden and Daniel Ellsberg. (16 January 2018) '"Is Whistleblowing Worth Prison or a Life in Exile?": Edward Snowden Talks to Daniel Ellsberg'. *The Guardian*. <https://www.theguardian.com/world/2018/jan/16/is-whistleblowing-worth-prison-or-a-life-in-exile-edward-snowden-talks-to-daniel-ellsberg?CMP=share_btn_fb>. Accessed 26 March 2018.

94 Ann E. Marimow and Miranda S. Spivack. (10 July 2008) 'Takoma Park Officials Frown Upon Foie Gras'. *The Washington Post*. <http://www.washingtonpost.com/wp-dyn/content/article/2008/07/09/AR2008070901547.html>. Accessed 7 August 2012; Dan Morse. (24 July 2007) 'City Council Strongly Backs Bid to Impeach Bush, Cheney'. *The Washington Post*. <http://www.washingtonpost.com/wp-dyn/content/article/2007/07/23/AR2007072301791.html >. Accessed 7 August 2012.

95 Shoemaker, 'Legacy of the Secret War'.

96 Warner, *Shooting at the Moon: The Story of America's Clandestine War in Laos*, p. 376.

97 Handicap International. (n.d.) 'History'. <http://www.handicap-internati onal.org.uk/about_us/our_history>. Accessed 7 August 2012; Aid Watch. (2003) 'Handicap International'. <http://www.observatoire-humanitair e.org/fusion.php?l=GB&id=21>. Accessed 7 August 2012.

98 Shoemaker, 'Legacy of the Secret War'.

99 Shoemaker, 'Legacy of the Secret War'. USAID did provide a $600 Ocean Freight Reimbursement for some of shovel, representing the 'only U.S. governmental aid for UXO work in Laos between 1975 and 1991'. See also: Barbara Crossette. (25 November 1987) '4 Aid Laos against Bombis and Other Horrors'. *The New York Times*. p. A9.

100 Prokosch, *The Technology of Killing: A Military and Political History of Antipersonnel Weapons*, pp. 135–45.

101 Shoemaker, 'Legacy of the Secret War'; Nat Hentoff. (30 May 1985) 'The FBI as Co-Conspirator'. *The Washington Post*. <https://www.washing tonpost.com/archive/politics/1985/05/30/the-fbi-as-co-conspirator /42ac8673-79ea-45ba-91fe-5186bbce297f/?utm_term=.d868c4e65b9 2>. Accessed 28 October 2017; Ivan Greenberg. (2010) *The Dangers of Dissent: The FBI and Civil Liberties since 1965*. Lanham, Lexington Books. pp. 271–2.

102 J. Ashley Roach. (1984) 'Certain Conventional Weapons Convention: Arms Control or Humanitarian Law?' *Military Law Review*. 105. p. 14.

103 North Vietnamese delegate to the Lucerne Conference of Government Experts, in: Prokosch, *The Technology of Killing: A Military and Political History of Antipersonnel Weapons*, p. 155.

104 'Protocol Additional to the Geneva Conventions of 12 August 1949, and Relating to the Protection of Victims of International Armed Conflicts (Protocol I), 8 June 1977' (8 June 1977). <http://www.icrc.org/ihl.nsf/f ull/470?opendocument>. Accessed 13 November 2011. Article 35, 2.

105 Legacies of War (2017) 'Overview: Who We Are'. <http://legaciesofwa r.org/about/overview/>. Accessed 22 March 2017.

106 Unless otherwise noted, biographical details on Channapha Khamvongsa are from interviews with her in March and August 2017.

107 Channapha Khamvongsa. (2017) 'Our Story'. *Legacies of War*. <http://le gaciesofwar.org/about/our-story/>. Accessed 12 January 2017.

108 Thomas Fuller. (5 April 2015) 'One Woman's Mission to Free Laos from Millions of Unexploded Bombs'. *The New York Times*. <https://www.ny times.com/2015/04/06/world/asia/laos-campaign-to-clear-millions-o f-unexploded-bombs.html?_r=0>. Accessed 12 January 2017.

109 Human Rights Watch. (2008) *Flooding South Lebanon: Israel's Use of Cluster Munitions in Lebanon in July and August 2006*. Washington DC, Human Rights Watch.

110 John Borrie. (2009) *Unacceptable Harm: A History of How the Treaty to Ban Cluster Munitions Was Won*. Geneva, UNIDIR.

111 Channapha Khamvongsa. (2010) 'Statement before the House Foreign Affairs Committee Subcommittee on Asia, the Pacific and the Global Environment'. <http://legaciesofwar.org/resources/congressional-heari ng-uxo-laos/channapha-khamvongsa-statement/>. Accessed 17 March 2017.

112 Elise Labott. (6 September 2016) 'Obama Announces $90 Million to Clear Laos' Unexploded Bombs'. *CNN*. <http://www.cnn.com/2016/09/06 /asia/laos-obama-aid-package/index.html>. Accessed 17 March 2017.

113 Elise Labott. (25 January 2016) 'Obama to Push to Clear Leftover Vietnam-era Bombs'. *CNN*. <http://edition.cnn.com/2016/01/24/politics/j ohn-kerry-laos-secret-war/>. Accessed 17 March 2017.

114 Fuller, 'One Woman's Mission to Free Laos from Millions of Unexploded Bombs'.

115 Statistics from Landmine and Cluster Munition Monitor: http://www. the-monitor.org

116 Channapha Khamvongsa. (7 September 2016) 'Channapha Khamvongsa: After War, A New Legacy of Peace in Laos'. <https://obamawhitehouse. archives.gov/blog/2016/09/07/channapha-khamvongsa-after-war-new-l egacy-peace-laos>. Accessed 17 March 2017.

117 Labott, 'Obama Announces $90 Million to Clear Laos' Unexploded Bombs'.

118 Human Rights Watch. (1 December 2017) 'US Embraces Cluster Munitions: Reverse Course on Internationally Banned, Reviled Weapons'. <https://www.hrw.org/news/2017/12/01/us-embraces-cluster-munition s>. Accessed 26 March 2018.

119 John Hudson. (31 August 2016) 'Last Remaining U.S. Maker of Cluster Bombs Stops Production'. *Foreign Policy*. <https://foreignpolicy.com/201 6/08/31/last-remaining-u-s-maker-of-cluster-bombs-stops-production/>. Accessed 17 March 2017.

120 Fuller, 'One Woman's Mission to Free Laos from Millions of Unexploded Bombs'.

121 Human Rights Watch, 'US Embraces Cluster Munitions: Reverse Course on Internationally Banned, Reviled Weapons'.

Chapter 3

1 Human Rights Watch (HRW) and Physicians for Human Rights (PHR). (1993) *Landmines: A Deadly Legacy*. New York, HRW. pp. 165–73.

2 In: Mark Jenkins. (January 2012) 'Cambodia's Healing Fields'. *National Geographic*. <http://ngm.nationalgeographic.com/2012/01/landmines/je nkins-text>. Accessed 14 July 2017.

3 Kenneth R. Rutherford. (2011) *Disarming States: The International Movement to Ban Landmines*. Oxford, Praeger Security International. pp. 20–31.

4 John Pilger. (17 April 2000) 'How Thatcher Gave Pol Pot a Hand'. *New Statesman*. <http://www.newstatesman.com/politics/politics/2014/04/how-thatcher-gave-pol-pot-hand>. Accessed 14 July 2017.

5 Human Rights Watch. (1991) *Land Mines in Cambodia: The Cowards' War*. New York: Human Rights Watch and Physicians for Human Rights. p. 2.

6 Paul Davies and Nic Dunlop. (1994) *War of the Mines: Cambodia, Landmines and the Impoverishment of a Nation*. London, Pluto Press.

7 James M. Scott. (1996) *Deciding to Intervene: The Reagan Doctrine and American Foreign Policy*. Durham, North Carolina, Duke University Press; Beth A. Fischer. (1997) *The Reagan Reversal: Foreign Policy and the End of the Cold War*. Columbia, Missouri, University of Missouri Press; Odd Arne Westad. (2005) *The Global Cold War: Third World Interventions and the Making of Our Times*. Cambridge, Cambridge University Press.

8 HRW and PHR, *Landmines: A Deadly Legacy*, pp. 165–73.

9 Yale University Cambodian Genocide Program. (2017) 'Cambodian Genocide Program'. <http://gsp.yale.edu/case-studies/cambodian-genocide-program>. Accessed 24 July 2017.

10 In: Jane Sharada Mahoney and Philip Edmonds. (1992) 'Editor's Introduction'. *Step by Step: Meditations on Wisdom and Compassion*. Berkeley, Parallax Press. p. 9.

11 Scott, *Deciding to Intervene: The Reagan Doctrine and American Foreign Policy*; Fischer, *The Reagan Reversal: Foreign Policy and the End of the Cold War*; Westad, *The Global Cold War: Third World Interventions and the Making of Our Times*; Fiona Terry. (2002) *Condemned to Repeat? The Paradox of Humanitarian Action*. Cambridge, Cambridge University Press. pp. 114–15, 121.

12 Terry, *Condemned to Repeat? The Paradox of Humanitarian Action*, p. 116.

13 John Burgess. (2015) *Temple in the Clouds: Faith and Conflict at Preah Vihear*. Bangkok, River Books; McGrath, *Landmines and Unexploded Ordnance: A Resource Book* p. 57; Terry, *Condemned to Repeat? The Paradox of Humanitarian Action*, pp. 118, 141–2.

14 Terry, *Condemned to Repeat? The Paradox of Humanitarian Action*, p. 114.

15 Details on K5, unless otherwise noted are drawn from, see: HRW and PHR, *Landmines: A Deadly Legacy*, pp. 165–73; Margaret Slocomb. (2001) 'The K5 Gamble: National Defence and Nation Building under the People's Republic of Kampuchea'. *Journal of Southeast Asian Studies*. 32(2). pp. 195–210; Ruth Bottomley. (2003) *Crossing the Divide: Landmines, Villages and Organizations*. Oslo, PRIO. pp. 14–17.

16 Terry, *Condemned to Repeat? The Paradox of Humanitarian Action*, p. 144.

17 Terry, *Condemned to Repeat? The Paradox of Humanitarian Action*, p. 144.

18 Matthew Bolton. (2010) *Foreign Aid and Landmine Clearance: Governance, Politics and Security in Afghanistan, Bosnia and Sudan.* London, I.B. Tauris. p. 74; Nikolai Jul Steensen. (2014) 'Norwegian People's Aid: A Study of the Mine Division from 1992–2002'. University of Oslo Master's Thesis. <https://www.duo.uio.no/bitstream/handle/1085 2/42488/Steensen-NPA-Master.pdf?sequence=1>. Accessed 26 September 2017.

19 US Department of State. (1994) 'Chapter V: Demining – The U.S. Response'. *Hidden Killers 1994: The Global Landmine Crisis.* <https://w ww.state.gov/www/global/arms/rpt_9401_demine_ch5.html>. Accessed 16 July 2017.

20 Dinah PoKempner. (1995) *Cambodia at War.* New York, Human Rights Watch. p. 104.

21 Burgess, *Temple in the Clouds: Faith and Conflict at Preah Vihear.*

22 ICRC, *Anti-personnel Landmines: Friend or Foe? A Study of the Military Use and Effectiveness of Anti-Personnel Mines.*

23 BBC. (26 November 2007) 'Controversial Legacy of Mad Mitch'. *BBC News.* <http://news.bbc.co.uk/2/hi/uk_news/scotland/7111303.stm>. Accessed 24 July 2017; BBC 2 Scotland. (2007) *Mad Mitch and The Last Battle of the British Empire.* <https://www.youtube.com/watch?v=R4 H95a2NYg8>.

24 Monin and Gallimore, *The Devil's Gardens: A History of Landmines,* p. 177.

25 Croll, *Landmines in War and Peace,* p. 168.

26 I must acknowledge that my thinking in the remainder of this chapter is heavily influenced by the scholarship of my spouse, Emily Welty, who has written extensively about the positive role religious actors can have in peacebuilding. See: Mohammed Abu-Nimer, Amal Khoury and Emily Welty. (2007) *Unity in Diversity: Interfaith Dialogue in the Middle East.* Washington DC, US Institute for Peace; Emily Welty. (2014) 'Faith-Based Peacebuilding and Development: An Analysis of the Mennonite Central Committee in Uganda and Kenya'. *Journal of Peacebuilding and Development.* 9(2). pp. 65–70; Emily Welty. (2016) 'The Theological Landscape of the Nuclear Nonproliferation Treaty: the Catholic Church, the World Council of Churches and the Bomb'. *Global Policy.* 7(3). pp. 396–404.

27 Unless otherwise footnoted, or drawn from interviews with Reth and Sister Denise, information about JRS's work in Thailand and Cambodia is from: JRS. (2012) *People We Met along the Way: JRS Cambodia.* Siem Reap, JRS; Hannah Cole, Molly Mullen, Tess O'Brien and Denise Coghlan. (2011) *Ambassadors before They Knew It: Song Kosal and Tun Channareth, Cambodia Campaign to Ban Landmines, 1994-2011.* Siem Reap, JRS.

28 Tun Channareth, in: Maxwell A. Cameron, Robert J. Lawson and Brian W. Tomlin. (1998) 'To Walk without Fear'. *To Walk without Fear: The Global Movement to Ban Landmines.* Maxwell A. Cameron, Robert J. Lawson and Brian W. Tomlin (Eds). Oxford, Oxford University Press. p. 14.

29 Jerry White and Kenneth Rutherford. (1998) 'The Role of the Landmine Survivors Network'. In: *To Walk without Fear: The Global Movement to Ban Landmines.* Maxwell A. Cameron, Robert J. Lawson & Brian W. Tomlin (Eds). Oxford, Oxford University Press. p. 101.

30 Sheree Bailey and Tun Channareth. (2008) 'Beyond the Rhetoric: The Mine Ban Treaty and Victim Assistance'. In *Banning Landmines: Disarmament, Citizen Diplomacy and Human Security.* Jody Williams, Stephen D. Goose and Mary Wareham (Eds). Lanham, Rowman & Littlefield. pp. 143–62.

31 Rutherford, *Disarming States: The International Movement to Ban Landmines*, pp. 20–31.

32 In: Walk without Fear Foundation. (2017) 'Tun Channareth'. <http://walkwithoutfear.ca/tun-channareth/>. Accessed 26 September 2017.

33 Amaya Valcarcel and Nick Jones. (2 February 2016) 'Interview with Denise Coghlan RSM on Asia Pacific Challenges'. <http://www.jrs.org.au/2532-2/>. Accessed 26 September 2017.

34 Unless otherwise cited, biographical details regarding Figaredo are drawn from: Jose Maria Rodriguez Olaizola. (2016) *The Heart of the Lonely Tree.* Battambang, Apostolic Prefecture of Battambang.

35 In: JRS, *People We Met along the Way: JRS Cambodia*, p. 46.

36 Terry, *Condemned to Repeat? The Paradox of Humanitarian Action*, p. 114.

37 Terry, *Condemned to Repeat? The Paradox of Humanitarian Action*, p. 114.

38 In: JRS, *People We Met along the Way: JRS Cambodia*, p. 46.

39 Terry, *Condemned to Repeat? The Paradox of Humanitarian Action*, pp. 143–4.

40 Terry, *Condemned to Repeat? The Paradox of Humanitarian Action*, p. 141.

41 Olaizola, *The Heart of the Lonely Tree*, pp. 82–4.

42 Olaizola, *The Heart of the Lonely Tree*, p. 126.

43 Biographical details on Maha Ghosananda are, unless otherwise cited, drawn from: Santidhammo Bhikkhu. (2009) *Maha Ghosananda: The Buddha of the Battlefield.* Bangkok, S.R. Printing Co; Maha Ghosananda. (1992) *Step by Step: Meditations on Wisdom and Compassion.* Berkeley, Parrallax Press; Simon Bloomfield. (27 March 2007) 'Maha Ghosananda'. *The Guardian.* <https://www.theguardian.com/news/2007/mar/28/guardianobituaries.religion> Accessed 20 July 2017.

44 Statistics from: Bhikkhu, *Maha Ghosananda: The Buddha of the Battlefield*, p. 39; Mahoney and Edmonds, 'Editor's Introduction', p. 12.

45 In: Bhikkhu, *Maha Ghosananda: The Buddha of the Battlefield*, pp. 27–9.

46 Bhikkhu, *Maha Ghosananda: The Buddha of the Battlefield*, p. 29.

47 Bhikkhu, *Maha Ghosananda: The Buddha of the Battlefield*, p. 6.

48 For more details on the Dhammayietras, see: R. Scott Appleby. (2008) 'Building Sustainable Peace: The Roles of Local and Transnational Religious Actors'. In *Religious Pluralism, Globalization, and World Politics.* Thomas Banchoff (Ed.). Oxford, Oxford University Press. pp. 125–54;

Kathryn Poethig. (2002) 'Movable Peace: Engaging the Transnational in Cambodia's Dhammayietra'. *Journal for the Scientific Study of Religion.* 41(1). pp. 19–28; Monique Skidmore. (1996) 'In the Shade of the Bodhi Tree: Dhammayietra and the Re-awakening of Community in Cambodia'. *Crossroads: An Interdisciplinary Journal of Southeast Asian Studies.* 10(1). pp. 1–32.

49 Bhikkhu, *Maha Ghosananda: The Buddha of the Battlefield*, p. 47.

50 Dith Pran. (1992) 'Foreword'. *Step by Step: Meditations on Wisdom and Compassion.* Berkeley, Parrallax Press. p. ix.

51 Ghosananda, *Step by Step: Meditations on Wisdom and Compassion*, p. 77.

52 Olaizola, *The Heart of the Lonely Tree*, pp. 104–6.

53 Rutherford, *Disarming States: The International Movement to Ban Landmines*, p. 28.

54 Human Rights Watch, *Land Mines in Cambodia: The Cowards' War.*

55 Human Rights Watch and Physicians for Human Rights. (1993) *Landmines: A Deadly Legacy.* New York, HRW. p. 3.

56 Rutherford, *Disarming States: The International Movement to Ban Landmines*, p. 28.

57 Rutherford, *Disarming States: The International Movement to Ban Landmines*, p. 20.

58 For detailed accounts of the ICBL and the diplomatic negotiations leading to the landmine ban treaty, see: Jody Williams. (2013) *My Name Is Jody Williams: A Vermont Girl's Winding Path to the Nobel Peace Prize.* Berkeley, University of California Press; Rutherford, *Disarming States: The International Movement to Ban Landmines*; Jody Williams, Stephen D. Goose and Mary Wareham (Eds). (2008) *Banning Landmines: Disarmament, Citizen Diplomacy and Human Security.* Lanham, Rowman & Littlefield; Leon V. Sigal. (2006) *Negotiating Minefields: The Landmines Ban in American Politics.* New York, Routledge; Richard A. Matthew, Bryan McDonald and Kenneth Rutherford (Eds). (2004) *Landmines and Human Security: International Politics and War's Hidden Legacy.* Albany, SUNY Press; Monin and Gallimore, *The Devil's Gardens: A History of Landmines*; Maxwell A. Cameron, Robert J. Lawson and Brian W. Tomlin (Eds). (1998) *To Walk without Fear: The Global Movement to Ban Landmines.* Oxford, Oxford University Press.

59 Williams, *My Name Is Jody Williams: A Vermont Girl's Winding Path to the Nobel Peace Prize*, p. 181.

60 In: JRS, *People We Met along the Way: JRS Cambodia*, p. 84.

61 Bhikkhu, *Maha Ghosananda: The Buddha of the Battlefield*, pp. 64–6, 73.

62 In: Bhikkhu, *Maha Ghosananda: The Buddha of the Battlefield*, pp. 93–4.

63 Details on the Phnom Penh conference are drawn from: Cole, Mullen, O'Brien and Coghlan, *Ambassadors before They Knew It: Song Kosal and Tun Channareth, Cambodia Campaign to Ban Landmines, 1994-2011*, pp. 18–19; Rutherford, *Disarming States: The International Movement to Ban*

Landmines, pp. 60–2, 161–2; Robert Lawson. (2002) 'Ban Landmines! The Social Construction of the International Ban on Anti-personnel Landmines 1991-2001'. PhD Thesis, Carleton University. <https://curve.carleton.ca/95141d64-2f23-4016-924f-acfccefa59ff>. Accessed 24 July 2017. pp. 104–6.

64 In: Cole, Mullen, O'Brien and Coghlan, *Ambassadors before They Knew It: Song Kosal and Tun Channareth, Cambodia Campaign to Ban Landmines, 1994-2011,* p. 19.

65 Cole, Mullen, O'Brien and Coghlan, *Ambassadors before They Knew It: Song Kosal and Tun Channareth, Cambodia Campaign to Ban Landmines, 1994-2011,* pp. 18–19.

66 Rutherford, *Disarming States: The International Movement to Ban Landmines,* p. 161.

67 Rutherford, *Disarming States: The International Movement to Ban Landmines,* pp. 60–1.

68 Williams, *My Name Is Jody Williams: A Vermont Girl's Winding Path to the Nobel Peace Prize,* p. 167.

69 e.g. Rutherford, *Disarming States: The International Movement to Ban Landmines,* p. 62.

70 Williams, *My Name Is Jody Williams: A Vermont Girl's Winding Path to the Nobel Peace Prize,* p. 186.

71 Tun Channareth. (6 October 1995) 'Lost in Vienna.' *CCW News.* 4.

72 In: Cole, Mullen, O'Brien and Coghlan, *Ambassadors before They Knew It: Song Kosal and Tun Channareth, Cambodia Campaign to Ban Landmines, 1994-2011,* p. 4.

73 Song Kosal, Tun Channareth, Sok Eng, Hem Phang, Klieng Vann and Soeun Chreuk, quoted in: Cole, Mullen, O'Brien and Coghlan, *Ambassadors before They Knew It: Song Kosal and Tun Channareth, Cambodia Campaign to Ban Landmines, 1994-2011,* pp. 24–5.

74 White and Rutherford, 'The Role of the Landmine Survivors Network', p. 101.

75 Rutherford, *Disarming States: The International Movement to Ban Landmines,* p. 172.

76 Rutherford, *Disarming States: The International Movement to Ban Landmines,* p. 81.

77 Tun Channareth, quoted in: Cole, Mullen, O'Brien and Coghlan, *Ambassadors before They Knew It: Song Kosal and Tun Channareth, Cambodia Campaign to Ban Landmines, 1994-2011,* p. 26.

78 Rutherford, *Disarming States: The International Movement to Ban Landmines,* p. 83.

79 Cole, Mullen, O'Brien and Coghlan, *Ambassadors before They Knew It: Song Kosal and Tun Channareth, Cambodia Campaign to Ban Landmines, 1994-2011,* p. 28.

80 White and Rutherford, 'The Role of the Landmine Survivors Network', pp. 106–7, 111–12.

81 Cameron, Lawson and Tomlin, 'To Walk without Fear', p. 14.

82 Jody Williams. (10 December 1997) 'Jody Williams – Nobel Lecture'. <http s://www.nobelprize.org/nobel_prizes/peace/laureates/1997/williams-lect ure.html>. Accessed 24 July 2017.

83 In: Cole, Mullen, O'Brien and Coghlan, *Ambassadors before They Knew It: Song Kosal and Tun Channareth, Cambodia Campaign to Ban Landmines, 1994-2011*, p. 30.

84 Rutherford, *Disarming States: The International Movement to Ban Landmines*, p. 130; Stephen D. Goose. (2008) 'Goodwill Yields Good Results: Cooperative Compliance and the Mine Ban Treaty'. In: *Banning Landmines: Disarmament, Citizen Diplomacy and Human Security*. Jody Williams, Stephen D. Goose and Mary Wareham (Eds). Lanham, Rowman & Littlefield. pp. 105–26; Yeshua Moser-Puangsuwan. (2008) 'Outside the Treaty Not the Norm: Nonstate Armed Groups and the Landmine Ban'. In: *Banning Landmines: Disarmament, Citizen Diplomacy and Human Security*. Jody Williams, Stephen D. Goose and Mary Wareham (Eds). Lanham, Rowman & Littlefield. pp. 163–78.

85 Mark Perry. (2020), 'Not Even the Military Thinks Landmines are a "Vital Tool"'. American Conservative. Retrieved from <https://www.theamericanconservative. com/articles/not-even-the-military-thinks-landmines-are-a-vital-tool/>.

86 Dennis Barlow, in: Rutherford, *Disarming States: The International Movement to Ban Landmines*, p. 3.

87 In: ICBL-CMC. (2017) 'Mr. Tun Channareth'. <http://www.icbl.org/en-gb/ about-us/who-we-are/ambassadors/mr-tun-channareth.aspx>. Accessed 26 September 2017.

88 Olaizola, *The Heart of the Lonely Tree*, p. 135.

89 Olaizola, *The Heart of the Lonely Tree*, pp. 122–3.

Chapter 4

1 Quotations from accident report in possession of the author.

2 Mary Kaldor. (2007) *New and Old Wars: Organized Violence in a Global Era*. 2nd Ed. London, Polity.

3 Mats Berdal. (2003) 'How "New" are "New Wars"? Global Economic Change and the Study of Civil War'. *Global Governance*. 9. p. 487.

4 Timothy Donais. (2005) *The Political Economy of Peacebuilding in Post-Dayton Bosnia*. London, Routledge. p. 119.

5 Ian Mansfield. (2015) *Stepping into a Minefield: A Life Dedicated to Landmine Clearance around the World*. Newport, Big Sky Publishing. p. 222.

6 GICHD. (June 2003) *The Role of the Military in Mine Action*. <http://ww w.gichd.ch/fileadmin/pdf/publications/Role_Military_MA.pdf>. Accessed 7 August 2012. p. 32, note 77, 33.

7 Mary Anderson. (1999) *Do No Harm: How Aid Can Support Peace – Or War*. London, Lynne Rienner. p. 37.

8 World Bank. (19 March 2004) 'Project Performance Assessment Report: Bosnia and Herzegovina'. Report No. 28288. p. v.

9 Office of the High Representative (OHR). (12 October 2000) 'Decision Removing Milos Krstic from His Position as a Member of the Demining Commission and Banning Him from Holding Any Official or Appointive Public Office'. <http://www.ohr.int/decisions/removalssdec/default .asp?content_id=317>. Accessed 28 October 2017; Office of the High Representative (OHR). (12 October 2000) 'Decision Removing Enes Cengic from His Position as a Member of the Demining Commission and Banning Him from Holding Any Official or Appointive Public Office'. <http://www.ohr.int/decisions/removalssdec/default.asp?content_id=318> . Accessed 28 October 2017; Office of the High Representative (OHR). (12 October 2000) 'Decision Removing Berislav Pusic from His Position as a Member of the Demining Commission and Banning Him from Holding Any Official or Appointive Public Office'. <http://www.ohr.int/decisions/ removalssdec/default.asp?content_id=319>. Accessed 28 October 2017/.

10 Office of the High Representative (OHR). (30 June 2006) 'Notice of Decision by the High Representative to Lift the Ban Imposed on Enes Cengic by the High Representative Decision, dated 11 October 2000'. <http://www.ohr.int/?p=64891>. Accessed 28 October 2017; Office of the High Representative (OHR). (30 June 2006) 'Notice of Decision by the High Representative to Lift the Ban Imposed on Milos Krstic by the High Representative Decision, dated 11 October 2000'. <http://www.ohr. int/?p=64895>. Accessed 28 October 2017.

11 International Criminal Tribunal for the Former Yugoslavia (ICTY). (29 May 2013) 'Judgment Summary for Jadranko Prlic and Others'. <http:// www.icty.org/x/cases/prlic/tjug/en/130529_summary_en.pdf>. Accessed 30 May 2013. See also: SENSE Tribunal. (26 November 2007) 'Exchanges According to Berislav Pusic'. <http://www.sense-agency.com/icty/exchan ges-according-to-berislav-pusic.29.html?cat_id=1&news_id=10638>. Accessed 6 June 2011.

12 Court of Bosnia and Herzegovina. (28 August 2006) 'Custody Ordered for Radomir Kojic'. <http://www.sudbih.gov.ba/index.php?id=218&je zik=e>. Accessed 6 June 2011; Court of Bosnia and Herzegovina. (29 February 2007) 'Weekly Activities of the Court of BiH: Section I and II: (25 February 2008 – 29 February 2008)'. <http://www.sudbih.gov.ba/file s/docs/sedmicni_pregled/e/s_activities_(25_-_29_February_2008).pdf>. Accessed 6 June 2011.

13 Matthew Bolton and Hugh Griffiths. (September 2006) *Bosnia's Political Landmines: A Call for Socially Responsible and Conflict-Sensitive Mine Action*. London, Landmine Action. <http://www.landmineaction.org/reso urces/Bosnias_Political_Landmines.pdf>.

14 US Embassy Sarajevo, 'Demining: Allegations of Fraud and Malfeasance in USG Supported Programs'.

15 Reuters. (10 February 2007) 'NATO Troops in Pale Raid the House of a Suspected Supporter of Radovan Karadzic'. *ITN Source*. <http://www.itn

source.com/shotlist/RTV/2007/02/10/RTV210407>. Accessed 6 June 2011.

16 US Embassy Sarajevo. (31 January 2007) 'Bosnia – Prosecutor to Open Investigation of USG-Funded Demining Programs'. Ref. 07SARAJEVO0230; US Embassy Sarajevo. (14 February 2007) 'Bosnian Demining Investigation Update: Investigation Initiated, PM/WRA Visit, Kojic Raid'. 07SARAJEVO0369.

17 Anderson, *Do No Harm: How Aid Can Support Peace – Or War*, p. 69.

18 Truth and Reconciliation Commission. (29 October 1998) *Truth and Reconciliation Commission of South Africa Report*. 3. pp. 116–17, 182–3. <http://www.justice.gov.za/trc/report/finalreport/Volume%203.pdf>. Accessed 2 August 2011.

19 International Campaign to Ban Landmines. (1999) 'Kuwait'. *Landmine Monitor Report*. <http://www.the-monitor.org/index.php/publications/ display?act=submit&pqs_year=1999&pqs_type=lm&pqs_report=kuw ait&pqs_section=>. Accessed 7 August 2012; International Campaign to Ban Landmines. (1999) 'Humanitarian Mine Action'. *Landmine Monitor Report*. <http://www.the-monitor.org/index.php/publications/display?u rl=lm/1999/english/exec/Execweb1-03.htm>. Accessed 7 August 2012.

20 Eddie Banks. (August 2003) 'In the Name of Humanity'. *Journal of Mine Action*. 7(2). <http://maic.jmu.edu/journal/7.2/focus/banks/banks.htm>. Accessed 13 November 2011; Ann Fitz-Gerald and Derrick J. Neal. (2000) 'Dispelling the Myth Between Humanitarian and Commercial Mine Action Activity'. *Journal of Mine Action*. 4(3). <http://maic.jmu.edu/Jour nal/4.3/features/myth/myth.htm>. Accessed 13 November 2011.

21 CBS Studios, Inc. (16 July 1982) 'Star Trek II: The Wrath of Khan'. <http:// www.chakoteya.net/movies/movie2.html>. Accessed 20 November 2011.

22 Dijana Pejic. (August 2003) 'From Puppets to Empowerment: The Bosnia and Herzegovina Genesis Project'. *Journal of Mine Action*. 7(2). <http:// maic.jmu.edu/journal/7.2/focus/pejic/pejic.htm>. Accessed 20 November 2011.

23 The information presented here on the Genesis Project comes from a research project and a series of writing assignments I did for UNICEF's mine action programme in Bosnia. The text here has been adapted from other reports I wrote, including UNICEF. (April 2006) *Mine Risk Education and Mine Victim Assistance: Integrated Mine Action Program in Bosnia and Herzegovina: Final Report to the Government of Italy 2002-2006*. Sarajevo, Bosnia and Herzegovina, UNICEF; Bolton. (23 June 2005) 'Puppets Help Children Get the Message on Landmines'. *The Examiner* (Independence, MO). p. 4A; Matthew Bolton. (2005) 'Bosnia and Herzegovina: UNICEF-Sponsored Campaign Saves Kids from Landmines'. *UNICEF*. http://www .unicef.org/ceecis/reallives_3419.html>. Accessed 12 July 2011.

24 Rebecca West. (1994 [1940]) *Black Lamb and Grey Falcon: A Journey through Yugoslavia*. New York, Penguin.

25 Annette Abelsen. (26 April 2007) 'Cooperation and Assistance in Clearing Mined Areas – Priorities for Norway in Resource Allocation'. <http://ww w.regjeringen.no/en/dep/ud/about_mfa/organisation/departments/dep artment_un_peace_humanitarian/seksjon-for-humanitare-sporsmal/aab/ speeches/minedareas.html?id=467173>. Accessed 4 August 2011.

26 Unless otherwise footnoted, the following data comes from: Bolton, *Foreign Aid and Landmine Clearance: Governance, Politics and Security in Afghanistan, Bosnia and Sudan*. Chapter 6.

27 Darvin Lisica and David Rowe. (2004) 'Strategic Analysis of Mine Action in Bosnia and Herzegovina'. Available from the Bosnia and Herzegovina Mine Action Center. Sarajevo. p. 53.

28 Mansfield, *Stepping into a Minefield: A Life Dedicated to Landmine Clearance around the World*, p. 233.

29 Bolton, *Foreign Aid and Landmine Clearance: Governance, Politics and Security in Afghanistan, Bosnia and Sudan*. Chapters 6–7.

30 GICHD. (June 2003) *The Role of the Military in Mine Action*. Geneva, GICHD. p. 33.

31 Elvira Jukic. (25 April 2014) 'Bosnia De-Mining Boss Grilled over Corruption Claims'. *BalkanInsight*. <http://www.balkaninsight.com/en/ article/bosnia-mining-director-questioned-over-corruption>. Accessed 21 May 2017; NPA. (2014) *Clearing the Mines: Report by the Mine Action Team for the Third Review Conference of the Antipersonnel Mine Ban Treaty*. Oslo, NPA. pp. 11, 25–6.

32 K. H. 'Political Minefield'. *The Economist*. <http://www.economist.com/ blogs/charlemagne/2014/02/corruption-greece>. Accessed 21 May 2017; Anthee Carassava. (9 May 2014) 'Greek Land Mine Scandal Sparks Far-reaching Investigation'. *Los Angeles Times*. <http://www.latimes.com/w orld/europe/la-fg-greece-scandal-20140509-story.html>. Accessed 21 May 2017.

33 Matthew Bolton. (23 May 2014) 'Floods in Bosnia Create New Landmine Risk'. *The I.B. Tauris Blogs*. <https://theibtaurisblog.com/2014/05/23/flood s-in-bosnia-create-new-landmine-risk/>. Accessed 21 May 2017.

34 NPA. (2015) *Clearing the Mines: Report for the Fourteenth Meeting of States Parties of the Anti-Personnel Mine Ban Convention*. Oslo, NPA. pp. 29–30.

35 Darko Momić. (13 January 2016) 'Dušan Gavran osuđen na deset mjeseci zatvora'. *Press*. <http://pressrs.ba/info/vijesti/dusan-gavran-osuden-na-deset-mjeseci-zatvora-12-01-2016>; S. M. (12 January 2016) 'Dušan Gavran osuđen na 10 mjeseci zatvora'. *Slobodna Bosna*. <https://www.sl obodna-bosna.ba/vijest/25985/kazna_ili_nagrada_dusan_gavran_osudj en_na_10_mjeseci_zatvora.html>.

36 Rodolfo Toe. (4 April 2016) 'Demining in Bosnia Slowed By Lack of Funds'. *BalkanInsight*. <http://www.balkaninsight.com/en/article/demi ning-in-bosnia-slowed-by-lacking-funds-04-01-2016>.

37 Audit Office of the Institutions of Bosnia and Herzegovina. (October 2016) 'Performance Audit Report. Efficiency of the Demining System in Bosnia and Herzegovina'. No. 01-02-03-10-16-1-1101/16.

38 Ishaan Tharoor. (16 September 2015) 'The Refugees' Path to Europe Marked by New Threat: Land Mines'. *The Washington Post*. <https://w ww.washingtonpost.com/news/worldviews/wp/2015/09/16/refugees-face -new-threat-on-journey-to-europe-land-mines/?utm_term=.bc6aa1b0c5 30>. Accessed 24 October 2017.

39 NPA, *Clearing the Mines: Report for the Fourteenth Meeting of States Parties of the Anti-Personnel Mine Ban Convention*, p. 29.

Chapter 5

1 iCasaulties.org. (2009) 'Operation Enduring Freedom'. <http://icasualties. org/OEF/Fatalities.aspx>. Accessed 12 July 2017; Mike R. Vining. (2017) 'SSG Justin J. Galewski'. EOD Warrior Foundation. <http://www.eodwarri orfoundation.org/memorial/warrior/justin-galewski>. Accessed 12 July 2017.

2 Action on Armed Violence. (2019) 'Afghanistan'. <https://aoav.org.uk/expl osiveviolence/afghanistan/>. Accessed 7 October 2019.

3 Mine Action Programme of Afghanistan. (March 2017) 'MARA Fast Facts'. <http://dmac.gov.af/wp-content/uploads/2017/04/MAPA-Fast-Fac ts-Jan-March-2017-_3_-7.pdf>. Accessed 12 July 2017.

4 John Prados. (1996) *Presidents' Secret Wars: CIA and Pentagon Covert Operations from World War II through the Persian Gulf*. Rvsd Ed. Chicago, Elephant Paperbacks.

5 Christina Lamb. (20 February 1989) 'US Discloses Details of Afghan Humanitarian Aid'. *Financial Times*. p. 2; Peter I. Bergen. (2002) *Holy War, Inc.: Inside the Secret World of Osama bin Laden*. New York, Touchstone. p. 71.

6 Steve Coll. (2004) *Ghost Wars: The Secret History of the CIA, Afghanistan and bin Laden, From the Soviet Invasion to September 10, 2001*. London, Penguin Books; George Crile. (2004) *Charlie Wilson's War*. New York, Grove Press; Barnett R. Rubin. (2002) *The Fragmentation of Afghanistan*. 2nd Ed. New Haven, Yale University Press; Fiona Terry. (2002) *Condemned to Repeat? The Paradox of Humanitarian Action*. Ithaca, Cornell University Press. pp. 55–82; Selig S. Harrison. (1990) 'Afghanistan'. In *After the Wars: Reconstruction in Afghanistan, Indochina, Central America, Southern Africa and the Horn of Africa*. Anthony Lake. (Ed.). Washington DC, Overseas Development Council; Helga Baitenmann. (January 1990) 'NGOs and the Afghan War: The Politicisation of Humanitarian Aid'. *Third World Quarterly*. 12(1); Charlie Wilson. (October 1989) 'Continue U.S. Aid to Afghanistan'. *The World & I*.

7   In Steve Coll. (19 July 1992) 'Anatomy of a Victory: CIA's Covert Afghan War'. *Washington Post.*

8   Susan Orlean. (15 February 2010) 'Riding High: Mules in the Military'. *The New Yorker.* p. 67.

9   RONCO. (1 February 1990) 'Quarterly Report: Commodity Export Program Afghanistan: AID REP Project No. 306-0205-C-00-9384-00, October 1, 1989 through December 31, 1989'. Available from USAID Development Experience Clearinghouse. Document PD-ABJ-491. rcr12-3; USAID. (1 June 1989) 'Afghanistan: Briefing for the Deputy Administrator-designate'. Available from USAID Development Experience Clearinghouse. Document PN-ABR-629. p. 8; Adam Pertman. (18 February 1989) 'Gorbachev Asks US to Halt Afghan Aid; $250m Nonmilitary Effort Detailed'. *The Boston Globe.* p. 1; Dan Hayter. (April 2003) 'The Evolution of Mine Detection Dog Training'. *Journal of Mine Action.* 7(1). <https://www.jmu.edu/cisr/journal/7.1/features/hayter/hayter.htm>. Accessed 25 July 2017.

10 George Crile. (2003) *Charlie Wilson's War: The Extraordinary Story of How the Wildest Man in Congress and a Rogue CIA Agent Changed the History of Our Times.* New York, Grove Press. p. 370.

11 Mansfield, *Stepping into a Minefield: A Life Dedicated to Landmine Clearance around the World*, p. 36.

12 Mansfield, *Stepping into a Minefield: A Life Dedicated to Landmine Clearance around the World*, p. 115.

13 For more details about the landmine situation in Afghanistan see: Survey Action Center. (2006) *Landmine Impact Survey – Islamic Republic of Afghanistan.* Takoma Park, Survey Action Center. For details of how the landmine situation developed, see also: Monin and Gallimore, *The Devil's Gardens: A History of Landmines*, pp. 162–3, 171; Croll, *The History of Landmines*, pp. 125–6; Shawn Roberts and Jody Williams. (1995) *After the Guns Fall Silent: The Enduring Legacy of Landmines.* Washington, Vietnam Veterans of America Foundation; US Defense Intelligence Agency. (1988) 'Mine Warfare in Afghanistan: A Defense Research Assessment'. 88-DIA-0438 8G. Document 39223, Afghanistan Extras Unpublished Collection, Box 3, Folder 1986, George Washington University National Security Archive.

14 Rutherford, *Disarming States: The International Movement to Ban Landmines*, pp. 20–31.

15 USAID (24 October 1988) 'A.I.D. Strategy: Afghan Resettlement and Rehabilitation'. *Development Experience Clearinghouse.* Document PN-ABR-629. <http://www.dec.org/pdf_docs/PNABR629.pdf>. Accessed 1 May 2006. pp. 13–32.

16 RONCO. (June 1998) 'Humanitarian Demining: Ten Years of Lessons'. *The Journal of Humanitarian Demining.* 2(2). <https://www.jmu.edu/cisr/journal/2.2/field/ronco.htm>. Accessed 25 July 2017; Margaret Buse.

(June 2000) 'RONCO Executives Talk about Demining, Integration and the IMAS Contract: (An Interview with Lawrence Crandall, Stephen Edelmann and A. David Lundberg)'. *Journal of Mine Action*. 4(2). <http s://www.jmu.edu/cisr/journal/4.2/Features/ronco/ronco.htm>. Accessed 25 July 2017; Dave McCracken. (2001) 'Thailand: The Land of Smiles (But Be Careful Where You Step!)' *Journal of Mine Action*. 5(1). <https://w ww.jmu.edu/cisr/journal/5.1/Focus/Dave_McCracken/mcracken.htm>. Accessed 25 July 2017; Hayter, 'The Evolution of Mine Detection Dog Training'.

17   RONCO. (18 April 1991) 'Proposal to Transfer Management of MDD Program from RONCO Consulting Corporation to Afghan Technical Consultants, UNOCA'. Available from USAID Development Experience Clearinghouse. Document PD-ABJ-299. p. iii.

18   USAID. (16 November 1989) 'Briefing Book for the Visit of ANE/ Assistant Administrator Carol Adelman: December 1-8, 1989'. *Digital National Security Archives: Afghanistan: The Making of U.S. Policy, 1973-1990.* <http://nsarchive.chadwyck.com>. Accessed May 2006.

19   Human Rights Watch. (2005) 'III. The Battle for Kabul: April 1992-March 1993'. *Blood-Stained Hands: Past Atrocities in Kabul and Afghanistan's Legacy of Impunity.* <https://www.hrw.org/reports/2005/afghanistan0605/ 4.htm>. Accessed 24 July 2017.

20   Mansfield, *Stepping into a Minefield: A Life Dedicated to Landmine Clearance around the World*, pp. 135–6.

21   BBC. (4 May 2017) 'Afghan Warlord Hekmatyar Returns to Kabul after Peace Deal'. *BBC News.* <http://www.bbc.com/news/world-asia-3980 2833>.

22   Bolton, *Foreign Aid and Landmine Clearance: Governance, Politics and Security in Afghanistan, Bosnia and Sudan*. pp. 90–3; Matthew Bolton. (2008) 'Goldmine? A Critical Look at the Commercialization of Afghan Demining'. London School of Economics Centre for the Study of Global Governance 2008/1. <http://eprints.lse.ac.uk/23363/>. Accessed 16 July 2017.

23   C. Walker. (24 February 1989) '"Mad Mitch" Will Help to Clear Afghan Mines'. *The Times*; Adam Kelliher. (9 March 1989) 'Anti-personnel mines maim Afghans'. *United Press International.*

24   John F. Burns. (2 December 1989) 'British Group Clears Mines Of Kabul War'. *The New York Times.* p. 23.

25   Walker, '"Mad Mitch" Will Help to Clear Afghan Mines'.

26   Mansfield, *Stepping into a Minefield: A Life Dedicated to Landmine Clearance around the World*, p. 26.

27   Mansfield, *Stepping into a Minefield: A Life Dedicated to Landmine Clearance around the World*, p. 36.

28   Akbar Noor. (September 1996) 'Dealing with an Invisible Enemy: The Socio-Economic Impacts of Landmines on some Local Communities

in Afghanistan'. Islamabad, UNOCHA. p. 11. Available from: <http://www.afghandata.org:8080/xmlui/handle/azu/4860>. Accessed 24 July 2017; Mansfield, *Stepping into a Minefield: A Life Dedicated to Landmine Clearance around the World*, p. 131.

29 ICBL. (1999) 'Afghanistan'. *Landmine Monitor*. <http://archives.the-monitor.org/index.php/publications/display?url=lm/1999/afghanistan>. Accessed 24 July 2017.

30 Details on Taliban human rights abuses and war crimes are available in: Human Rights Watch. (2001) *Massacres of Hazaras in Afghanistan*. New York, Human Rights Watch; Ahmed Rashid. (2010) *Taliban: Militant Islam, Oil and Fundamentalism in Central Asia*. 2nd Ed. New Haven, Yale University Press.

31 Details on ACBL activities from: ACBL. (1998) 'Annual Report 1998'. <http://www.afghandata.org:8080/xmlui/handle/azu/7338>. Accessed 24 July 2017; ACBL. (2000) 'Annual Report 2000'. <http://www.afghandata.org:8080/xmlui/handle/azu/7339>. Accessed 24 July 2017.

32 Mansfield, *Stepping into a Minefield: A Life Dedicated to Landmine Clearance around the World*, p. 144.

33 Yeshua Moser-Puangsuwan. (2008) 'Outside the Treaty Not the Norm: Nonstate Armed Groups and the Landmine Ban'. In: *Banning Landmines: Disarmament, Citizen Diplomacy and Human Security*. Jody Williams, Stephen D. Goose and Mary Wareham (Eds). Lanham, Rowman & Littlefield. p. 168; Human Rights Watch. (October 2001) 'Landmine Use in Afghanistan'. <https://www.hrw.org/legacy/backgrounder/arms/landmines-bck1011.pdf>. Accessed 24 July 2017; ICBL, 'Afghanistan'.

34 Mansfield, *Stepping into a Minefield: A Life Dedicated to Landmine Clearance around the World*, p. 145.

35 Mansfield, *Stepping into a Minefield: A Life Dedicated to Landmine Clearance around the World*, p. 145.

36 Bolton, 'Goldmine? A Critical Look at the Commercialization of Afghan Demining'.

37 'Whoever kills a soul unless for a soul or corruption in the land – it is as if he had slain mankind entirely. And whoever saves one – it is as if he had saved mankind entirely'. Al-Qur'an 5:32.

38 Michael Ignatieff. (28 July 2002) 'Nation-Building Lite'. *The New York Times*. <http://www.nytimes.com/2002/07/28/magazine/28NATION.html?pagewanted=all>. Accessed 19 August 2012.

39 UNAMA. (18 January 2011) 'Deminers in the Firing Line'. <https://unama.unmissions.org/deminers-firing-line>. Accessed 25 July 2017.

40 For further information on Taliban attitudes to landmines, see: ICBL. (16 November 2016) 'Afghanistan: Mine Ban Policy'. Landmine and Cluster Munition Monitor. <http://the-monitor.org/en-gb/reports/2017/afghanistan/mine-ban-policy.aspx>. Accessed 24 July 2017; Moser-Puangsuwan, 'Outside the Treaty Not the Norm: Nonstate Armed Groups and the

Landmine Ban', p. 168; Croll, *Landmines in War and Peace*, p. 134; Paul
Wapner. (2004) 'The Campaign to Ban Antipersonnel Landmines and
Global Civil Society'. In *Landmines and Human Security: International
Politics and War's Hidden Legacy*. Richard A. Matthew, Bryan McDonald
and Kenneth Rutherford (Eds). Albany, SUNY Press p. 255; Geneva Call.
(2005) *Armed Non-State Actors and Landmines*. Geneva, Program for the
Study of International Organization(s). pp. 65–7; Shalinia Chawla. (June
2000) 'Diffusion of Landmines in Afghanistan'. *Strategic Analysis: A Monthly
Journal of the IDSA*. 24(3). <https://www.idsa-india.org/an-jun-400.html>

41 John Lundberg. (August 2005) 'Reflecting on 10 Years of RONCO
Operations in Mine Action'. *Journal of Mine Action*. 9.1. <http://maic.jm
u.edu/journal/9.1/Focus/lundberg/lundberg.htm>. Accessed 20 August
2012; RONCO. (April 2003) 'Mine Detection Dogs: An Integral Tool in
RONCO Mine Clearance Operations'. *Journal of Mine Action*. 7(1). <http
://maic.jmu.edu/journal/7.1/features/ronco/ronco.htm>. Accessed 19
November 2011.

42 Stacy L. Smith. (August 2006) 'RONCO's Response to Explosive Remnants
of War in Post-conflict Environments'. *Journal of Mine Action*. 10(1). <http
s://www.jmu.edu/cisr/journal/10.1/feature/smith/smith.shtml>. Accessed
14 July 2017.

43 Anon. (8 September 2005) 'DynCorp International to Remove Land
Mines In Afghanistan'. *Business Wire*.

44 James Warden. (24 April 2009) 'Road Projects Play Key Role in Battling
Afghan Insurgents'. *Stars and Stripes*. <http://www.stripes.com/news/
road-projects-play-key-role-in-battling-afghan-insurgents-1.90690>.
Accessed 19 November 2011.

45 Johanna Neuman and Joel Havemann. (15 February 2007) 'Bush Orders
More Troops Into Afghanistan'. *Los Angeles Times*. <http://www.uruknet.
de/?s1=1&p=30669&s2=16>. Accessed 19 November 2011.

46 US Embassy Kabul. (9 February 2007) 'Humanitarian Mine Action in
Afghanistan – Going Commercial'. Unclassified US State Department
Cable. Obtained by author.

47 For further details on this data see: Bolton, *Foreign Aid and Landmine
Clearance: Governance, Politics and Security in Afghanistan, Bosnia and
Sudan*, Chapter 5.

48 Ron Suskind. (17 October 2004) 'Faith, Certainty and the Presidency of
George W. Bush'. *New York Times Magazine*. <http://www.nytimes.com/2
004/10/17/magazine/17BUSH.html>. Accessed 27 June 2011.

49 US Department of State, Office of Inspector General. (November
2009) 'Report of Inspection: Humanitarian Mine Action Programs in
Afghanistan'. Report No. ISP-I-10-11. <http://oig.state.gov/documents/org
anization/133663.pdf>. Accessed 8 August 2012. pp. 18, 29, 30, 33.

50 George MacDonald Fraser. (1969) *Flashman: From the Flashman Papers,
1839-1842*. New York, Penguin. pp. 64, 102.

51 Christopher Hitchens. (2011) 'Fraser's Flashman: Scoundrel Time'. *Arguably: Essays by Christopher Hitchens.* New York, Twelve. pp. 358–9.

52 Michael Ignatieff. (2003) *Empire Lite: Nation-Building in Bosnia, Kosovo and Afghanistan.* London, Vintage. p. 95.

53 Crile, *Charlie Wilson's War: The Extraordinary Story of How the Wildest Man in Congress and a Rogue CIA Agent Changed the History of Our Times,* pp. 476–7.

54 Rory Stewart. (2006) *The Places In Between.* Orlando, Harcourt.

55 Britta Sandberg. (4 September 2009) 'Guards at US Embassy Organized Humiliating Sex Games'. *Spiegel Online International.* <http://www.spiegel.de/international/world/0,1518,646977,00.html>. Accessed 8 July 2011.

56 US Senate Committee on Armed Services. (28 September 2010) 'Inquiry into the Role and Oversight of Private Security Contractors in Afghanistan'. <http://www.humansecuritygateway.com/showRecord.php?RecordId=33965>. Accessed 7 March 2012. p. i.

57 US Senate Committee on Armed Services, 'Inquiry into the Role and Oversight of Private Security Contractors in Afghanistan', pp. iii–iv, 7, 23–4, 32–7.

58 Jude Sheerin. (9 October 2010) 'Afghan Security Firms "Hand in Glove" with Taliban'. *BBC News.* <http://www.bbc.co.uk/news/world-south-asia-11501762>. Accessed 7 March 2012.

59 US Senate Committee on Armed Services, 'Inquiry into the Role and Oversight of Private Security Contractors in Afghanistan', pp. ix–x.

60 BBC. (28 September 2016) 'Dorset Mondial Defence Pair Jailed over Arms Deal Bribe'. *BBC News.* <http://www.bbc.com/news/uk-england-dorset-37499406>. Accessed 14 July 2017; City of London Police. (28 September 2016) 'Two Men Have Been Jailed Following an International Investigation into Bribes'. <https://www.cityoflondon.police.uk/news-and-appeals/Pages/Two-men-have-been-jailed-following-an-international-investigation-into-bribes-.aspx>. Accessed 14 July 2017; Department of Justice. (4 November 2015) 'Former Department of Defense Contractor Pleads Guilty to Soliciting and Receiving Kickback Proceeds Related to U.S. Government Contract'. *Justice News.* <https://www.justice.gov/opa/pr/former-department-defense-contractor-pleads-guilty-soliciting-and-receiving-kickback-proceeds>. Accessed 14 July 2017; SIGAR. (2016) *SIGAR Oversight.* <https://www.sigar.mil/pdf/quarterlyreports/2016-04-30qr-section2.pdf>. Accessed 14 July 2017. pp. 48–9.

61 International Campaign to Ban Landmines. (2006) 'Afghanistan'. *Landmine Monitor Report 2006.* <http://www.the-monitor.org/index.php/publications/display?url=lm/2006/afghanistan.html>. Accessed 19 November 2011.

62 UNMACA. (18 June 2007) 'Deminers Continue Working for the Good of Communities Despite of Several Attacks'. ReliefWeb. <http://reliefweb.int/node/235254>. Accessed 5 July 2011.

Chapter 6

1 ICBL. (2004) 'Sudan'. *The Landmine Monitor*. <http://www.the-monitor.o
rg/index.php/publications/display?act=submit&pqs_year=2004&pqs_ty
pe=lm&pqs_report=sudan&pqs_section=#Heading16004>. Accessed
1 January 2012; ICBL (15 September 2011) 'Sudan: Support for Mine
Action'. *The Landmine and Cluster Munition Monitor*. <http://www.the
-monitor.org/index.php/cp/display/region_profiles/theme/1368>.
Accessed 1 January 2012.

2 For more information on road risk classification see: Greg
Crowther and Richard Moyes. (November 2006) *Anti-Vehicle Mines:
Understanding the Impact and Managing the Risk*. London, Landmine
Action. pp. 54–5.

3 Jim Pansegrouw, in: UNMIS. (7 December 2005) 'Press Briefing'. <http
://reliefweb.int/sites/reliefweb.int/files/resources/D0980CAB3F3D1E154
92570DE001FB2EF-unmis-sdn-7dec.pdf>. Accessed 31 July 2017.

4 Human Rights Watch. (13 December 1999) 'Food Aid to Sudanese Rebels
Opposed'. <http://www.hrw.org/news/1999/12/12/food-aid-sudanese-r
ebels-opposed>. Accessed 18 December 2011. See also: Adele Harmer.
(March 2004) 'Aid to Poorly Performing Countries: Sudan Case Study'.
Background Paper 5 for ODI Study on Poor Performing Countries. <http
://www.odi.org.uk/resources/details.asp?id=5016&title=aid-poorly-perfo
rming-countries-sudan-case-study>. Accessed 3 January 2012.

5 BBC. (31 August 2010) 'South Sudan to End Use of Child Soldiers'. *BBC
News*. <http://www.bbc.co.uk/news/world-africa-11135426>. Accessed 18
December 2011.

6 Human Rights Watch. (2009) *'There Is No Protection': Insecurity and
Human Rights in Southern Sudan*. New York, Human Rights Watch. p. 3.
<http://www.hrw.org/sites/default/files/reports/southsudan0209_web.pdf
>. Accessed 19 December 2011.

7 Council on Foreign Relations. (2019) 'Civil War in South Sudan'. *Global
Conflict Tracker*. <https://www.cfr.org/interactives/global-conflict-track
er#!/conflict/civil-war-in-south-sudan>. Accessed 12 October 2019.

8 Anon. (29 March 1862) 'Torpedoes at Columbus'. *Harper's Weekly*. 6. pp.
202–3.

9 Teddy Bottinelli in: Croll, *Landmines in War and Peace*, p. 79.

10 In: Croll, *Landmines in War and Peace*, p. 23.

11 In: Croll, *Landmines in War and Peace*, p. 23.

12 US Army, *Land Mines and Booby Traps*. FM5-31, Section IV.

13 Donald Rumsfeld. (6 June 2002) 'Press Conference by US Secretary of
Defence, Donald Rumsfeld'. <http://www.nato.int/docu/speech/2002/s0
20606g.htm>. Accessed 27 July 2017.

14 Derek Gregory. (2011) 'The Everywhere War'. *The Geographical Journal*.
177 (3). pp. 238–50.

15 Derek Gregory. (2010) 'War and Peace'. *Transactions of the Institute of British Geographers*. 35. pp. 154–86.

16 Elements of this section are drawn from: Matthew Bolton. (2015) 'From Minefields to Minespace: An Archeology of the Changing Architecture of Autonomous Killing in US Army Field Manuals on Landmines, Booby Traps and IEDs'. *Political Geography*. 46. pp. 41–53.

17 Matthew Bolton. (2008) 'Sudan's Expensive Minefields: An Evaluation of Political and Economic Problems in Sudanese Mine Clearance'. <http://po liticalminefields.com/2008/07/29/sudans-expensive-landmines>. Accessed 2 January 2012.

18 ICBL. (2016) 'South Sudan'. *Landmine Monitor*. <http://the-monitor.org/e n-gb/reports/2016/south-sudan>. Accessed 27 July 2017.

19 ICBL, 'South Sudan'.

20 ICBL. (2016) 'Afghanistan: Mine Action'. *Landmine and Cluster Munition Monitor*. <http://www.the-monitor.org/en-gb/reports/2016/afghanistan/m ine-action.aspx>. Accessed 31 July 2017.

21 Severine Autesserre. (2014) *Peaceland: Conflict Resolution and the Everyday Politics of International Intervention*. Cambridge, Cambridge University Press. pp. 219–30.

22 cf. David Keen. (2008) *The Benefits of Famine: A Political Economy of Famine & Relief in Southwestern Sudan, 1983-9*. Oxford, James Currey. p. 216.

23 X, Y and Z. (2007) Independent evaluation of one donor's projects in Sudan. p. 25. Obtained by author.

24 Independent Consultant Y. (27 January 2006) Evaluation of NGO X. Document obtained by author. p. 7.

25 For more on these estimates, see: Ilaria Bottigliero. (2000) *120 Million Landmines Deployed Worldwide: Fact or Fiction?* Barnsley, Leo Cooper; Croll, *Landmines in War and Peace*, pp. 153–4; Stuart Maslen. (2004) *Mine Action after Diana: Progress in the Struggle against Landmines*. London, Pluto Press. pp. 24–5.

26 UN in: Croll, *Landmines in War and Peace*, p. 154.

27 E.g. NPA, *Clearing the Mines: Report for the Fourteenth Meeting of States Parties of the Anti-Personnel Mine Ban Convention*.

28 ICBL. (2016) 'Croatia: Mine Action'. *Landmine Monitor*. <http://the-mon itor.org/en-gb/reports/2016/croatia/mine-action.aspx>.

29 Autesserre, *Peaceland: Conflict Resolution and the Everyday Politics of International Intervention*, pp. 240–3.

30 Matthew Bolton. (2008) 'Sudan's Expensivme Minefields: An Evaluation of Political and Economic Problems in Sudanese Mine Clearance'. <http://po liticalminefields.com/2008/07/29/sudans-expensive-landmines>. Accessed 2 January 2012.

31 Bolton, 'Sudan's Expensive Minefields: An Evaluation of Political and Economic Problems in Sudanese Mine Clearance'.

32 NPA internal document quoted in: Aid Watch. (6 March 2006) 'Norwegian People's Aid [Norsk Folkehjelp]'. <http://www.observatoire-humanitaire.org/fusion.php?l=GB&id=75>. Accessed 3 January 2012.

33 Larry Minear. (1991) *Humanitarianism under Siege: A Critical Review of Operations Lifeline Sudan*. Trenton, NJ, Red Sea Press. p. 85. Emphasis in original.

34 Halle Jørn Hanssen. (9 August 2005) 'Speech for Garang'. *Norwegian People's Aid*. <http://otto.idium.no/nf.no/?module=Articles;action=Art icle.publicShow;ID=2586>. Accessed 3 December 2011.

35 Watch, 'Norwegian People's Aid [Norsk Folkehjelp]'.

36 International Criminal Court. (27 April 2007) 'Situation in Darfur, Sudan in the Case of the Prosecutor v. Ahmad Muhammad Harun ("Ahmad Harun") and Ali Muhammad al Abd-al-Rahman ("Ali-Kushayb")'. ICC-02/05-01/07. <http://www.icc-cpi.int/iccdocs/doc/doc279813.PDF>. Accessed 28 November 2011.

37 Human Rights Watch. (8 December 2005) 'Entrenching Impunity: Government Responsibility for International Crimes in Darfur'. <http://www.hrw.org/en/reports/2005/12/08/entrenching-impunity>. Accessed 28 November 2011. pp. 24, 27, 57, 63, 67, 87.

38 BBC. 'Powell Declares Genocide in Sudan'. *BBC News*. <http://news.bb c.co.uk/2/hi/3641820.stm>. Accessed 28 November 2011.

39 Simon Allison. (2 November 2011) 'The Butcher of Nuba's New Job'. *Daily Maverick*. <http://dailymaverick.co.za/article/2011-11-02-the-butcher-o f-nubas-new-job>. Accessed 30 November 2011; Julie Flint and Alex de Waal. (2008) *Darfur: A New History of a Long War*. 2nd Ed. London, Zed Books. p. 124.

40 Meeting of the States Parties to the Convention on the Prohibition of the Use, Stockpiling, Production and Transfer of Anti-Personnel Mines and on their Destruction: Sixth Meeting, Zagreb. (2 December 2005) 'List of Participants'. <http://www.apminebanconvention.org/fileadmin/pdf/mbc/ MSP/6MSP/6MSP_List_of_participants.pdf>. Accessed 3 January 2012. Meeting of the States Parties to the Convention on the Prohibition of the Use, Stockpiling, Production and Transfer of Anti-Personnel Mines and on their Destruction: Seventh Meeting, Geneva. (22 September 2006) 'List of Participants'. <http://www.apminebanconvention.org/fileadmin/pdf/mbc/ MSP/7MSP/7MSP_List_of_Participants.pdf>. Accessed 3 January 2012.

41 UNMAO. (2006) 'Capacity Building'. <http://www.sudanmap.org/Capac ityBuilding.html>. Accessed 29 July 2008.

42 Patrick Worsnip. (6 June 2008) 'ICC Bid to Arrest Sudan Suspect Failed-spokeswoman'. *Reuters*. <http://www.reuters.com/article/2008/06/06/id USN06455243>. Accessed 30 November 2011.

43 Anon. (28 February 2007) 'Sudanese ICC Suspect Says Inspired by Saddam'. *Mail & Guardian*. <http://mg.co.za/article/2007-02-28-sudanese-icc-suspect-says-inspired-by-saddam>. Accessed 30 November 2011.

44 Simon Tisdall. (3 December 2008) 'Man Blamed for Darfur Says I Am at Peace with Myself'. *The Guardian*. <http://www.guardian.co.uk/wor ld/2008/dec/04/sudan-darfur-human-rights-war-crimes>. Accessed 30 November 2011.

45 BBC. (16 May 2011) 'Sudan: SPLM Rejects South Kordofan win for Ahmed Haroun'. *BBC News*. <http://www.bbc.co.uk/news/world-africa-13408877>. Accessed 30 November 2011; James Copnell. (10 May 2011) 'Sudan: Could Nuba Mountains Be Next Conflict?' *BBC News*. <http://ww w.bbc.co.uk/news/world-africa-13351773>. Accessed 30 November 2011.

46 Alan Boswell. (20 June 2011) 'Inside Sudan's Nuba Mountains: Tales of Terror Bleed Out'. *Time*. <http://www.time.com/time/world/article/0,859 9,2078615,00.html#ixzz1fClHPiAY>. Accessed 30 November 2011.

47 ICBL. (15 November 2011) 'Sudan: Mine Ban Policy'. *Landmine and Cluster Munition Monitor*. <http://www.the-monitor.org/custom/index .php/region_profiles/print_profile/377>. Accessed 1 January 2012.

48 International Campaign to Ban Landmines. (31 July 2012) 'Sudan: Cluster Munition Ban Policy'. <http://www.the-monitor.org/index.php/cp/display/ region_profiles/theme/2214>. Accessed 7 August 2012.

49 Al Jazeera. (1 April 2012) 'Sudan Governor to Troops: "Take No Prisoners."' *Al Jazeera*. <http://www.aljazeera.com/news/africa/2012/03 /2012331114433519971.html>. Accessed 7 August 2012.

50 Human Rights Watch. (11 December 2012) 'Under Seige: Indiscriminate Bombing and Abuses in Sudan's Southern Kordofan and Blue Nile States'. <http://www.hrw.org/reports/2012/12/11/under-siege>. Accessed 16 May 2013.

51 Reuters. (11 January 2011) 'U.N. Flew Indicted War Criminal to Sudan Meeting'. *Reuters*. <http://af.reuters.com/article/sudanNews/idAFN1117 006320110111?pageNumber=1&virtualBrandChannel=0>. Accessed 30 November 2011.

52 Gérard Prunier. (2008) *Darfur: A 21st Century Genocide*. 3rd Ed. Ithaca, Cornell University Press; Flint and de Waal, *Darfur: A New History of a Long War*.

53 Andrew Latham. (2000) 'Global Cultural Change and the Transnational Campaign to Ban Antipersonnel Landmines: A Research Agenda'. YCISS Occasional Paper No. 62. <http://www.yorku.ca/yciss/publications/OP62-Latham.pdf>. Accessed 21 May 2011; Richard Price. (Winter 1995) 'A Genealogy of the Chemical Weapons Taboo'. *International Organization*. 49(1). pp. 73–103.

54 Mia Farrow. (28 March 2008) 'What're a Few Thousand Mines …' *MiaFarrow.org* <http://miafarrownews.blogspot.com/2008/03/whats-f ew-thousand-mines.html>. Accessed 28 November 2011.

55 ICBL. (5 October 2011) 'Sudan: Mine Action'. *Landmine and Cluster Munition Monitor*. <http://www.the-monitor.org/index.php/cp/display/ region_profiles/theme/1370>. Accessed 5 December 2011; ICBL. (2012)

'Sudan: Mine Action'. *Landmine and Cluster Munition Monitor*. < http://archives.the-monitor.org/index.php/cp/display/region_profiles/theme/2213>. Accessed 31 July 2017.

56 Mine action researcher. (18 April 2008) Personal email to author.

57 Autesserre, *Peaceland: Conflict Resolution and the Everyday Politics of International Intervention*, p. 85.

58 Local demining NGO manager. (2006) Letter to international demining NGO. Obtained by author.

59 Autesserre, *Peaceland: Conflict Resolution and the Everyday Politics of International Intervention*, p. 118.

60 Autesserre, *Peaceland: Conflict Resolution and the Everyday Politics of International Intervention*, p. 82.

61 Autesserre, *Peaceland: Conflict Resolution and the Everyday Politics of International Intervention*, p. 116.

62 PRIO. (2009) 'Assistance to Mine-Affected Communities (AMAC)'. <http s://www.prio.org/Projects/Project/?x=1202>. Accessed 1 October 2017.

63 Kristian Berg Harpviken and Rebecca Roberts (Eds). (2004) *Preparing the Ground for Peace: Mine Action in Support of Peacebuilding*. PRIO Report 2/2004. Oslo, PRIO. p. i.

64 Rebecca Roberts and Mads Frilander. (2004) 'Preparing for Peace: Mine Action's Investment in the Future of Sudan'. *Preparing the Ground for Peace: Mine Action in Support of Peacebuilding*. PRIO Report 2/2004. Kristian Berg Harpviken & Rebecca Roberts (Eds.). Oslo, PRIO.

65 Rebecca Roberts. (June 2006) 'Developing National Mine Action Capacity in Sudan: The Impact of Conflict, Politics, and International Assistance'. <https://www.prio.org/utility/DownloadFile.ashx?id=515&type=publi cationfile>. Accessed 1 October 2017.

66 Roberts and Frilander, 'Preparing for Peace: Mine Action's Investment in the Future of Sudan', p. 15.

67 Salma El Wardany. (23 September 2011) 'Sudan Army, Opposition Fighters Clash in Southern Kordofan'. *Bloomberg*. <http://www.bloomber g.com/news/2011-09-23/sudan-clashes-resume-in-southern-kordofan-s tate-smc-reports.html>. Accessed 3 December 2011; Douglas H. Johnson. (2003) *The Root Causes of Sudan's Civil Wars*. Oxford, James Currey. p. 163.

68 IRIN. (12 November 2009) 'The Nuba Mountains – Straddling the North-south Divide'. *IRIN News*. <http://www.irinnews.org/report.aspx?reportid =86994>. Accessed 25 November 2011; See also: African Rights. (1995) *Facing Genocide: The Nuba of Sudan*. London, African Rights; Johnson, *The Root Causes of Sudan's Civil Wars*, pp. 131–5.

69 Johnson, *The Root Causes of Sudan's Civil Wars*, p. 132.

70 International Crisis Group. (21 October 2008) 'Sudan's Southern Kordofan Problem: The Next Darfur?' Crisis Group Africa Report No. 145. pp. i, 2. <http://www.crisisgroup.org/~/media/Files/africa/horn-of-africa/sudan/

Sudans%20Southern%20Kordofan%20Problem%20The%20Next%20D
arfur.pdf>. Accessed 25 November 2011.

71 Survey Action Center. (January 2009) 'Landmine Impact Survey – Sudan:
South Kordofan State'. <http://www.sac-na.org/pdf_text/sudan/SK_Repo
rt_Apr09.pdf>. Accessed 1 January 2012; Survey Action Center. (2009)
Landmine Impact Survey: Republic of the Sudan. Washington DC, Survey
Action Center. <http://www.sac-na.org/pdf_text/sudan/SDN_FinalRep
ort.pdf>. Accessed 1 January 2012.

72 International Crisis Group, 'Sudan's Southern Kordofan Problem: The
Next Darfur?' pp. i–ii.

73 International Crisis Group, 'Sudan's Southern Kordofan Problem: The
Next Darfur?' p. 11.

74 Tempas Camilo Moses. (7 August 2007) Personal interview with author in
Juba.

75 DanChurchAid. (5 November 2005) 'Humanitarian Mine Action in
Sudan'. <http://www.danchurchaid.org/sider_paa_hjemmesiden/what
_we_do/issues_we_work_on/hma/read_more/humanitarian_mine_act
ion_in_sudan>.

76 Roberts and Frilander, 'Preparing for Peace: Mine Action's Investment in
the Future of Sudan', p. 18.

77 Roberts and Frilander, 'Preparing for Peace Mine Action's Investment in
the Future of Sudan', pp. 5, 18.

78 Peter Moszynski. (27 November 2005) 'Mine Action in the Midst of
Internal Conflict: The Case of Sudan'. *Mine Action in the Midst of Internal
Conflict*. Report on the workshop organized by Geneva Call and the
International Campaign to Ban Landmines Non-State Actors Working
Group in Zagreb. Geneva, Geneva Call. p. 31.

79 John Garang de Mabior. (2003) 'Keynote Address'. *Mine Ban Education
Workshop in Southern Sudan: Report of Proceedings and Recommendations*.
Geneva, Geneva Call. p. 4. <http://www.genevacall.org/wp-content/up
loads/dlm_uploads/2013/11/20031001_mine_ban_education_worksh
op_southern_sudan_proceedings1.pdf>. Accessed 26 September 2017.

80 Save the Children Sweden. (December 2004) 'Organizational Capacity and
Impact Assessment to Selected Partners in Sudan'. Unpublished document
obtained by author.

81 ICBL. (2016) 'Sudan: Mine Ban Policy'. *Landmine and Cluster Munition
Monitor*. <http://the-monitor.org/en-gb/reports/2016/sudan/mine-ban-po
licy.aspx>.

Chapter 7

1 Details on the Dallas incident are from: Simone McCarthy. (9 July 2016)
'What Does Dallas's "Bomb Robot" Mean for the Future of Policing?'

Christian Science Monitor. <https://www.csmonitor.com/USA/USA-Update/2016/0709/What-does-Dallas-s-bomb-robot-mean-for-the-future-of-policing>. Accessed 10 September 2017; Sara Sidner and Mallory Simon. (12 July 2016) 'How Robot, Explosives Took Out Dallas Sniper in Unprecedented Way'. *CNN.* <http://www.cnn.com/2016/07/12/us/dallas-police-robot-c4-explosives/index.html>. Accessed 10 September 2017.

2 McCarthy, 'What does Dallas's "bomb robot" mean for the future of policing?'

3 In: Sidner and Simon, 'How Robot, Explosives Took Out Dallas Sniper in Unprecedented Way'.

4 Peter M. Asaro. 'How Just Could a Robot War Be?' In *Proceedings of the 2008 Conference on Current Issues in Computing and Philosophy.* pp. 50–64. <http://www.cybersophe.org/writing/Asaro%20Just%20Robot%20War.pdf>. Accessed 3 August 2012.

5 Peter Asaro, in: The Alyona Show. (23 February 2012) 'The Ethics of Robotics'. <http://www.youtube.com/watch?feature=player_embedded&v=NoPxP5G44Rk>. Accessed 3 August 2012.

6 Associated Press. (4 April 2004) 'U.S. Bets on Land Mine Technology'. *Wired.* <http://www.wired.com/techbiz/media/news/2004/04/62940>. Accessed 10 January 2012; Human Rights Watch. (August 2005) 'Development and Production of New Landmines'. In *Back in Business? U.S. Landmine Production and Exports.* <http://www.hrw.org/legacy/backgrounder/arms/arms0805/3.htm>. Accessed 10 January 2012; Christopher Moraff. (3 October 2006) 'Along Came a Spider'. *The American Prospect.* <http://prospect.org/article/along-came-spider>. Accessed 10 January 2012; International Campaign to Ban Landmines. (2 November 2011) 'United States: Mine Ban Policy'. *Landmine and Cluster Munition Monitor.* <http://www.the-monitor.org/index.php/cp/display/region_profiles/theme/1445>. Accessed 10 January 2012.

7 In: Moraff, 'Along Came a Spider'.

8 US Army. (14 May 2012) '13--Spider Additional Quantities: Solicitation Number: W15QKN-12-T-B003'. <http://landminesinafrica.files.wordpress.com/2012/07/more-spider-mines-ordered-5-14-12.pdf>. Accessed 31 July 2012.

9 Human Rights Watch. (2020) 'US: Trump Administration Abandons Landmine Ban'. Retrieved from <https://www.hrw.org/news/2020/01/31/us-trump-administration-abandons-landmine-ban>.

10 Leonard Greene. (3 May 2010) 'Robo-partner Makes Sure NYPD Is Always Well-"Armed."' *The New York Post.* <http://www.nypost.com/p/news/local/robo_partner_makes_sure_nypd_is_9Z2LS9H1fIsM3cCradwwDJ>. Accessed 7 August 2012.

11 Northrop Grumman. (2012) 'Robotic Platforms and Sub-systems'. <http://www.is.northropgrumman.com/by_solution/remote_platforms/index.html>. Accessed 10 January 2012; Tuan Nguyen. (31 July 2008) 'Meet

the Real-Life Wall-E'. *ABC News*. <http://abcnews.go.com/Technology/A headoftheCurve/Story?id=5484694&page=1#.TwyzaByCWIs>. Accessed 10 January 2012.

12 Northrop Grumman. (2012) 'F6A – The Industry's Most Versatile Platform: Accessories'. <http://www.is.northropgrumman.com/by_solutio n/remote_platforms/product/f6b/f6a_accessories/index.html>. Accessed 10 January 2012.

13 McGrath, *Landmines and Unexploded Ordnance: A Resource Book*, p. 148.

14 Ian Roderick. (2010) 'Considering the Fetish Value of EOD Robots: How Robots Save Lives and Sell War'. *International Journal of Cultural Studies*. 13(3). pp. 235–53.

15 P. W. Singer. (2009) *Wired for War: The Robotics Revolution and Conflict in the 21st Century*. New York, Penguin Books. p. 31.

16 P. W. Singer in: Al Jazeera. (2011) 'Robot Wars'. *Fault Lines*. <http://bcove. me/jrbx7oi1>. Accessed 3 August 2012.

17 In: Stephen Graham. (14 February 2013) 'Foucault's Boomerang: The New Military Urbanism'. *openDemocracy*. <https://www.opendemocracy.net /opensecurity/stephen-graham/foucault%E2%80%99s-boomerang-ne w-military-urbanism>. Accessed 10 September 2017.

18 Michel Foucault. (1995) *Discipline and Punish: The Birth of the Prison*. Alan Sheridan (Trans.) 2nd Ed. New York, Vintage Books.

19 Croll, *Landmines in War and Peace*, p. 171.

20 NYPD. (20 September 2010) 'Midtown Manhattan Security Initiative'. <http://www.nyc.gov/html/nypd/html/pr/pr_2010_midtown_security_in itiative.shtml>. Accessed 10 January 2011. See also: Pam Martens. (23 October 2011) 'Wall Street Firms Spy on Protesters in Tax-Funded Center'. *truthout*. <http://www.truth-out.org/wall-street-firms-spy-protesters-t ax-funded-center/1319394553>. Accessed 10 January 2011.

21 Tom Namako. (30 November 2010) 'PATH tunnels get $600M ring of steel'. *New York Post*. <http://www.nypost.com/p/news/local/manh attan/path_tunnels_get_ring_of_steel_EWttW8dN6UKpaA2iSbpGRI>. Accessed 7 August 2012.

22 NYPD, 'Midtown Manhattan Security Initiative'. See also: Martens, 'Wall Street Firms Spy on Protesters in Tax-Funded Center'.

23 Matthew Bolton and Victoria Measles. (2013) 'Barricades Dot Net: Post-Fordist Policing in Occupied New York City'. In: *Occupying Political Science: The Occupy Wall Street Movement from New York to the World*. Emily Welty, Matthew Bolton, Chris Malone and Meghana Nayak (Eds). New York, Palgrave Macmillan. pp. 163–90.

24 Duncan Osborne. (11 August 2011) 'NYPD May Employ Surveillance Drones'. *Gay City News*. <http://www.chelseanow.com/articles/2011/08/1 1/gay_city_news/news/doc4e4414474e153994147714.txt>. Accessed 11 January 2012.

25 Nick Paumgarten. (14 May 2012) 'Here's Looking at You'. *The New Yorker*. p. 48.

26 Dan Gettinger. (15 June 2015) 'Robot Cops near You'. <http://dronecenter. bard.edu/police-robots-in-the-u-s/>. Accessed 10 September 2017.
27 Anon. (21 December 2011) 'Underwater Drones Help NYPD Secure Harbor'. *Homeland Security News Wire*. <http://www.homelandsecurityne wswire.com/dr20111221-underwater-drones-help-nypd-secure-harbor>. See also: Al Baker. (4 December 2011) 'Underwater Drones Giving More Eyes to Police Harbor Unit as Searches Grow'. *The New York Times*. <http ://www.nytimes.com/2011/12/05/nyregion/drone-submarines-add-eyes-for-nyc-harbor-police.html?_r=3>. Accessed 11 January 2012.
28 Bureau of Investigative Journalism. (2019) 'Current Statistics'. <https://w ww.thebureauinvestigates.com/projects/drone-war>. Accessed 12 October 2019.
29 Medea Benjamin. (2012) *Drone Warfare: Killing by Remote Control*. New York, OR Books.
30 P. W. Singer. (April 2009) 'PW Singer on Military Robots and the Future of War'. <http://www.ted.com/talks/pw_singer_on_robots_of_war.html>. Accessed 1 August 2012.
31 Armin Krishnan. *Killer Robots: Legality and Ethicality of Autonomous Weapons*. Burlington, Ashgate. p. 147.
32 David Cortright. (9 January 2012) 'License to Kill'. *CATO Unbound*. <http ://www.cato-unbound.org/2012/01/09/david-cortright/license-to-kill/>. Accessed 1 August 2012.
33 Loz Blain. (n.d.) 'South Korea's Autonomous Robot Gun Turrets: Deadly from Kilometers Away'. *gizmag*. <http://m.gizmag.com/article/17198/>. Accessed 12 January 2012.
34 DoDaam Systems. (n.d.) 'Super aEgis II'. <http://dodaam.com/ sub_0202_1_3.php>. Accessed 12 January 2012; DoDaam Systems. (n.d.) 'Athena'. <http://dodaam.com/sub_0202_1_4.php>. Accessed 12 January 2012.
35 Andrew S. Erickson, Lyle J. Goldstein and William S. Murray. 'Chinese Mine Warfare: A PLA Navy "Assassin's Mace" Capability'. Naval War College China Maritime Studies. 3. pp. 20, 25. <http://www.usnwc.edu/ Research---Gaming/China-Maritime-Studies-Institute/Publications/docu ments/CMS3_Mine-Warfare.aspx>. Accessed 11 January 2012.
36 Anon. (25 September 2011) 'Autonomous Kill Bots Continue A Trend'. *Strategy Page*. <http://www.strategypage.com/htmw/htweap/articles/20110 925.aspx>. Accessed 12 January 2012.
37 Singer, 'PW Singer on military robots and the future of war'.
38 David E. Sanger. 'Obama Order Sped Up Wave of Cyberattacks Against Iran'. *The New York Times*. <http://www.nytimes.com/2012/06/01/world /middleeast/obama-ordered-wave-of-cyberattacks-against-iran.html? _r=1&hp>. Accessed 2 August 2012.
39 Guilbert Gates. (1 June 2012) 'How a Secret Cyberwar Program Worked'. *The New York Times*. <http://www.nytimes.com/interactive/2012/06/01/ world/middleeast/how-a-secret-cyberwar-program-worked.html?ref= middleeast>. Accessed 2 August 2012; Anon. (20 September 2010) 'A

Worm in the Centrifuge'. *The Economist*. <http://www.economist.com/node/17147818>. Accessed 2 August 2012.

40 Tim Blackmore. (2005) *War X: Human Extensions in Battlespace*. Toronto, University of Toronto Press.

41 In: Sarah A. Topol. 'Attack of the Killer Robots'. *BuzzFeed*. <https://www.buzzfeed.com/sarahatopol/how-to-save-mankind-from-the-new-breed-of-killer-robots?utm_term=.vgKKzjPrOq#.mg4DNzRyL7>. Accessed 26 September 2017.

42 Eric Bland. (18 May 2009) 'Robot Warriors Will Get a Guide to Ethics'. *NBC News*. <http://www.nbcnews.com/id/30810070/#.UZxPeoWAZpE>. Accessed 22 May 2013.

43 Patrick Lin, George Bekey and Keith Abney. (20 December 2008) 'Autonomous Military Robotics: Risk, Ethics, and Design'. <http://ethics.calpoly.edu/ONR_report.pdf>. Accessed 1 August 2012.

44 Noah Shachtman. (18 October 2007) 'Robot Cannon Kills 9, Wounds 14'. *Wired.com*. <http://blog.wired.com/defense/2007/10/robot-cannon-ki.html>. Accessed 1 August 2012.

45 Reuters. (11 June 2012) 'U.S. Navy Drone Crashes in Maryland, No Injuries'. *Chicago Tribune*. <http://articles.chicagotribune.com/2012-06-11/news/sns-rt-us-usa-drone-crashbre85a1f3-20120611_1_drone-crashes-crash-site-unmanned-spy-plane>. Accessed 1 August 2012.

46 Drone Wars UK. (18 March 2017) '3. Drone Crash Database'. <https://dronewars.net/drone-crash-database/>. Accessed 17 September 2017.

47 For a more detailed version of this argument, see: Peter Asaro. (Forthcoming 2012). 'On Banning Autonomous Lethal Systems: Human Rights, Automation and the Dehumanization of Lethal Decision-Making'. Special Issue on New Technologies and Warfare, *International Review of the Red Cross*.

48 Singer, 'PW Singer on military robots and the future of war'.

49 Humanitarian Disarmament Campaigns Summit. (21 October 2012) 'Communique'. <http://www.4disarmament.org/2012/10/23/humanitarian-disarmament-campaigns-summit/>. Accessed 26 August 2017.

50 Philip Alston. (28 May 2010) *Report of the Special Rapporteur on extrajudicial, summary or arbitrary executions, Philip Alston: Addendum: Study on targeted killings*. A/HRC/14/24/Add.6. <https://documents-dds-ny.un.org/doc/UNDOC/GEN/G10/137/53/PDF/G1013753.pdf?OpenElement>. Accessed 28 August 2017.

51 Singer, *Wired for War: The Robotics Revolution and Conflict in the 21st Century*, pp. 170–8.

52 ICRAC. (December 2009) 'Mission Statement'. <http://icrac.net/statements>. Accessed 3 August 2012.

53 Noel Sharkey. (17 August 2007) 'Robot Wars Are a Reality'. *The Guardian*. <http://www.guardian.co.uk/commentisfree/2007/aug/18/comment.military>. Accessed 3 August 2012.

54 Sarah A. Topol. (26 August 2016) 'Attack of the Killer Robots'. *BuzzFeed*.
    <https://www.buzzfeed.com/sarahatopol/how-to-save-mankind-from-th
    e-new-breed-of-killer-robots?utm_term=.dpJ5R6XbqE#.symNZb5w6P>.
    Accessed 18 September 2017.
55 Topol, 'Attack of the Killer Robots'.
56 HRW. (2012) *Losing Humanity: The Case against Killer Robots*. New York,
    HRW. pp. 1–5.
57 HRW, *Losing Humanity: The Case against Killer Robots*, p. 5.
58 US DoD. (21 November 2012) 'Autonomy in Weapon Systems'. Directive
    No. 3000.09. <https://fas.org/irp/doddir/dod/d3000_09.pdf>. Accessed 17
    September 2017.
59 HRW. (April 2016) 'Killer Robots and the Concept of Meaningful Human
    Control: Memorandum to Convention on Conventional Weapons (CCW)
    Delegates'. <https://www.hrw.org/sites/default/files/supporting_resources/rob
    ots_meaningful_human_control_final.pdf>. Accessed 17 September 2017.
60 Mark Gubrud. (27 November 2012) 'DoD Directive on Autonomy in
    Weapon Systems'. *ICRAC*. <https://icrac.net/2012/11/dod-directive-on-a
    utonomy-in-weapon-systems/>. Accessed 17 September 2017.
61 Campaign to Stop Killer Robots. (26 April 2013) 'Campaign Launch in
    London'. <http://www.stopkillerrobots.org/2013/04/campaign-launch-in-
    london/>. Accessed 17 September 2017.
62 Christof Heyns. (9 April 2013) 'Report of the Special Rapporteur on
    extrajudicial, summary or arbitrary executions, Christof Heyns'. A/
    HRC/23/47. p. 1. <http://www.ohchr.org/Documents/HRBodies/HRCo
    uncil/RegularSession/Session23/A-HRC-23-47_en.pdf>. Accessed 17
    September 2017.
63 Heyns, 'Report of the Special Rapporteur on extrajudicial, summary or
    arbitrary executions, Christof Heyns', p. 17.
64 Campaign to Stop Killer Robots. (28 May 2013) 'Consensus: Killer Robots
    Must Be Addressed'. <http://www.stopkillerrobots.org/2013/05/nations-t
    o-debate-killer-robots-at-un/>.
65 ICRAC. (14 November 2013) 'ICRAC Delivers Statement to States Parties
    to the Convention on Conventional Weapons at the UN in Geneva'.. Accessed 17
    September 2017.
66 Kenneth Anderson and Matthew Waxman. (2012) 'Law and Ethics for
    Robot Soldiers'. *Policy Review*. <http://www.hoover.org/research/law-and-
    ethics-robot-soldiers>. Accessed 18 September 2017.
67 Noel Sharkey. (2012) 'The Evitability of Autonomous Robot Warfare'.
    International Review of the Red Cross. 94(886). pp. 787–99.
68 Anderson and Waxman. (2012) 'Law and Ethics for Robot Soldiers'.
69 James Jay Carafano. (6 August 2015) 'Don't Kill The Killer-Robots--Just
    Yet'. <http://www.heritage.org/defense/commentary/dont-kill-the-killer-
    robots-just-yet>. Accessed 18 September 2017.

70 Matthew Bolton and Cayman Mitchell. (29 August 2014) 'The Peloponnesian War and Killer Robots: Norms of Protection in Security Policy'. *e-International Relations*. <http://www.e-ir.info/2014/08/29/the-peloponnesian-war-and-killer-robots-norms-of-protection-in-security-policy/>. Accessed 17 September 2017.

71 Sarah Knuckey. (14 May 2014) 'Do Women Have Anything to Say about Autonomous Weapons?' *Just Security*. <https://www.justsecurity.org/10424/women-autonomous-weapons/>.

72 Campaign to Stop Killer Robots. (February 2016) 'Binder of Women'. <http://www.stopkillerrobots.org/wp-content/uploads/2013/03/Women Experts_1Feb2016.pdf>. Accessed 17 September 2017.

73 Article 36. 'Say No to #ManPanels'. <http://www.manpanels.org/>. Accessed 17 September 2017.

74 Mary Wareham. (16 May 2014) 'Campaign to Stop Killer Robots statement by Mary Wareham, Human Rights Watch to the Convention on Conventional Weapons Meeting of Experts'. <http://www.stopkillerrobots. org/wp-content/uploads/2013/03/KRC_Statement_CCW_16May2014_As Delivered.pdf>. Accessed 17 September 2017.

75 Campaign to Stop Killer Robots. (22 August 2019) 'Russia, United States Attempt to Legitimize Killer Robots'. <https://www.stopkillerrobots. org/2019/08/russia-united-states-attempt-to-legitimize-killer-robots>. Accessed 12 October 2019.

76 Colum Lynch. (6 May 2016) 'At the United Nations, Umoja Translates as Bureaucratic Chaos'. *Foreign Policy*. <http://foreignpolicy.com/2016 /05/06/at-the-united-nations-umoja-translates-as-bureaucratic-chaos/>. Accessed 18 September 2017.

77 Peter Teffer. (7 September 2017) 'Killer Robots Debate Shortened by Unpaid Bills'. *EU Observer*. <https://euobserver.com/science/138914>. Accessed 18 September 2017.

78 Campaign to Stop Killer Robots. (30 May 2017) 'Diplomatic Efforts Falter'. <http://www.stopkillerrobots.org/2017/05/diplomatsfalter/>. Accessed 18 September 2017.

79 Lynch, 'At the United Nations, Umoja Translates as Bureaucratic Chaos'.

80 UN Secretariat. (30 September 2017) 'Status of Contributions of BWC, CCW, CCM, OTW as at 30 September 2017'. <https://www.unog.ch/8025 6EDD006B8954/%28httpAssets%29/B9ABE4E09C2366F6C12581AE0 04A4182/$file/Status+of+Contrib+BWC+CCW+CCM+OTW_30+Sep+ 2017.pdf>. Accessed 3 November 2017.

81 Campaign to Stop Killer Robots, 'Diplomatic Efforts Falter'.

82 In: Topol, 'Attack of the Killer Robots'.

83 Campaign to Stop Killer Robots, 'Diplomatic Efforts Falter'.

84 Topol, 'Attack of the Killer Robots'.

85 Future of Life Institute. (n.d.) 'Autonomous Weapons: An Open Letter from AI & Robotics Researchers'. <https://futureoflife.org/open-letter-autonomous-weapons/>. Accessed 18 September 2017.

86 Meghan Hennessey. (13 August 2014) 'Clearpath Robotics Takes Stance against 'Killer Robots'.' <https://www.clearpathrobotics.com/2014/08/clearpath-takes-stance-against-killer-robots/>. Accessed 18 September 2017.

87 Joachim Dagenborg and Gwladys Fouche. (11 March 2016) 'Norway wealth fund's ethics watchdog warns firms not to make killer robots'. *Reuters*. <https://www.reuters.com/article/norway-swf-arms/exclusive-norway-wealth-funds-ethics-watchdog-warns-firms-not-to-make-killer-robots-idUSL5N16H3AQ>. Accessed 18 September 2017.

88 Future of Life Institute. (n.d.) 'An Open Letter to the United Nations Convention on Certain Conventional Weapons'. <https://futureoflife.org/autonomous-weapons-open-letter-2017>. Accessed 18 September 2017.

89 Campaign to Stop Killer Robots. (22 January 2019) 'Global Poll Shows 61% Oppose Killer Robots'. <https://www.stopkillerrobots.org/2019/01/global-poll-61-oppose-killer-robots/>. Accessed 12 October 2019.

90 In: Campaign to Stop Killer Robots. (12 November 2018) 'UN Head Calls for a Ban'. <https://www.stopkillerrobots.org/2018/11/unban/>. Accessed 12 October 2019.

91 Campaign to Stop Killer Robots, 'Russia, United States Attempt to Legitimize Killer Robots'.

92 António Guterres. (25 May 2017) 'Life in War Zones Remains Grim, with Cities Turned into Death Traps, Civilian Suffering "Pushed to the Limits", Secretary-General Tells Security Council'. <https://www.un.org/press/en/2017/sc12841.doc.htm>. Accessed 18 September 2017.

93 Mary Wareham. (12 May 2016) 'When Cities Become Death Traps'. <https://www.hrw.org/news/2016/05/12/when-cities-become-death-traps>. Accessed 18 September 2017.

94 See: Matthew Bolton. (2016) 'Time for a Discursive Rehabilitation: A Brief History of General and Complete Disarmament'. In *Rethinking General and Complete Disarmament in the Twenty-First Century*. D. Plesch and K. Miletic (Eds). New York, UN Office for Disarmament Affairs. pp. 3–14.

95 Mary Wareham. (18 September 2017) 'Preventing Suffering through "Humanitarian Disarmament" Countries to Begin Signing Nuclear Weapons Treaty This Week'. <https://www.hrw.org/news/2017/09/18/preventing-suffering-through-humanitarian-disarmament>. Accessed 18 September 2017.

Epilogue

1 UN. (7 July 2017) '(29th meeting) UN Conference to Negotiate a Legally Binding Instrument to Prohibit Nuclear Weapons, Leading towards Their Total Elimination'. *UN Web TV*. <http://webtv.un.org/search/29th-meeting-un-conference-to-negotiate-a-legally-binding-instrument-to-prohibit-n

uclear-weapons-leading-towards-their-total-elimination/5496837948001/?
term=nuclear%20weapons&sort=date>.

2 Setsuko Thurlow. (2003) 'Setsuko Thurlow's Personal Testimony as Told to
   Physicians for Global Survival in 2003'. *Hibakusha Stories*. <http://hibakus
   hastories.org/meet-the-hibakusha/meet-setsuko-thurlow/>.

3 Thurlow, 'Setsuko Thurlow's Personal Testimony as Told to Physicians for
   Global Survival in 2003'.

4 Setsuko Thurlow. (8 July 2017) 'Hiroshima Survivor Speaks as U.N
   Delegates Vote to Prohibit Nuclear Weapons'. <https://www.youtube.com/
   watch?v=JGd5OioiLak>.

5 John Hersey. (1989) *Hiroshima*. Reprint Edition. New York, Vintage.

6 Robert Croonquist. (n.d.) 'Meet Setsuko Thurlow: Hiroshima A-bomb
   Survivor'. *Hibakusha Stories*. <http://hibakushastories.org/meet-t
   he-hibakusha/meet-setsuko-thurlow/>; Anon. (30 April 2011) 'James
   McKitrick Thurlow'. *Toronto Star*. <http://www.legacy.com/obituaries/t
   hestar/obituary.aspx?n=james-mckitrick-thurlow&pid=150611603>.

7 In: Elizabeth Renzetti. (5 August 2017) 'In Hiroshima, One August
   Morning in 1945 Was Dark as Night – and This Woman Can't Forget It'.
   The Globe and Mail. <https://beta.theglobeandmail.com/news/world/hiros
   hima/article35881700>. Accessed 23 September 2017.

8 In: Nicholas Thompson. (21 September 2009) 'Inside the Apocalyptic
   Soviet Doomsday Machine'. *Wired*. <https://www.wired.com/2009/09/
   mf-deadhand/>. Accessed 23 September 2017.

9 Eric Schlosser. (2013) *Command and Control: Nuclear Weapons, the
   Damascus Accident, and the Illusion of Safety*. New York, Penguin.

10 SIPRI. (3 July 2017) 'Global Nuclear Weapons: Modernization Remains
   the Priority'. <https://www.sipri.org/media/press-release/2017/gl
   obal-nuclear-weapons-modernization-remains-priority>. Accessed 10
   September 2017.

11 ICAN. (n.d.) 'The Legacy of Nuclear Testing'. <http://www.icanw.org/the
   -facts/catastrophic-harm/the-legacy-of-nuclear-testing/>.

12 US Department of Energy Nevada Operations Office. (December 2000)
   'United States Nuclear Tests: July 1945 through September 1992'. DOE/
   NV—209-REV 15. p. xv. Available from: <https://web.archive.org/web/2
   0061012160826/http://www.nv.doe.gov/library/publications/historical/DO
   ENV_209_REV15.pdf>. Accessed 25 September 2017.

13 US Department of Justice. (17 March 2016) 'Radiation Exposure
   Compensation System: Awards to Date'. Available from: <https://web.ar
   chive.org/web/20160318033248/https://www.justice.gov/civil/awards-date
   -03172016>. Accessed 25 September 2017.

14 Thurlow, 'ICAN Statements to the Negotiating Conference: Opening
   Statement'.

15 UN, '(29th Meeting) UN Conference to Negotiate a Legally Binding
   Instrument to Prohibit Nuclear Weapons, Leading towards Their Total
   Elimination'.

16 Nobel Prize. (2017) 'International Campaign to Abolish Nuclear Weapons (ICAN) - Facts'. <http://www.nobelprize.org/nobel_prizes/peace/laureates /2017/ican-facts.html>. Accessed 3 November 2017.

17 In: ICAN. (26 October 2017) 'Atomic Bomb Survivor to Jointly Accept Nobel Peace Prize on ICAN's Behalf'. <http://www.icanw.org/campaign -news/atomic-bomb-survivor-to-jointly-accept-nobel-peace-prize-on -icans-behalf/>. Accessed 3 November 2017.

18 My reflections here are influenced by Albert Camus. (1991) *The Myth of Sisyphus: And Other Essays*. New York, Vintage.

INDEX